Adaptation in Contemporary Culture

ADAPTATION IN CONTEMPORARY CULTURE

Textual Infidelities

Edited by
Rachel Carroll

continuum

Continuum International Publishing Group

The Tower Building   80 Maiden Lane
11 York Road   Suite 704
London SE1 7NX   New York, NY 10038

www.continuumbooks.com

British Library Cataloguing-in-Publication Data
A catalogue record for this book is available from the British Library.

ISBN: 978-0-8264-4456-1 (Hardback)
         978-0-8264-2464-8 (Paperback)

Library of Congress Cataloging-in-Publication Data
A catalog record for this book is available from the Library of Congress.

Typeset by Newgen Imaging Systems Pvt Ltd, Chennai, India
Printed and bound in Great Britain by CPI Antony Rowe, Chippenham, Wiltshire

Contents

Acknowledgements

I would like to thank Ruth Helyer for her invaluable contribution to the development of this project in its early stages.

Contributors

Frances Babbage is Senior Lecturer in Drama at the University of Sheffield. She has published on performance, adaptation and rewriting in *Modern Drama, Comparative Drama, New Theatre Quarterly, Contemporary Theatre Review* and *New Comparisons*. She is author of *Augusto Boal* (Routledge, 2004), and her forthcoming publications include *Re-visioning Myth: Feminist Strategies in Contemporary Drama* (Manchester University Press).

Terryl Bacon is an artist and film-maker, and Senior Lecturer in Media and Cultural Studies at the University of the West of England. Her research centres on gender and identity in new media, film and photography. Her published papers and exhibitions include 'The construction of identity in the digital era: renegotiating relationship' (Centre for Creative Media Research, Bournemouth, 2005) and the visual essay 'Disembodied intimacy', shown at *Imaging Social Movements* (Edge Hill, Ormskirk, 2004).

Rachel Carroll is Principal Lecturer in English Studies at the University of Teesside. Her research interests are in gender and sexuality in contemporary fiction and film. She has published in *Genders, Journal of Adaptation in Film and Performance* and *Textual Practice*, and is currently working on a monograph entitled *Rereading Heterosexuality: Feminism, Queer Theory and Contemporary Fiction* (Edinburgh University Press, forthcoming).

Catherine Constable is an Associate Professor at the University of Warwick. Her research interests are in film theory, philosophy, postmodern theory and contemporary Hollywood cinema. She is the author of *Thinking in Images: Film Theory, Feminist Philosophy and Marlene Dietrich* (British Film Institute, 2005) and *Adapting Philosophy: Jean Baudrillard and The Matrix Trilogy* (Manchester University Press, 2009).

Govinda Dickman is Lecturer in Digital Media and Video Documentary at the University of the West of England. He is a film-maker, postmedia artist, and internationally broadcast documentary editor. He has talked, made films about, or published on social and collaborative film-making; cinematic realism and phenomenology vs. the dialectics of mechanically indexical media; film and spirituality; the aesthetics and politics of Hollywood cinema; and embodiment and corporeality (Palgrave, forthcoming).

Rebecca D'Monté is Senior Lecturer in Drama at the University of the West of England. She has co-edited two books: *Female Communities 1600–1800: Literary Visions and Cultural Realities* (with Nicole Pohl, Macmillan, 1999), and *Cool Britannia: British Political Drama in the 1990s* (with Graham Saunders, Palgrave, 2007). She has written articles on, among others, Margaret Cavendish, Dodie Smith, Esther McCracken, Judy Upton and Sarah Kane. At present she is preparing monographs on women dramatists, 1930–1960, and on British theatre during the Second World War.

Josephine Dolan is Senior Lecturer in Film Studies at the University of the West of England. Her research spans a range of media, including literature, film and radio, and is organized around questions of identity – national, gender, class, race and childhood. Her publications include work on the writer Daphne du Maurier and the British film star Anne Neagle, and she is currently working on two areas of interest: the biopic genre, and representations of older women in contemporary media culture.

Heather Emmens is a doctoral student in the English Department at Queen's University, Kingston, Canada. She researches contemporary lesbian and gay literature, including television adaptations of queer novels.

Pete Falconer is a doctoral student in the Department of Film and Television Studies at the University of Warwick. His main research interests are in Hollywood cinema and its genres. His primary focus is on Westerns, but he has also published work on horror movies.

Suzy Gordon is Senior Lecturer in Film Studies at the University of the West of England. Her research focuses largely on the intersections between psychoanalysis, feminism and film theory. Her work has been published in *Screen*, *Angelaki* and *Feminist Media Studies*, and her monograph *Film, Feminism and Melanie Klein* is forthcoming (Routledge).

Ruth Helyer is a Principal Lecturer at the University of Teesside. Her research interests are in contemporary fiction and film (particularly American), visual culture and gender studies (particularly masculinity).

Joe Kember is Senior Lecturer in Film at the University of Exeter. He has published widely on aspects of early cinema, Victorian popular entertainments, and related theories of modernity, and he is the co-investigator with the AHRC-funded project, 'Moving and Projected Images in the South-west 1800–1914'. His most recent book, *Marketing Modernity: Victorian Popular Shows and Early Cinema*, is published by the University Of Exeter Press (2009).

Iris Kleinecke-Bates is Lecturer in Film Studies at the University of Hull. Her current research is on notions of memory and nostalgia and the representation of the past on British television. She is the author of an article on *The Forsyte Saga* in *Screen*.

Christopher Marlow is Senior Lecturer in English at the University of Lincoln. He has published in the fields of early modern literature and postmodern fiction, and is particularly concerned with poststructuralist approaches to neglected or unusual texts. He is also interested in the representation of friendship and masculinity in literature, especially in early modern university drama.

Cathlena Martin, a PhD candidate at the University of Florida, researches children's culture through literature, comics, film and new media. Her dissertation work focuses on the changing nature of children's literature and culture in a digital age through the convergence of print and digital texts. She teaches communication arts at Samford University, and professional communication and business writing at the University of Florida, online through distance learning. Her publications include chapters in edited collections on topics such as *Peter Pan* and video games, play in *Ender's Game*, and using wikis in the college classroom.

Estella Tincknell is Reader in Media and Cultural Studies at the University of the West of England. She is the co-editor of *Film's Musical Moments* (2006), author of *Mediating the Family: Gender, Culture and Representation* (2005), and joint author of *The Practice of Cultural Studies* (2004). She has contributed to *Critical Survey*, *Feminist Media Studies*, *Gender and Education*, *Journal of Sociology of Education*, *Journal of European Cultural Studies* and *Journal of Popular Film and Television*, and she is on the editorial board of *Body and Society*. She is currently writing *Re-Viewing Jane Campion: Angels, Voices and Demons* (Palgrave Macmillan).

Brenda R. Weber is Assistant Professor in Gender Studies at Indiana University. She has published in such journals as *Genders*, *The International Journal of Men's Health*, *Feminist Studies*, and *Configurations*. Her book projects are *Makeover TV: Selfhood, Citizenship, and Celebrity* (Duke University Press, 2009) and *Figuring Fame: Women, Gender, and the Body in the Transatlantic Production of Literary Celebrity*.

Karen Wells is Lecturer in Development Studies and International Childhood Studies at Birkbeck College, London. Her research interests are in material and visual cultures, and childhood. She has published in *Space and Culture*, *Journal of Visual Communication*, *Social and Cultural Geography*, *Ethnic and Racial Studies* and *Journal of Consumer Culture*. Her book *Childhood in a Global Context* is published by Polity Press (2009).

Paul Wells is Director of the Animation Academy at Loughborough University and he has published widely in the field, including *Understanding Animation*, *Animation: Genre and Authorship*, *Animation and America* and *Fundamentals of Animation*. He was the series consultant for the BBC's *Animation Nation* documentaries, he conducts workshops worldwide based on his animation scriptwriting book, and he has co-written *Re-Imagining Animation* with film-maker and graphic designer Johnny Hardstaff.

CHAPTER ONE

Introduction: Textual Infidelities

RACHEL CARROLL

All adaptations express or address a desire to return to an 'original' textual encounter; as such, adaptations are perhaps symptomatic of a cultural compulsion to repeat. The motivations informing the production and consumption of adaptations may seem intent on replication but, as the chapters in this collection demonstrate, every 'return' is inevitably transformative of its object – whether that object be the original text or the memory of its first encounter. A film or television adaptation of a prior cultural text – no matter how 'faithful' in intention or aesthetic – is inevitably an *interpretation* of that text: to this extent, every adaptation is an instance of textual *in*fidelity. *Adaptation in Contemporary Culture* considers adaptation not only as a significant film and television genre, but also as a cultural practice which exemplifies key trends in postmodern culture. The diversity of texts explored in this collection is indicative of an attempt to reconfigure the ways in which adaptation is conceptualized by considering it within an extended range of generic, critical and theoretical contexts: literary, film, television and other visual texts are examined both as 'origins' and 'adaptations', and new insights are offered into the construction of genres, canons and 'classics'. *Adaptation in Contemporary Culture* aims to expand the range of texts considered under the rubric of 'adaptation': adaptations of both 'classic' and contemporary texts by British and American authors – from Jane Austen, Edgar Allen Poe and Charles Dickens to Bret Easton Ellis, P. D. James and Sarah Waters – are analysed alongside film remakes, video games, biopics, fan fiction and celebrity culture.

Key critical paradigms for adaptation studies – fidelity, intertextuality, historicity and authorship – provide the conceptual focus for each section of the collection. Fidelity, as a contested concept, has proved a defining concern for adaptation studies. **Part I: Remaking Fidelity** revisits the critical and theoretical issues implicit in the assumption that a media adaptation should be judged by its faithfulness to a literary original. Fidelity is taken out of its more familiar context – the film and television adaptation of the classic literary text – and considered within an expanded field of adaptation, including the theatrical adaptation and the film remake. The subjective investments and productive potential of fidelity as a mode of cultural engagement are examined, with the figure of the 'fan' emerging as a significant cultural agent. The traditional focus on adaptation as a 'page to screen' process tends to privilege the literary origin. **Part II: After-images** emphasizes the significance of visual contexts when considering adaptation. The diversity of transmedia intertextuality is explored with reference to the genre film remake, photography, animation and the video game. Adaptations of classic texts enable contemporary audiences to revisit the past; as such they can be situated within the broader context of postmodern appropriations of history. **Part III: Reproducing the Past**, adaptations are situated within historical and theoretical frameworks, including queer theory and critical whiteness studies, which enable a critical interrogation of the 'reproductive' work of adaptation. Issues of origin and authorship have been recurring concerns within adaptation studies. **Part IV: Afterlives** explores the incorporation of authors – as literary 'properties' or celebrities – into the culture of adaptation. Deference to the authorial signature is one way in which the 'faithful' adaptation has traditionally announced itself; here the figure of the author becomes the *object* of adaptation. In this final section, questions of fidelity are examined in relation to 'reauthorship', the biopic and celebrity culture.

Remaking Fidelity

In 'Heavy bodies, fragile texts: stage adaptation and the problem of presence', Frances Babbage explores Punchdrunk Theatre's 'promenade' performance of Edgar Allen Poe's short stories, entitled *The Masque of the Red Death*. This production is considered within the context of theatrical literary adaptation more broadly, with Bram Stoker's *Dracula* providing an illustrative case study of the challenges of adaptation for the stage. Dispensing with the traditions of realism which prevail in so many film and television adaptations, *The Masque of the Red Death* enacts a 'live encounter' with the source text/s which is inevitably fragmented and uniquely subjective. Arguing against the repression of subjective response as 'academically unbecoming', Babbage examines this innovative instance of adaptation as providing a space for the participant's memories of the original to be revisited and renewed. While *The Masque of the Red Death* departs radically from the (realist) representational strategies of fidelity, Gus van Sant's 1998 film *Psycho* demonstrates a fidelity to Hitchcock's 1960 original which some viewers and critics found perverse.

In 'Reflections on the surface: remaking the postmodern with van Sant's *Psycho*', Catherine Constable examines the contradictions inherent in the critical denunciation of van Sant's film; her analysis of the film's production and reception reveals the complexity of fidelity as a mode of adaptation practice, and the paradoxes of fidelity as a critical criterion. Through close attention to the relationship between van Sant's film and its multiple 'originals' – the film, the screenplay and the shooting script – Constable demonstrates how the self-reflexivity of the 1998 *Psycho* is productive of new meanings.

Analogies between the remake and the adaptation are also the concern of 'Affecting fidelity: adaptation, fidelity and affect in Todd Haynes's *Far From Heaven*', in which Rachel Carroll reflects on the critical recuperation of these once-compromised film and television genres. Haynes's 2002 film *Far From Heaven* – a homage to Douglas Sirk's 1955 melodrama *All That Heaven Allows* – offers another instance of 'perverse fidelity', albeit one which met with a more favourable reception. Consideration of the affective dimension of fidelity in relation to a gendered film genre – the 'women's picture' – is here employed to question the ritual renunciation of fidelity as a 'critically suspect sentiment'.

Intertextual allusion is a cinematic practice entirely in keeping with van Sant and Haynes's auteur status, and yet the degree of fidelity exhibited by their unconventional film remakes seems more akin to the sentiments associated with fandom. In 'The folding text: *Doctor Who*, adaptation and fan fiction', Christopher Marlow notes how the 2005 revival of the BBC's long-running and highly popular science-fiction drama witnessed the passage of some significant 'fans' into positions of authorial power. Marlow demonstrates how issues of 'canon' and authorship, in relation to cult texts and their audiences, have been transformed by the proliferation of fan fiction as hosted by new media platforms. Aptly enough for a drama which routinely confounds concepts of linear time, *Doctor Who* similarly complicates the conventional temporal structures of adaptation. Employing a Derridean reading, Marlow suggests how the most recent iteration of *Doctor Who* folds into itself the sometimes transgressive fictional extrapolations of its fans; in this way, the 'new' *Doctor Who* – itself scripted and directed by fans who have 'crossed over' – has origins in sources which are themselves adaptations.

After-images

Marlow explores the ways in which a popular revival of a cult genre must address two audiences simultaneously: the expert and the unknowing. In '*3:10* again: a remade Western and the problem of authenticity', Pete Falconer examines the genre movie as adaptation, with reference to a 2007 remake of a classic Hollywood Western. Here questions of fidelity pertain not simply to the 'source text' but more broadly to the conventions of a genre with which the original audience would be familiar but into which the less knowing audience must be inducted. From the vantage point of a film remake, Falconer offers insights into 'period' adaptation, reflecting on the tensions between fidelity to a historical past and fidelity to the conventions of a classic genre.

The authenticity of the Western remake would seem to reside less in its deference to a prior authorial signature than in its fidelity to a specific mode of representation, here dictated by genre. In 'Child's play: participation in urban space in Weegee's, Dassin's and Debord's versions of *Naked City*', Joe Kember explores the intertextual relationship between a series of texts produced in the 1940s and 1950s, which appeared in contexts ranging from the tabloid press to the avant garde manifesto. The continuity which Kember discerns is not attributed simply to a common source text – Weegee's celebrated photographic portfolio – but rather to a shared repertoire of 'playful, experimental or even transgressive' representational strategies for the depiction of urban experience; drawing on Henri Lefebvre's 'rhythmanalysis', Kember traces a signature tension between motifs of immersion and detachment as a defining feature of the *Naked City* text/s.

Twenty-first-century children's play provides the context for Cathlena Martin's exploration of transmedia intertextuality in 'Charlotte's website: media transformation and the intertextual web of children's culture'. As a classic of children's literature, E. B. White's 1952 novel *Charlotte's Web* has been adapted for the screen as both animated and live-action feature films; Martin places its adaptation to video game in the context of current debates about remediation. For the child consumer immersed in convergence culture, *Charlotte's Web* becomes an intertext with multiple manifestations whose brand identity is affirmed by familiar graphics and common marketing strategies, rather than authorial origin.

The kinds of anthropomorphic strategies employed in media adaptations of *Charlotte's Web* are investigated by Paul Wells in '"Stop writing or write like a rat": becoming animal in animated literary adaptations'. Animated adaptations of Maurice Sendak's *Where the Wild Things Are*, P. L. Travers's *Mary Poppins* and George Orwell's *Animal Farm* are situated within a critical paradigm of 'bestial ambivalence'; employing Deleuze and Guattari's concept of 'becoming animal', Wells investigates the complex ways in which such adaptations mediate the relationship between human and animal.

Reproducing the Past

In 'Historicizing the classic novel adaptation: *Bleak House* (2005) and British television contexts', Iris Kleinecke-Bates explores the role of television in mediating popular understandings of the past and, more particularly, the impact of classic adaptations of Dickens on perceptions of the Victorian era. Focusing on the 2005 BBC television adaptation of

Bleak House, she examines the historicity of television as a medium and the changing conventions of period drama. Iris Kleinecke-Bates suggests that the acclaimed 'soap opera' format of the 2005 adaptation can be seen as a signifier both of fidelity to the original publication conditions of the source text and of nostalgia for television's own history in its return to earlier traditions of period drama serialization. Iris Kleinecke-Bates notes how the 2005 *Bleak House* marked a departure from the heritage aesthetic which prevailed in classic adaptations in the 1980s and early 1990s.

The cultural politics of this genre is the focus of Karen Wells's examination of a contemporary heritage film for children in 'Embodying Englishness: representations of whiteness, class and Empire in *The Secret Garden*'. Wells places Agnieskza Holland's 2003 film adaptation of Frances Hodgson Burnett's 1911 novel in the multicultural context of its contemporary child audience; she argues that a 'scopic regime of race' is at work in the film which serves to heighten representations of whiteness while diminishing Burnett's questioning of class and imperial hierarchies.

In 'Taming the velvet: lesbian identity in cultural adaptations of *Tipping the Velvet*', Heather Emmens explores a doubly mediated adaptation of the past: the BBC 2002 television adaptation of Sarah Waters's 1998 neo-Victorian fiction. Drawing on Judith Butler's analysis of cultural repetitions as having both 'disruptive' and 'domesticating' effects, Emmens examines the cultural politics of lesbian representability with particular reference to what she terms the 'femme-inization' of lesbian visibility in mainstream popular culture. Emmens argues that the Andrew Davies's-scripted adaptation not only supplanted Waters's authorship but also rescripted her queer text for consumption by an implied male heterosexual audience. The tensions between disruption and domestication are further investigated with reference to popular appropriations of Davies's adaptation, in the form of a tabloid newspaper's pornographic 'tribute' to *Tipping the Velvet*, and a comic television pastiche.

The gendered and racial politics of reproductive sexuality are explored by Terryl Bacon and Govinda Dickman in '"Who's the Daddy?": the aesthetics and politics of representation in Alfonso Cuarón's adaptation of P. D. James's *Children of Men*'. Speculative fictions rewrite the present as the putative past of a fictional future; analysing Cuarón's film as 'remediating' the present, Bacon and Dickman interrogate the ostensible liberalism of its stance on race, postmodernity and globalization. Situating *Children of Men* within current cinematic trends, they examine the 'spectacularization' of James's narrative as effected by immersive camera techniques and CGI simulation. More specifically, Bacon and Dickman interrogate the racial and gendered displacements at work in the adaptation whereby responsibility for a dystopian future – figuratively extrapolated from a contemporary present – is shifted from white men to women and racial 'others'.

Afterlives

In 'Origin and ownership: stage, film and television adaptations of Daphne du Maurier's *Rebecca*', Rebecca D'Monté explores the afterlives of du Maurier's 1938 fiction, itself a reworking of Charlotte Brontë's 1847 novel *Jane Eyre*. D'Monté considers the 1940 stage and film adaptations within the contexts both of prevailing theatrical and cinematic conventions – the drawing-room drama and the female Gothic respectively – and contemporary historical conditions, specifically wartime anxieties about the preservation of national and gendered identities. By contrast, the 1920s setting of the 1997 television adaptation is examined as symptomatic of the heritage trend in classic adaptation, and as constructing an earlier post-war period as the location for a more explicit depiction of sexual transgression. As the author of both a 'reauthored' fiction – itself extensively reworked by subsequent writers – and of an 'unfaithful' stage adaptation of her own novel, du Maurier exemplifies the complexities of authorship as a category of cultural production.

In 'The post-feminist biopic: re-telling the past in *Iris*, *The Hours* and *Sylvia*', Josephine Dolan, Suzy Gordon and Estella Tincknell explore the reproduction of the past as mediated not only by film genre – ranging from heritage pictorialism to Sirkian melodrama – but also by the biopic as a mode of public history. Issues of gender, authorship and agency are foregrounded in their analysis of biopics of women writers adapted from male authored biographical texts. The pre-feminist 1950s prove a key reference point for these films, whose 'post-feminist' location in relation to second-wave feminism is examined. Dolan, Gordon and Tincknell argue that the depiction of Iris Murdoch, Virginia Woolf and Sylvia Plath in these films serves not only to reiterate a problematic association between female creativity and 'madness', but also to posit a nominally reconstructed masculinity as the casualty of female agency.

In 'For the love of Jane: Austen, adaptation and celebrity', Brenda R. Weber considers the extension of the proliferating Austen adaptation canon to the undocumented 'text' of her life. She explores the persistent fascination with Austen's romantic life as expressed within the 'second canon' of Austen-inspired material; the fidelity of late-twentieth- and twenty-first-century 'Janeites' is situated in the context of contemporary cultures of fandom and celebrity. In response to the heteronormative imperatives at work in much fictional speculation on Austen's 'life-text', Weber argues that Austen's sorophilia – as depicted in the 2008 television biopic *Miss Austen Regrets* – can be understood as the model for her narrative evocations of affective attachment.

The afterlives of adapted texts and authors are the focus of this final section; the collection concludes with a chapter dedicated to a novel which figures itself as the afterlife of imaginary films. In '*Glamorama*, cinematic narrative and contemporary fiction', Ruth Helyer reads Bret Easton Ellis as 'an author adapted by his own texts'. His 1991 novel

Glamorama – as yet unadapted for the screen, unlike his notorious *American Psycho* – is examined as a 'cinematic narrative' which self-consciously evokes and emulates cinematic narrative techniques. More-over, Helyer suggests that it depicts a postmodern 'reality' so thoroughly mediated by film and celebrity culture that its protagonists are reduced to 'models' with no original; perpetually performing their identities, they act out their roles as if for an adaptation of their own lives.

Part I

Remaking Fidelity

CHAPTER TWO

Heavy Bodies, Fragile Texts: Stage Adaptation and the Problem of Presence

FRANCES BABBAGE

It is dark. I stretch out an arm and hit a wall: cool, slippery. My fingers discover a door, turn a handle – but it is locked. Briefly, I am alarmed: there is no one else here and it's quiet – muffled – my face is covered, my breathing amplified. And although I don't really believe it, I allow myself to think: what if I am trapped in here? And I think: I should not be in here. I turn abruptly and give a little gasp as I bump into a body. It moves – thankfully – and clutches my arm, and together we stumble through a curtained alcove and I am somewhere new.

    The light is more generous now. It is a bedroom: a woman's, I decide, although minus its occupant. Something about the clutter: the jumble of bottles – perfume? – and impression of lace. I look away from tumbled bed-sheets to walls almost obscured by scraps of paper, all pinned to the faded flock. I make out the diminutive writing on one card: a recipe to cure consumption ('Take one peck of small garden snails and a quart of earthworms', it begins). Those bottles – not perfume, but medicine: Piso's Consumption Cure; Dr Kilmer's Indian Cough Cure Consumption Oil. I turn to my companion from the other room, but there is no one there. I could be alone throughout this, I think: just me, my thoughts and a succession of rooms, unpeopled, yet not lifeless. Leaving by a different door I am almost knocked over by a man running past, pursued by another in a top hat shouting: 'Sir – I demand the satisfaction of a gentleman.' Masked figures hurry after these two down a corridor: I follow.[1]

This is Punchdrunk Theatre's *The Masque of the Red Death*, staged at Battersea Arts Centre in 2007–08: or rather, my experience of it. It is a truism of theatre that no two spectators, present the same night, witness the same show. Here the claim is literally true: Punchdrunk, formed in 2000, specialize in productions where an entire building is transformed into a labyrinthine installation through which spectators move freely over the course of a few hours. Performance experience is fragmented on many levels: you may catch a narrative when the scene is finishing, or, as I did, find yourself in rooms which seem palpably only recently abandoned. You may decide to leave a scene halfway through, itself just a fragment of a larger narrative the actors do not choose to share. There may be sequences you hear about yet never find, whilst others you stumble on repeatedly. One may be improvised uniquely for you alone. You can observe; you can interact, with characters and material things (there is an abundance of 'things'). You can do almost anything, except remove the anonymous mask you receive on arrival – or, perhaps, depart before Punchdrunk want you to.

In this chapter I examine two principal questions. First, how far can a performance form like this – a vast installation-cum-promenade that invites spectators to receive scenes in any order and demands they miss some altogether – be considered to 'adapt' literary texts? What becomes of narrative in such circumstances, and does this matter? Second, what relationships might exist between private prior acquaintance with a source text and the opportunities for reception which the live encounter provides? In addressing that second question I refer directly to my own, necessarily subjective, engagement with the 'texts' of Punchdrunk and Poe, and set this alongside other equally impressionistic responses from others who attended during the show's seven-month sell-out run. Beyond these, I refer to the 'authoritative' assessments of media critics. A quantity of perspectives are considered, yet in their multiplicity the impression that forms becomes less coherent, not more so. How can one evaluate work where spectator engagement has been so fundamentally diverse – indeed, where no consensus exists on what took place? Given that difficulty, whilst I consider the wider implications of such an approach for the creation and reception of theatrical adaptation and risk initial conclusions, my analysis never quite parts company with experience and opinion that is intuitive, unverifiable, and possibly fanciful.

The immersive experience offered by Punchdrunk's *Masque* is not without precedent in the history of stage adaptation. The theatre company Grid Iron, formed in 1995, also specialize in site-specific promenade performance in unusual locations: productions have included an adaptation of Angela Carter's story 'The Bloody Chamber' for Edinburgh's underground vaults in 1997 and Jim Crace's novel *The Devil's Larder* for the Old City Morgue in Cork in 2005 (www.gridiron. org.uk). Another company, Wildworks, emerged from an artistic collaboration titled *Three Islands Project*, an ambitious adaptation of the Gabriel Garcia Marquez story 'A Very Old Man with Enormous Wings', realized on three separate occasions in large-scale outdoor production on Malta, Cyprus and at home in Cornwall between 2003 and 2005 (www.wildworks.biz). Such projects are not representative of theatrical adaptation as wider practice, yet since I deal here with fundamental issues concerning dramatic treatments of literature – with 'problems' that reinvention of prose for performance must always confront – I preface discussion of my central example, Punchdrunk, by situating this alongside more familiar adaptation practices.

The tradition of adapting non-dramatic literature for the stage is longstanding. Today it is rare that listings for any major theatre in the country, in any season, do not include at least one adaptation; most have more.[2] The status of production *as* adaptation is not always foregrounded; understandably, marketing will highlight the perceived strongest draw. But where adaptation is announced as such, today's theatre audiences have come to accept – to expect – ever more inventive dramaturgical strategies from its creators. No longer is a novel rejected for adaptation, for instance, on grounds of the quantity of settings in the original; nor is the typical solution to this problem the resituating of dramatic action within limited, practically realizable locations. I give one example to show how conceptions of stage adaptation have shifted over recent decades, with reference to a source – not Poe, but equally Gothic – presenting numerous difficulties for theatrical transposition.

Bram Stoker's *Dracula*, (in)famous novel of the Victorian *fin-de-siècle*, has been repeatedly adapted to the cinema screen – indeed, so significant a presence has the Count found here that, as Linda Hutcheon notes, 'films about Dracula today are as often seen as adaptations of other earlier films as they are of Bram Stoker's novel' (2006: 21). This is not equally true of *Dracula*'s adaptations for the theatre, although there are many. The ephemerality of live performance, and the smaller numbers reached, mean that collective cultural memory of stage adaptation's history – in general and in this instance – will always be less strongly marked. The problems *Dracula* poses for stage or screen are manifold. There is its epistolary structure, seemingly giving access to the viewpoints of multiple narrators; the plot – journeying from Transylvania to London, Whitby and back again – presents another difficulty; the sheer quantity of characters, still another. Beyond any of these is the challenge of finding form for that which defies representation, because it is otherworldly. The immediacy and intimacy of stage-spectator contact, which is theatre's strength, may conversely make this medium less able than film to give effective shape to a figure as shadowy as the vampire.

The first licensed staging of *Dracula*, by actor-manager Hamilton Deane and opening in London in 1924, compressed Stoker's unwieldy narrative into three acts, two set in Jonathan Harker's study and one in Mina Harker's boudoir. Omitted as 'unstageable' were the entire first section of the novel recording Harker's harrowing experiences in Transylvania, and the pursuit of Dracula to his native land. These decisions, although radical, were not detrimental to the production's success: it ran for a record-breaking 391 performances at three London theatres, followed by a still more profitable Broadway transfer. The notoriety Deane's adaptation achieved was partly due to a sensational epilogue which saw the Count 'staked' in his coffin, a magician's disappearing box allowing him to 'crumble bloodlessly into dust before the audience's eyes' (Skal 1993: 63). The moment was highly effective, if efficacy can be measured by the reported statistic that, on average, seven spectators fainted each night (Ludlam 1977: 180). The critics proved less susceptible. *Punch*'s reviewer mocked the 'grave conscientious[ness]' of the actors, incongruous within what should have been allowed to become 'full-blooded' melodrama, concluding that such scenes must always be 'more seriously alarming between the pages of a book than they are in the three-dimensional medium of the stage' (Skal 1993: 10).

More recent dramatizations have taken advantage of familiarity with anti-illusionist stage conventions to adopt alternative strategies in tackling the challenges posed. Liz Lochhead's 1985 version, first staged at Edinburgh's Royal Lyceum, made striking use of a composite set in which Dracula's castle remained present and visible throughout, at times more, at times less clearly lit: the distinction between Transylvania and England, alien and familiar, was literally made hazy, reinforcing the play's refusal to align the threatened crisis unproblematically with a foreign 'other'. A decade later, Hull Truck Theatre Company staged a new *Dracula* adaptation by Jane Thornton and John Godber at their own theatre in Hull, and like Lochhead found a radical 'solution' to the structural challenges inherent in the source text. This version had a cast of just six and played on what was *'essentially an empty stage. A few old chairs, upstage a raised area connected by ramps. Candles, cobwebs, a plethora of coffins'* (Thornton and Godber 1998: 1). Through imaginative manipulation of this sparse set, the 'impossible' became stageable: for example, Dracula could now descend head first down the 'castle wall' evoked by a lifted ramp – an unforgettable image in Stoker's book and one that Deane had desired as a prologue for his 1924 adaptation but which was judged 'too expensive and cumbersome for touring' (Skal 1993: 3).

Hull Truck's production can be placed within a contemporary tradition of physical theatre – influenced by such practitioners as Jerzy Grotowski and Jacques Lecoq – whereby the actor is made emphatically the channel through which narrative interactions, events, even locations are conveyed. Direct representation of place or scenic shift is judged not just unnecessary but potentially an actual impediment to establishing a stage-spectator relationship in which liveness and creativity are paramount. It is not difficult to make the leap from this 1995 *Dracula* to another, staged by Northern Ballet Theatre at the West Yorkshire Playhouse in 2005. David Nixon's production employed a simple *mise-en-scène* of Gothic architectural images which served as evocative backdrop for a performance language composed of movement, light and shadow, and costume designed to extend the expressive capacities of the dancer's body. Adaptation of novel to ballet necessarily allows much licence, especially since, as Patrick Flanery has argued, the latter has traditionally been considered 'something like the antithesis of literature'; anticipating subtraction of the verbal dimension, audiences of dance theatre will expect a production that assumes a distinctively new shape (Flanery 2008).

These overtly 'physical theatres' have not ousted more realistic representation, nor do they threaten to do so: nonetheless, their influence on the contemporary stage is profound. Today, the actor/performer, as opposed to the character, will likely be the heart of an adaptation. Typically, polysemic designs or a bare space are substituted for illustrative stage sets. No list of key players should omit Théâtre de Complicité, Shared Experience or Kneehigh Theatre, all leaders in this field and part of a growing body of companies whose reinventions of prose texts for performance collectively celebrate the actor's capability seemingly to embody any narrative, any image. Increasingly, the principles that underpin contemporary anti-illusionist theatre allow – indeed, actively encourage – freedoms in adaptation that, by implication, invite us to find more representative treatments unsatisfactory, their expressive potential literally encumbered by the weight of their properties.

Given this trend in contemporary stage adaptation to cast off ever more decisively the 'trappings' of realistic representation, it is intriguing that Punchdrunk should adopt what is in one sense the reverse approach. In their work, the stage set is brought back with a vengeance, establishing as complete an illusion as the company can muster: director Felix Barrett's designers apply a 'cinematic level of detail' to the host space, aiming 'to immerse the audience in the world of the play' (www. punchdrunk.org.uk). The place of performance becomes the central character of the drama. Of course, the performers themselves still matter, and they make strong impressions on us – the tantalizing fragments of dialogue and fiercely physical, erotic sequences of partner dance, choreographed by Maxine Doyle and now a Punchdrunk trademark – but such scenes can flash past spectators, somewhat; the invitation to linger in and dwell upon the event is fundamentally bound to one's relationship with the extraordinary created space. In that relationship, the stated intent of 'immersion' is not fully achieved, I suggest, if this implies one is wholly submerged in the illusion to the point where the structures beyond and beneath this disappear from consciousness. Part of the pleasure in participation derives from recognition of the marriage of features already present in the building with the dressings imposed upon it, a union in which it becomes difficult to judge 'real' from 'fake'. The layering of place that results and which characterizes site-specific performance as a genre has been described by Mike Pearson and Cliff McLucas, directors of Welsh performance company Brith Gof, as indicative of tensions between 'the host and the ghost'. For McLucas, these terms seek to articulate 'the relationship between place and event. The host site is haunted for a time by a ghost that the theatre-makers create. Like all ghosts it is transparent and the host can be seen through the ghost' (Kaye 2000: 128). Pearson elaborates on this:

> Site-specific performances rely upon the complex superimposition and co-existence of a number of narratives and architectures, historical and contemporary. These fall into two groups: those that pre-exist the work – of the host – and those which are of the work – of the ghost. (Taylor 1997: 95–6)

Useful as this host/ghost dynamic proves as a way to articulate the operations and effects of performance that exploits unusual and challenging sites, or uses conventional theatre buildings in an unconventional way, in examining Punchdrunk's *Masque* we must add another layer. There are narratives in play here that derive neither from host nor ghost, but are brought by the spectators themselves. I do not speak (although I could) of the ways in which spectator engagement might be shaped by personal acquaintance with company or building (and Battersea Arts Centre, the 'host', would be deeply familiar to many attending). I refer to the narratives of Poe, as these exist in the imagination and memories of audience members. Some may come 'innocently' – that is, with no such prior knowledge – and the extent to which the event acquaints them with Poe's work is, regrettably, the subject of another essay. But what space can be found, in this production, for the Poe that many of us must bring in our heads?

Despite its title, Punchdrunk's production adapts not one but several of Poe's 'tales of terror': 'The Fall of the House of Usher', 'The Cask of Amontillado', and 'William Wilson', among others. Poe's brides were there – Berenice, Ligeia, Eleonora – those doomed, skeletal creatures I sometimes struggle to tell apart. 'The Masque of the Red Death' provides the framing story, appropriately so since it leads its reader through a succession of rooms, each more extraordinary than the last. In this tale, a plague has fallen on the country. The rooms are chambers in the palace of Prince Prospero and while the disease rages beyond its walls, the Prince and his friends enjoy a decadent party. They believe themselves safe from the plague until a mysterious guest arrives dressed in graveclothes and corpse-like mask 'besprinkled with the scarlet horror' (Poe 1986: 258). Death has stolen in amongst the revellers, Poe says, 'like a thief in the night' (Poe 1986: 260).

I have always loved Poe's stories, being guiltily fond of his deranged heroes and moribund, mutilated heroines.[3] I have seen these filmed, incomparably in the 'Poe cycle' of American International Pictures, vehicles for an increasingly self-parodic Vincent Price. I have listened to them translated into opera, in works by Peter Hammill (1991) and Philip Glass (1987). I have watched them in the theatre, memorably Steven Berkoff's 1974 version of 'Usher' (I saw it in the 1990s), as well as amateur adaptations of 'Hop-Frog', 'The Tell-Tale Heart' and 'The Black Cat'. But in all cases, whatever liberties were taken with narrative, however great the impact of the formal transposition, the adaptations were conventional to the point that they sought to (re)tell a story, as well as rouse our senses and enshroud us in atmosphere. Punchdrunk's production was different. 'Adaptation' is not the company's term – 'dramatic intervention and interpretation' is the single phrase they use referring to the relationship of performance to prior text(s) – but I apply it here nevertheless, borrowing Hutcheon's definition of adaptation as 'an extended, deliberate, announced revisitation of a particular work of art', 'a derivation that is not derivative', coming 'second without being secondary' (Hutcheon 2006: 170, 9). By these terms, the definition fits. The show's programme suggests two, equally valued subjects: the first, Poe; the second, Punchdrunk. As noted, there is almost nothing there about adaptation: it is for us to fill in the gaps, the implication being that the created event represents a dynamic fusion of two complementary artistic forces (albeit with only one party's consent).

As adaptation, Punchdrunk's production is distinctive in that it does not attempt to tell the stories it references. Attending it was like fingering my own copy of Poe's tales pulled from a fire, as if left with no more than remnants, pages charred and quantities missing, but the text in my hands still vividly evocative of that which, somehow, I consider Poe to be: the stories as *I* recall them; the unquantifiable 'spirit' of the material. The openly subjective character of this analogy prompts me to return to the binaries of 'fidelity' and 'betrayal', terms that have been largely discredited within adaptation studies – and rightly so, as the problems they raise are too numerous to recount. But we should not dismiss those terms out of hand, even given the difficulties they present, since when encountering adaptation as 'knowing' audience – in other words, experiencing it *as* adaptation – one's response can be profoundly subjective: 'that's not how I saw it' is a reaction so instinctive and understandable that it should not be repressed by being judged academically unbecoming. After all, is it not a risk that in refusing to invite such terms openly into discussion they haunt it all the more?

In my own three hours with Punchdrunk, in all its fragmentation, missed moments and repetitions, I felt drawn decisively into the world of Poe's fiction. The experience reflected the 'Poe' with whom I am familiar: extravagant, obsessive, ludicrous, poetic, morbid, perverse. The lavish provision of the visual and physical, with a relative sparsity of text, seemed an apt translation of Poe's own preference for unusual 'effect' above reliance on action and incident (Poe 1986: 481). At the same time, this approach revealed cavalier disregard for another of Poe's aesthetic principles: the vital importance of literary structure. An effective 'plot', for Poe, is one where 'no one of its component parts shall be susceptible of *removal* without *detriment* to the whole' (Poe 1986: 457); his works – if we believe him – were constructed with almost mathematical precision (Poe 1986: 480–92). But the company not only played fast and loose with Poe's tales – extracting only small fragments and adding much invention – but largely relinquished control of the way spectators received these: we witnessed some moments but not all, and recognized that some would be differently improvised by performers each night, if repeated at all. By no means would I term Punchdrunk's work unstructured. On the contrary, its organization was highly sophisticated. Rather, in place of controlled narrative composition, the company substitute event composition – and for that event to be possible, narrative 'wholeness' was sacrificed, perhaps gleefully abandoned.

A seasoned spectator of Punchdrunk, which I am not, might take a more cynical line on the production's treatment of Poe. Many who saw *Masque* had attended the company's *Faust* the year before, and so broadly knew what to expect.[4] One, who found *Faust* 'wonderful', appeared already jaded: for him, *Masque* was a version of the same, still wonderful, he allowed, but ultimately 'more of the wonderful same' (Rebellato 2008). One might begin to suspect that the particularities of the source material could be less important for the company than the manner of production: could any source – literary or otherwise – be given a 'Punchdrunk treatment'?

I had not seen the company's work before, however, and was powerfully affected by it. I admired the scale of the achievement, and still do: it was a stunning, generous installation, vast in scale yet obsessed with minutiae, its performances skilled, witty, frequently audacious. But more importantly, I appreciated what it did with Poe. Actually, to get to the heart of it, I appreciated most what it *did not* do with Poe. Punchdrunk did not present 'Roderick Usher' and leave me to judge his likeness to a preconceived idea. I cannot say if the woman I saw dressed by her maid was Berenice or Rowena, nor if it was she who sought the cure for consumption (she was certainly pale). The performers did not enact 'The Tell-Tale Heart' to the accompaniment of a ticking clock. They did not 'enact' much at all. They gave beginnings, but not an end. They did not drown out the fragile, hazy impressions of Poe's tales that I have in my mind; they left space for my own (pre)-readings. This sounds like faint praise: am I merely saying that they did not *spoil* Poe for me?

Actually, I want to argue that for Punchdrunk not to ruin 'my' Poe is no insignificant achievement. Literature, and the experience of reading, is one pleasure; dramatic performance brings rewards that are equally profound. This twin fascination draws us towards adaptation, but simultaneously instils terror of it. I have sympathy with Philip Hensher, writing here in reference to the BBC's 2005 production of *Bleak House*:

> The main reason for not watching this dramatisation, or . . . any dramatisation of *Bleak House* ever again is knowing that one would sit there with gritted teeth waiting for some magnificently unnecessary moment [in Dickens' narrative], groaning with pain at its omission or suffering an only temporary relief. (Hensher 2005)

Hensher's is an extreme position, its implication being that the only conceivably acceptable 'retelling' would – as in the Borges story, 'Pierre Menard, Author of the Quixote' – have to be one where no single word of the original was either added to, or removed. I would not go so far. The conviction that theatrical sensibility can meet literature in ways that are unique and valuable maintains my patience with adaptation as a practice, but keeps me largely more engaged by and enthusiastic for its marginal experiments than its dominant centre.

One study that could help us theorize dramatic adaptation does not directly address the subject at all. Elaine Scarry's *Dreaming by the Book* (1999) considers the means by which poets and writers of prose facilitate the reader's process of mental composition: much of the book is devoted to examining the kind of textual strategies that bring literature 'to life' in the minds of its recipients. Scarry argues that the challenge faced by such authors is to build impressions of vivacity and substance in the non-material realm of the imagination. Her point is not that, as readers, we construct entire mental stage sets for *Madame Bovary*, or *Silas Marner*, but rather that – to take the latter – we memorably 'see' the soft yellow ringlets of the child Eppie, as Marner does, and with him recognize these as replacement for the golden guineas that were stolen from him. Works of literature – repetitive black marks on a white page – thus strive to achieve texture, shade, movement, weight, in our reception of them. But if as Scarry suggests this is the challenge for poetry and prose, I would argue that dramatic adaptation of such texts meets that challenge in reverse: here, the problem becomes one of preventing an excess of noise, colour and corporeality – an overabundance of presence – from trampling too heavily upon the mental images that haunt spectators who (re-)receive such texts through performance. This in essence is the problem of which Hensher complains: 'The main reason for not wanting to watch this *Bleak House* is simply that one doesn't want it in one's head.' He claims further that the 'better the dramatisation, the worse the danger that another imagination will interpose itself between the author's and the reader's: one nothing to do with either' (Hensher 2005). Hensher writes of televised adaptation, and here maybe the clash of visions he dreads is especially jarring. Drama on film tends towards realism, crowding the screen with 'information' that this aesthetic demands but which was not required in the literary original. As Jonathan Miller has commented, '[i]n some mysterious way, the description of a scene [in a novel] appears to be fully occupied by what it describes and never appears to lack what it fails to mention' (Giddings, Selby and Wensley 1990: 18).

Unlike drama on film, drama on stage necessarily favours more selective representation of the 'real'. My commentary on successive treatments of *Dracula* sketched a trajectory whereby adaptations seemed progressively more agile, confident in their ability to convey the 'essence' of a source and discard all that is deemed inessential. But that depends on how one chooses to remember a show. Thinking back now on all three *Draculas*, I retain more powerfully from the memory an excitement at what could have been, rather than what was. The boldest leaps come back to land, sometimes with a too-audible thump. In moments of Hensheresque frustration, we might feel that even the smartest, most spirited takes on a text are literally just that: they 'take' something that mattered, or at least intrude painfully upon it. One could adopt Hensher's line: if it means that much to you, don't watch it. But I want to argue for adaptation that can excite and inspire, and yet serve a know-ing audience with kindness. Pursuing my reversal of Scarry, such an adaptation would begin to undo its own completeness: it would con-trive to destabilize and undermine the very structures – temporal, spa-tial, bodily, aural – that stage production must necessarily erect. This deconstruction could admit the possibility of more subtle negotiation between the physical here-and-now of the theatre, and the intangible 'non-place' of multifarious images and preconceptions rooted in the minds of a potential audience.

I have argued that Punchdrunk's Poe achieved a balance between what was given and what withheld. Nevertheless, a show like this one will always be a controversial model for adaptation. Some spectators who were not already familiar with Poe reported that they found it 'hard to understand' (Pilbeam 2008), 'too fragmentary to grip' (Worth 2008), with 'many hints but not enough certainties' (Francis 2008); one who did know the tales still 'had trouble finding any Poe folks at all in the murky bowels' of the Battersea Arts Centre (Isherwood 2008). Yet if this production's treatment of its source did not leave an innocent audience much wiser, this need not constitute criticism; I would not argue that an adaptation's merit lies in its ability to make us feel we 'know' literature we have not read. But despite these problems and dis-satisfactions, I propose that participatory site-specific performance, here exemplified by Punchdrunk, is a form that might provocatively 'adapt' texts and textuality in ways that delicately circumvent the excess of presence that too often overburdens adaptations for the stage.

In conclusion, I return briefly to our physical mode of engagement with Punchdrunk and the implications of this for the event as adapta-tion. Spectators are masked; it is dark, intentionally disorientating; you may arrive in a group, but find yourself alone. Reviewing the produc-tion favourably, Michael Billington introduced the caveat that 'whereas the joy of most theatre is that one participates in a collective experience, here the stress is on individually determined journeys' (Billington 2007). The point is fair, but perhaps the degree of isolation one encounters is simultaneously that which supports and makes space for cherished individual attachments to the source. And whilst one is essentially alone during the event, there is a kind of community that comes afterwards. So many people have spoken about this show, written about it, added to blogs about it, all eager to share what 'their' three hours meant to them. I conclude with the thoughts of other spectators, in other words, with more of the impressionistic, individualistic responses which I acknow-ledged at the outset as inseparable from this debate:

> It felt so complete . . . so detailed, full and empty . . . at times I felt physically dirty; I could feel desperation and life within rooms . . . as well as death. (Gasparetto 2008)

A woman washing bloody rags, medical detritus . . . A wardrobe with no back that led into space and out through a fireplace into a room with a large table. A Narnia moment – my favourite of the whole experience. It haunted me for several days as I remembered the atmosphere, the detail of the furnishings and costumes, but I have no memory of a story, of a tale. (Nowell 2008)

[T]here are moments of unforgettable quiet; you go into a room – fire in the grate, oil lamp glinting on sepia photographs – to find a Victorian matron playing a piano, nothing seems to be happening, but her life rustles around her. (Clapp 2007)

I felt I had stepped into the text and was able to be a character, viewed by other spectators but not the actors themselves. I felt my experience was totally my own and unshared. (Mensah 2008)

Notes

Thanks also to Bridget Escolme, Clare Finburgh, Wendy Frost, John Keefe, Rob Neumark Jones and Fernanda Prata, whose comments on Punchdrunk's production have helped shape this chapter but are not directly quoted here.

1. I attended *The Masque of the Red Death* on 16 January 2008. My account is impressionistic, as I did not make notes during the performance itself (it would scarcely have been possible); the writing I describe from the card is only what subsequent research suggests might well have been there.
2. Leeds' West Yorkshire Playhouse, for example, has four adaptations in the 2008 Autumn/ Winter season: George Orwell, Edward Gorey, J. M. Barrie and Kester Aspden are sources.
3. See for example Poe's Berenice, whose teeth are extracted while she is still alive.
4. Rebecca Pilbeam (2008) comments that having seen *Faust* she 'knew the show would play through twice so . . . didn't have to panic too much about missing anything first time round', and she noted that the audience received 'the white masks we had also worn for *Faust*'.

Bibliography

Berkoff, Steven (1990), *Agamemnon and The Fall of the House of Usher*. Charlbury: Amber Lane Press.

Billington, Michael (2007), *The Guardian*, 4 October.

Clapp, Susannah (2007), 'Into the velvet darkness. . .'. *The Observer*, 7 October.

Deane, Hamilton and Balderston, John L. (1993), *Dracula*. David Skal, (ed. and annotated). New York: St Martin's Press.

Flanery, Patrick (2008), 'Adapting classics'. (Pre-performance lecture given at Sheffield's Lyceum Theatre for Northern Ballet Theatre's *A Tale of Two Cities*. 1 October 2008.) Unpublished.

Francis, Penny (2008), Personal interview. (Attended performance of 12 December 2007.)

Gasparetto, Angela (2008), Personal interview. (Attended performance of 29 February 2008.)

Giddings, Robert, Keith Selby and Chris Wensley (1990), *Screening the Novel.* London: Macmillan.

Grid Iron Theatre Co. website: *www.gridiron.org.uk.* (Accessed 8 December 2008.)

Hensher, Philip (2005), 'You'll never catch me watching it'. *The Guardian,* 7 November.

Hutcheon, Linda (2006), *A Theory of Adaptation.* London and New York: Routledge.

Isherwood, Charles (2008), 'When audiences get in on the act'. *The New York Times,* 10 February.

Lochhead, Liz (1989), *Mary Queen of Scots Got Her Head Chopped Off and Dracula.* London: Penguin.

Ludlam, Harry (1977), *A Biography of Bram Stoker.* London: Nel Books.

Mensah, Ena (2008), Personal interview. (Attended performance of 21 March 2008.)

McLucas, Clifford (2000), 'Ten feet and three-quarters of an inch of theatre' in Nick Kaye (ed.), *Site-Specific Art.* London: Routledge, pp. 125–37.

Nowell, Tess (2008), Personal interview. (Attended performance of 2 April 2008.)

Pearson, Mike (1997), 'Special worlds and secret maps: a poetics of perform-ance' in Anna-Marie Taylor (ed.), *Staging Wales: Welsh Theatre 1979–1997.* Cardiff: University of Wales Press, pp. 85–99.

Pilbeam, Rebecca (2007), Personal interview. (Attended performance of 11 October 2007.)

Poe, Edgar Allan (1986), *The Fall of the House of Usher and Other Writings.* David Galloway (ed.). Harmondsworth: Penguin.

Punchdrunk Theatre Co. website: *www.punchdrunktheatre.org.uk.* (Accessed 8 December 2008.)

Rebellato, Dan (2008), Personal interview. (Attended performance of 19 November 2007.)

Scarry, Elaine (1999), *Dreaming By the Book.* Princeton, New Jersey: Princeton University Press.

Stoker, Bram (1997), *Dracula.* Nina Auerbach and David Skal (ed. and anno-tated). New York and London: Norton.

Thornton, Jane and John Godber (1998), *Dracula.* London: Warner/Chappell Plays.

Wildworks Theatre Co. website: *www.wildworks.biz.* (Accessed 8 December 2008.)

Worth, Libby (2008), Personal interview. (Attended performance of 6 March 2008.)

CHAPTER THREE

Reflections on the Surface: Remaking the Postmodern with van Sant's *Psycho*

CATHERINE CONSTABLE

The critical reception of Gus van Sant's *Psycho* (1998) was overwhelmingly negative. General audiences and academics alike perceived the remake as an outrageous insult to a much-loved classic, Hitchcock's *Psycho*, made in 1960.[1] Indeed, the '*Psycho*: Saving a Classic' website 'urged audiences to express their dissatisfaction [with van Sant's film] by boycotting the opening weekend' (Verevis 2006: 58). Academic writing on *Psycho 98* was equally derisory, Thomas Leitch noting only three exceptions to the general rule.[2] William Rothman's despairing comment, 'the more I dwell on van Sant's *Psycho*, the more it can seem that cinema ... has run its course, that the art of film is declaring bankruptcy' (1999: 29), is an extreme version of a general dismissal of the film itself as aesthetically bankrupt. The critical context gives a certain logical inexorability to James Naremore's conclusion that *Psycho 98* should never have been made: 'A better solution would have been to simply remaster the original 35 mm print and exhibit it around the world' (1999–2000: 12).

Reviews and articles typically dismissed *Psycho 98* as a bad copy of the Master's original. Unfortunately, the terms for its dismissal were provided by Universal's own publicity campaign, which positively flaunted the criterion of fidelity, thereby inviting invidious comparisons with the first film. Leitch summarizes the key conditions governing the film's production (2003). Famously, van Sant was said to have followed Joseph Stefano's dialogue line by line, and John Russell's camera work shot by shot. The remake was made for $20,000,000, the inflation-adjusted equivalent of *Psycho 60*'s $800,000 budget. Finally, van Sant was said to have insisted on adhering to Hitchcock's very tight, 6-week shooting schedule. It seems feasible to suggest that the publicizing of van Sant's embracing such a series of textual and technical constraints was meant to put *Psycho 98* on a par with Hitchcock's own experiments with technical limitations, most obviously the ten-minute take in *Rope* (1948).

The language of fidelity used in the promotional material also generates a model for mapping changes to the original as laudable attempts to restore its full impact/glory. In this way, the remake's restoration of deleted lines from the screenplay, such as Cassidy's line to Marion that bed is 'the only playground to beat Las Vegas', and recreation of impossibly expensive shots from the shooting script, such as the opening helicopter shot across the city, are regarded as expressions of loyalty to 'the original'. However, such loyalty is misguided since it is clear that the vaunted 'original' has proliferated into (at least) three different texts: the film, the screenplay and the shooting script. The publicity surrounding *Psycho 98* thus made it much more than the simple updating of a classic: it set up a quest for a fetishized 'authenticity' that can be seen as a paradoxical attempt to be more Hitchcock than Hitchcock.

The publicity campaign's fetishization of an impossible authenticity plays into fans' and academics' conception of *Psycho 60* as a unique, original text and social event. The valorization of the originality of the first film sustains a series of binary oppositions – original/copy, authentic/imitation – through which the second will always be judged to be lacking. Constantine Verevis argues that the evaluation of *Psycho 98* as a 'cheap imitation' is entirely logical given that most of the critical literature on the remake conceptualizes 'remaking as a one-way process: a movement from authenticity to imitation, from the superior self-identity of the original to the debased resemblance of the copy' (2006: 58). It should also be added that *Psycho 60* has an indisputable claim to 'superior self-identity' in its critical valorization as the epitome of the holistic aesthetics espoused by Cahiers du Cinema, which Sam Ishii-Gonzalès summarizes: 'Rohmer and Chabrol once claimed, "In Hitchcock's work form does not embellish content, it creates it." Form is not added to meaning that is pre-existent. Meaning is discovered in the elaboration of form' (2001–2: 153). The conjunction of form with meaning creates an indissoluble link, a model of each film as an indivisible totality. Ishii-Gonzalès concludes: 'This, for Hitchcock, was the power of "pure cinema"' (2001–2: 153).

The strong sense of the absolute integrity of Hitchcock's texts informs much of the critical literature on *Psycho 98*. The articles follow the 'one-way process' defined by Verevis, most setting out to demonstrate the ways in which the remake as bad copy is fundamentally flawed. Naremore's article is a good example of the double bind in which *Psycho 98* is caught: where it is the same as *Psycho 60* it is merely 'slavish imitation', and 'wherever van Sant diverges from the original he makes bad choices' (1999–2000: 5–6). Interestingly, most of the academic articles that address the text of *Psycho 98* in any detail simply provide lists of the ways in which it diverges from, and thereby loses the aesthetic integrity and/or authorial brilliance of, the original. Ishii-Gonzalès' introduction to his article is a clear example. He aims to demonstrate 'how alterations made to the original structure [of the parlour scene] in the "shot-by-shot" remake manage to divest this sequence not only of its emotional intensity and its thematic resonance but also of Hitchcock' (2001–2: 149). It is worth noting that in this instance writing on the remake closely resembles writing on literature-to-film adaptations, deploying what Robert Stam describes as 'an elegiac discourse of loss, lamenting what has been "lost" in the transition . . . while ignoring what has been gained' (2005: 3).

Importantly, the elegiac discourse constructed around *Psycho 98* often takes a specific form: the lamentation of the loss of depth and the construction of the remake as utterly superficial. Thus, for Adrian Martin, van Sant's film demonstrates that 'you can mechanically copy all the surface moves of a screen classic and still drain it of any meaning, tension, artistry, and fun' (2001–2: 133). Martin's view of the central actors' performances as 'hopelessly wooden and superficial' (2001–2001: 134) is shared by many other critics. Rothman argues that Vince Vaughn's 'obvious weirdness' means that his Norman lacks the emotional depth of Anthony Perkins' (1999: 30); while Leitch argues that Anne Heche's 'sunnier, flightier Marion' lacks the 'gravity of Leigh's' (2003). In these two readings the move to the pure surface is respectively characterized as the loss of the secret – Norman's psychosis as hidden depths – and the loss of gravity/gravitas in the form of Leigh's stolid sincerity and integrity. McDowell augments these analyses by suggesting that the superficiality of the performances prohibits the audience from investing emotionally in the characters (2008).

Rothman's analysis of textuality and meaning expands the imagery of depth and hidden secrets in order to argue that *Psycho 98* lacks the philosophical significance of the original film: 'Behind the surface of Hitchcock's films, or, rather, on the surface but "hidden" by being in plain view, are . . . motifs or signs or symbols . . . whose presence participates crucially in the film's philosophical meditations' (1999: 33). Rothman identifies the presence of 'Hitchcock's "////" motif' (1999: 32) at the end of *Psycho 60*, occurring in the dissolve from Mrs Bates' mummified face to the external façade of the courtroom – its four white pillars forming the four bars '////'. Van Sant reprises the dissolve but changes Mrs Bates' hairstyle from a tight bun recalling Madelaine and Carlotta in *Vertigo* to 'wild, long hair', thereby ensuring that 'the spirits of those ghostly Hitchcock women' are not recalled. As a result, the first shot of the 'dissolve is . . . devoid of . . . mystery' (1999: 32–3). Worse still, in the second shot the courthouse lacks columns and does not reprise the vital '////' motif. Across Hitchcock's work the motif is said to act as a metaphor for the imprisonment of the characters within the diegetic world as well as the audiences' inability to access that world, providing a visual demarcation of the barrier of the screen itself (Rothman 1999: 32).

While the meta-critical/philosophical dimensions accruing to the '////' motif are clearly absent from *Psycho 98*, Rothman goes further, arguing that the two shots comprising the dissolve can only be regarded as utterly devoid of meaning:

> The superimposition of one shot stripped of its original significance over another shot likewise devoid of significance turns Hitchcock's complex and profound gesture not into a gesture of Van Sant's own, however . . . diminished in meaning and expressiveness . . . Rather Van Sant's dissolve is not meaningful or expressive. It does not have the force of a gesture at all. (1999: 33)

Leitch rightly points out the flaw in the logic of this argument: 'Granting that Van Sant's camerawork does not mean the same as Hitchcock's, why does it follow that it does not mean anything at all?' (2003). The answer lies in Rothman's utilization of a particular model of textual depth: in eradicating the mysterious and hidden dimensions of *Psycho 60*, van Sant's copy offers a proliferation of pure surfaces that constitutes the annihilation of meaning. Ultimately, of course, the depths of the Hitchcock text are guaranteed by the presence of the Master, the 'Genius' who 'resides between or beneath the shots' (Ebert quoted in Cohan 2001–2: 130). The widespread prevalence of this vision of Hitchcock in the critical material leads Leitch to argue that one of the distinct achievements of *Psycho 98* is its flushing out of 'unreconstructed Auteurism'! (2003)

For me, the most interesting feature of Rothman's writing is the precise crystallization of a particular series of images of textual depth, which hold sway across much of the critical discourse on *Psycho 98*. For such critics, the film's superficiality is understood as an involuntary voiding of depth, an accidental elimination of the power of the Master's original. In contrast, I will argue that the film explicitly plays out and plays with the loss of the secret and the impossibility of hidden depths. At the same time the film is not simply an example of postmodern aesthetics, a Baudrillardian vision of superficiality and style: it is a reflection on becoming a surface that both draws on and remakes aspects of postmodern theory.

The loss of the secret can be seen in the very different publicity campaigns surrounding the two films. Famously, Hitchcock urged audiences for *Psycho 60* not to reveal the 'tiny, little horrifying secrets' of the story, particularly the ending of the film (Williams 2000: 364–5). The story is structured around two secrets: the death of the central female protagonist one-third of the way into the film, and the revelation that Norman as Mother is her killer. Leitch, Robin Wood and numerous other critics have addressed the shocking impact on viewers of *Psycho* in 1960 of the revelation of the first secret (1989: 143–6; 2003). In contrast, as is frequently noted, the publicity for *Psycho 98* assumes audience knowledge of Marion's death. Indeed, the location of her murder is shown on the poster of the bloodied hand clutching at a shower curtain with the accompanying tag line: 'Check in. Relax. Take a shower.' The remake plays to the knowledgeable audience in that the murder is anticipated – to the point of being the subject of a macabre joke – and the murderer known. It is this that gives *Psycho 98* a particularly Baudrillardian problematic in that it remakes a film structured by secrets, indeed as a secret, while explicitly acknowledging that there are no secrets any more. For Baudrillard, it is the absence of the hidden that leads him to characterize the postmodern as obscene.

Psycho 98 begins with two logos: the turning globe of 'Universal' and the 'Imagine' droplet. The second is remade in that the typically translucent water droplet is coloured red, sliding down the screen before dripping into a red/black pool, whose concentric ripples play across the word 'Imagine'. The transformation of the logo draws attention to the importance of colour in the remake, the scarlet blood acting as a reminder of its distance from the black and white aesthetics of *Psycho 60*. The quantity of blood in the red/black pool is also suggestive of a higher level of violence, an acceleration that references the development of the slasher horror genre. For Carol Clover, *Psycho 60* is the film that begins the very first cycle of slasher horror films, setting up a template for the genre in terms of characterization, setting and weaponry (1992: 24–34). Verevis draws on Clover's work to argue that *Psycho 98* should be seen in the context of all the other remakes of *Psycho 60*: from John Carpenter's *Halloween* (1978) to Brian de Palma's *Dressed to Kill* (1980) (2006: 63–5, 68–9). The remake of the 'Imagine' logo attests to the audience's foreknowledge of events to come, while the quantity of scarlet gore also alludes to the multiplicity of remakes through which *Psycho 60* has been more generally disseminated into popular culture.

Famously, *Psycho 60* opens with a dissolve from the vertical lines of the credit design to the high-rise buildings of an urban skyline identified as 'Phoenix, Arizona'. Three further dissolves link the opening long shots of the city, culminating in a high-angle long shot of a hotel building as the camera zooms in towards a particular open window. There is a cut to a medium shot, virtually straight on to the window, and the camera tracks forward, sliding across the sill into the darkness of the hotel room. The contrast between the two types of camera movement – the zoom and the track – emphasizes the difference between the spaces: the public façades of the whitewashed buildings and the intimate darkness of private space. The next shot is a pan right that reveals the presence of the lovers, Marion and Sam, on the bed. They are discussing the necessity of meeting in secret. Hitchcock's opening can therefore be seen to set up a series of oppositions: public/private, light/dark, open/secret.

In contrast, *Psycho 98* begins with a helicopter shot that circles across the city and travels towards the selected hotel, apparently entering the open window and moving across the brightly lit hotel room to reveal the lovers on the bed. The use of the expensive helicopter shot combined with digital editing techniques to create the impression of a single, seamless shot means that the opening acts as a bravura statement celebrating the capacity of new technologies. In this regard, it conforms to Baudrillard's conception of the remake as the technical perfecting of the cinematic image: 'perfect remakes, or extraordinary montages that emerge from a more combinatory culture, of large photo-, kino-, historicosynthesis [sic.] machines' (1994: 45). Importantly, for Baudrillard, combining different elements does not result in aesthetic creation. Instead, technological perfection renders the remake, indeed most contemporary cinema, machinic rather than imaginative: 'Cinema has become hyper-realist, technically sophisticated, effective . . . All the films . . . fail to incorporate any element of make-believe (l'imaginaire). As if cinema were basically regressing towards infinity, towards . . . a formal empty perfection' (Charbonnier 1993: 30).

Van Sant's creation of a bravura single shot and use of consistently bright lighting clearly abolishes the oppositions between public/private, light/dark that structure Hitchcock's opening. The lighting in the first film indicates the sordid secrecy of the lovers' meetings, which is compounded by their discussion. Marion's unwelcome offer of a respectable dinner is made while she dresses on the other side of the room. The couple come back together when Marion suddenly propels herself into her lover's arms, saying 'Oh Sam, let's get married', her arms fastening tightly around his neck as she offers to lick the stamps on the envelopes containing his ex-wife's alimony payments. Leigh's performance conveys her great desire for marriage and respectability, suggesting that her affections are deep and sincere. In contrast, Anne Heche and Viggo Mortensen play the opening scene as light comedy, bantering about the possibility of a respectable dinner while remaining physically close to each other. Marion's later offer to 'lick the stamps' while appreciatively viewing Sam standing naked in front of the window transforms the previously heartfelt admission into innuendo!

For Baudrillard, remakes eliminate 'the psychological, moral, and sentimental blotches' of the original, thereby annihilating textual depth (1994: 45). The moral framework of *Psycho 60* is provided by Marion's desire for marriage and respectability, which perversely leads her to commit the immoral act of stealing the money. The film's opening creates a multiform sense of depth offering privacy, darkness, intimacy and interiority – the argument between Sam and Marion revealing his antipathy towards marriage and her desire for it. In contrast, the opening shot of *Psycho 98* exemplifies the logic of Baudrillard's hyperreal, in that the perfecting of visual technique is synonymous with the obliteration of structural oppositions. The absence of arguments and revelations also proscribes any psychological model of hidden depths.

The key issue is whether the display/play of surfaces offered by *Psycho 98* is more than Baudrillard's vision of meaningless, empty perfection.

Critics have argued that the colour palette of bright pastels used in *Psycho 98* acts as a visual indicator of its overt artifice and superficiality (MacDowell 2008). These colours predominate in Marion's wardrobe, which includes a candy pink suit and bright orange sun dress. However, the character is repeatedly associated with the colour orange, from her first appearance in peach/orange underwear to later appearances in her sun dress with key accessories: the orange-tinted sunglasses and vivid parasol. The scene in which Marion changes into her sun dress also serves to anticipate the character's association with birds, a symbolism that is set up much later in *Psycho 60*. While Heche changes, birdsong can be heard over the musical reprise. Moreover, while she sits on the bed, head in a bird-like tilt as she contemplates the stolen money, a white dove can be seen fluttering into the tree outside the window in the background. The metonymic juxtaposition of Heche and the dove, coupled with her performance style, unfairly slated as 'herky-jerky bird-like movements' (Rothman 1999: 29), underscore the inevitability of her death at the hands of the taxidermist Norman Bates.

Importantly, changes to the dialogue and the use of colour motifs in *Psycho 98* have the effect of reconstructing Marion's motivation from a bourgeois desire for marriage in the first film into a fantasy of escape. While she is sitting in her car at the pedestrian crossing, the voice-over plays out Marion's construction of Sam's reaction to her arrival. The first line is identical to that of *Psycho 60*: 'Marion, what in the world, what are you doing up here?' The question is followed by two new lines: 'Where in the world did you get all that money? Yeah – it's more than I need to get out of town.' The new lines reconstruct her flight according to the logic of the road movie, in that it becomes a fantasy of escaping the mundane banality of the everyday. Having been spotted by her boss, Marion drives away quickly. Both films have a dissolve from a close-up of Marion driving, to a long shot of the car travelling the open road, followed by another dissolve to a close-up of Marion as she nearly falls asleep at the wheel. The long shot in *Psycho 60* retains elements of the urban landscape in the pylons visible at the edge of the road. In contrast, van Sant offers a long shot of the car heading towards hills fringed by the warm orange hues of the setting sun, the tinted landscape picking up the key colour associated with Heche's Marion. Schneider reads this moment as an example of van Sant's own authorial signature emerging within *Psycho 98*: 'In this respect, [Marion] is not unlike the protagonists of Van Sant's other films who either live on, take to, or fantasize about the road in pursuit of . . . [a] more promising future (*To Die For, Good Will Hunting*)' (2001–2: 145). Importantly, Marion's fantasy of escape is constructed through the reprise of motifs from other films – foregrounding its status as a cultural construction.

While a few critics appreciated Heche's achievement, namely the creation of an entirely different Marion (Leitch 2003), the assessment of Vince Vaughn's performance as an impoverished copy was virtually unanimous. Rothman argues that 'Vaughn lacks Tony Perkins's trademark boy-next-door quality, so we are precluded from imagining . . . that behind the mask of the familiar, . . . there is a figure who is not what he seems' (1999: 32). This analysis foregrounds the disjunction between seeming and being that organizes Perkins' career-defining performance: the youthful, inexperienced, gauche adolescent, too embarrassed to name the bathroom and too bashful to dine with Marion in her bedroom, versus the Mother/killer within. It is clear that Vince Vaughn's performance is not organized in the same way. Rothman comments that 'Vaughn's nervous giggles give away from the outset that he is missing a screw or two' (1999: 32). Vaughn's receding hairline and lined face means that Norman's refusal to dine in the bedroom can no longer be read as youthful bashfulness, becoming instead a ploy that elicits a frowning, assessing stare from Marion. Vaughn displays Norman's madness through inappropriate laughter and the relentless twisting and untwisting of his hands, constructing the character via a series of surface tics rather than the suggestion of interior depths. Moreover, as a 'physically imposing, six-foot-five-inch leading-man' (Schneider 2001–2: 146), Vaughn's Norman can scarcely be said to hide his potential for being a physical threat.

The changes to the presentation of Norman in *Psycho 98* profoundly alter his motives for killing Marion, because he is systematically stripped of psychic depth. Žižek notes that the film's depiction of Norman successfully masturbating while viewing Marion undressing undermines the most basic model of psychodynamic pressure because the killing no longer constitutes a displacement of sexual climax (2004: 268). Indeed, Marion's murder cannot be viewed as the expression of repressed otherness: either the playing out of the fantasy of being Mother, or the return of repressed homosexuality, a homophobic reading facilitated by the casting of Anthony Perkins (MacDowell 2008). Lacking depth or oppositional otherness, the motive for murder is presented according to the logic of a continuum – as an exaggeration of heterosexual masculinity.

This reading is reinforced by the casting of Vaughn, 'whose resolutely macho heterosexual identity was well-established from previous films (e.g. *Swingers*, 1996)' (Schneider 2001–2: 146). Moreover, the physical differences between the two leading actors are so extreme – Heche's gamine slightness versus Vaughn's pumped-up vastness – that the pair offer an almost parodic presentation of normative, heterosexual gender roles.[3] Their physical disparity is duplicated in the picture that Norman removes from the wall in order to spy on Marion. Fragonard's *The Bolt* features a central man whose rippling back muscles are visible beneath his shirt as he holds a slight, struggling woman in his left arm while reaching to bolt the door out of the bedroom with his right hand. In the original painting, which dates from the late eighteenth century, the female character is dressed in golds and creams. However, the film alters the painting's colour composition, dressing her in oranges and reds and thereby doubly linking the female victim to Marion.[4]

An examination of the key changes to the shower scene show that it can no longer be read as the return of the repressed. Hitchcock famously presents Norman as a shadow on the other side of the translucent white shower curtain, using backlighting to construct him as a dark silhouette once the barrier is pulled away. The silhouette conjoins Norman with his disguise, the shape of the wig altering the contours of his face and head, thereby expressing his psychic fusion and confusion with Mother. Indeed, the use of the silhouette with its connotations of the darker double suggests the unconscious forces responsible for the crime. In *Psycho 98* the refractive shower curtain distorts Norman's outline into multiple lines of colour and light. Once the curtain is opened, Norman is not shot in silhouette. Instead, close-ups show his face through a multiplicity of veils provided by the water from the showerhead, a wispy, blonde wig and a layer of grey make-up. The assimilation of the wig into a series of layers reconstructs Norman's cross-dressing as a disguise that is clearly assumed. The play of veils/masks foregrounds the ways in which Norman's disguise is no longer a question of psychic depth, but rather one of the generic conventions of the presentation of the killer in the slasher movie.

The shower scene in *Psycho 98* contains a number of additional shots. The first medium shot of Marion in front of the shower curtain does not herald the entrance of the killer, acting instead as a teaser for the audience. More controversially, van Sant inserts two new long shots of stormy skies featuring fast time-lapse clouds while Marion is being stabbed. These clearly reference his own work, specifically the presentation of the open road in *My Own Private Idaho* (1991) (MacDowell 2008). Within the diegetic world of the film, the two shots link back to the long shot of Marion driving towards the hills, acting as subjective expressions of her fantasy of escape. Importantly, the shower scene uses a match of colour and movement to convey the loss of this transcendental fantasy of total freedom, however hackneyed, at the moment of death. Thus, the blue-greys of the scurrying time-lapse clouds match the rapidly receding strands of colour in the extreme close-up of Marion's iris dilating at the point of unconsciousness. Her final collapse is followed by a reprise of Hitchcock's famous graphic match, the dissolve from the extreme close-up of the blood swirling down the plug hole to the extreme close-up of Marion's dead eye. In *Psycho 60* the camera's rotation on the second close-up emphasizes the visceral physicality of Marion's obliteration, her identity swirling away down the drain. By contrast, van Sant doubles the camera's rotation on the second extreme close-up, drawing attention to the two very different metaphors for extinguishing life offered in *Psycho 98*.

The juxtaposition of the two different metaphors culled from different films is an example of the 'combinatory culture' of the remake that Baudrillard dismisses as incapable of creating new meanings (1994: 45). Ultimately, the technical and machinic perfection of the remake constructs it as pure surface – the signifier without the signified, form without content. For Rothman, van Sant's reprise of Hitchcock's gestures transforms them into non-gestures that are devoid of significance. Both theorists, somewhat surprisingly, share the conception of the move to surface as the voiding of depth and thus of all meaning. In contrast, I have followed a double line of argument: demonstrating the ways in which *Psycho 98* offers a relentless superficiality through the advertising of the secret, the circumventing of opposition, and the voiding of psychoanalytic depths; while also setting up different symbolic motifs through its deployment of bright pastel colours, performance style and road-movie references. *Psycho 98* displays the way in which playing with the surface creates the possibility of new meanings, changing the stolid, bourgeois Marion into a postmodern subject whose fragile fantasy of escape is constructed via movie references. Finally, the film, like its shower curtain, acts as a refractive lens, enabling us to look back to *Psycho 60* and appreciate it anew as a collaborative achievement for Hitchcock, Leigh and Perkins.

Notes

1. From this point onwards I will adopt Verevis' technique of distinguishing between the film and its remake by referring to them as *Psycho 60* and *Psycho 98* (Verevis 2006). This enables me to avoid replicating the evaluative binary original/copy.
2. The three critics were Paula Cohen, Steven Schneider and Constantine Verevis, whose articles appeared in the *Hitchcock Annual 2001–2* (Leitch 2003).
3. Schneider uses van Sant's casting of Heche to offer a queer reading of the murder as the result of Norman's rage at Marion's lesbian indifference to him (2001–2: 145–7).
4. I must thank Rose Cooper and Andrew Pollard for successfully identifying the picture and providing information on colour composition.

Bibliography

Baudrillard, J. (1994), *Simulacra and Simulation*, S. F. Glaser (trans.). Ann Arbor: University of Michigan Press.

Charbonnier, C. (1993), 'I like the cinema: interview with Jean Baudrillard', in M. Gane and G. Salemohamed (trans.), *Baudrillard Live: Selected Interviews*, M. Gane (ed.). London and New York: Routledge, pp. 29–35.

Clover, C. (1992), *Men, Women and Chainsaws: Gender and the Modern Horror Film*. Princeton, NJ: Princeton University Press.

Cohen, P. M. (2001–2), 'The artist pays homage', in *Hitchcock Annual*, 127–32.

Dressed to Kill (1980). USA, dir. Brian de Palma.

Durgnat, R. (2002), *A Long Hard Look at 'Psycho'*, London: BFI.

Good Will Hunting (1997). USA, dir. Gus van Sant.

Halloween (1978) USA, dir. John Carpenter.

Ishii-Gonzalès, S. (2001–2), 'An analysis of the parlour scene in *Psycho* x 2', in *Hitchcock Annual*, 149–54.

Leitch, T. (2000), '101 ways to tell Hitchcock's *Psycho* from Gus Van Sant's', *Literature/Film Quarterly*, vol. 28, issue 4 (online journal).

— (2003), 'Hitchcock without Hitchcock', *Literature/Film Quarterly*, vol. 31, issue 4 (online journal).

MacDowell, J. (2008), *What is the value of Van Sant's 'Psycho'?* Paper presented at the Cultural Borrowings Conference, The University of Nottingham. A different version of this paper can be found at www.offscreen.com/biblio/phile/essays/value_psycho/

Martin, A. (2001–2), 'Shot-by-shot follies', in *Hitchcock Annual*, 133–9.

My Own Private Idaho (1991). USA, dir. Gus van Sant.

Naremore, J. (1999–2000), 'Remaking *Psycho*', in *Hitchcock Annual*, 3–12.

Psycho (1960). USA, dir. Alfred Hitchcock.

Psycho (1998). USA, dir. Gus van Sant.

Rope (1948). USA, dir. Alfred Hitchcock.

Rothman, W. (1999), 'Some thoughts on Hitchcock's authorship', in *Alfred Hitchcock: Centenary Essays*, R. Allen and S. Ishii-Gonzalès (eds). London: BFI, pp. 29–44.

Schneider, S. J. (2001–2), 'Van Sant the provoca(u)teur', in *Hitchcock Annual*, 140–48.

Stam, R. (2005), 'Introduction: the theory and practice of adaptation', in R. Stam and A. Raengo (eds), *Literature and Film: A Guide to the Theory and Practice of Film Adaptation*. Oxford: Blackwell, pp. 1–52.

Swingers (1996). USA, dir. Doug Liman.

To Die For (1995). USA, dir. Gus van Sant.

Verevis, C. (2006), *Film Remakes*. Edinburgh: Edinburgh University Press.

Williams, L. (2000), 'Discipline and fun: *Psycho* and postmodern cinema', in C. Gledhill and L. Williams (eds), *Reinventing Film Studies*. London: Arnold, pp. 351–78.

Wood, R. (1989), *Hitchcock's Films Revisited*. New York: Columbia University Press.

Žižek, S. (2004), 'Is there a proper way to remake a Hitchcock film?', in *Past and Future Hitchcock*, R. Allen and S. Ishii-Gonzalès (eds). London and New York: Routledge, pp. 257–74.

CHAPTER FOUR

Affecting Fidelity: Adaptation, Fidelity and Affect in Todd Haynes's *Far From Heaven*

RACHEL CARROLL

Todd Haynes's 2002 film *Far From Heaven* has been widely construed as a contemporary auteur's tribute to Douglas Sirk's 1955 'women's picture' *All That Heaven Allows,* a film which has taken on the status of a classic of its genre in the canon of film history. Writing in *Remakes,* Constantine Verevis has noted how 'the forging of a canon of films and film makers by auteur critics [has] enabled allusion to film history ... to become a major expressive device' (2006: 62) in contemporary film; indeed, the radical reinscription of hidden sexual and racial histories effected by Haynes in *Far From Heaven* would seem to confirm its status as a creative intervention, rather than commercial replication, of a past cultural text. However, as notable as the film's departure from the narrative parameters of 1950s melodrama is Haynes's extraordinary fidelity to the cinematic sensibility of the Sirkian original. To place this paradox in the critical discourse of adaptation studies, *Far From Heaven* is both 'faithful' and 'free'. Questions of authorship, canon and cultural memory are integral to an understanding of the significance of Haynes's return to a historical film genre, issues which are equally central to the consideration of literary adaptations. By considering *Far From Heaven* in the context of adaptation studies I wish to suggest some affinities between the critical recuperation of the remake and the emergence of adaptation studies as a significant field in contemporary film, media and literary studies. More specifically, by reflecting on fidelity as manifested in *Far From Heaven* I wish to revisit the contested status of fidelity within adaptation studies; I will explore the relationship between fidelity and affect, and suggest that the fate of fidelity is implicated in a gendered cultural politics. The fidelity demonstrated in Haynes's *Far From Heaven* – which is at once affecting and affected without forfeiting its sincerity – is indicative of a mode of cultural production and consumption which is neither passive nor derivative, but active and productive.

The remake and the adaptation can both be considered genres of film or television production which have suffered a compromised critical status. The commercial motivations at work in recreating a work with an established audience or readership, and its apparently derivative relationship to a prior cultural production, have served to cast into doubt the artistic integrity of these genres; where originality and creative autonomy prevail as criteria of evaluation, the remake and the adaptation tend, by definition, to be found wanting. However, both genres have been subject to critical reappraisal. Where studies of adaptation are concerned, the extensive and expanding published work on adaptations, emerging both from film and media studies and from literary studies, has not merely achieved the critical recuperation of the study of (mostly literary) adaptations; it has also seemingly begun to inaugurate adaptation studies as a disciplinary field. The frequency with which studies of adaptation rehearse the history of its origins, revisit formative critical debates and reiterate a canon of founding works is suggestive of the evolution of a nascent disciplinary infrastructure. While work on the remake is, as yet, less extensive than that on adaptation (see Verevis 2006; Horton and McDougal 1998; Forrest and Koos 2002), instructive parallels can be drawn in terms of the strategies employed in the service of critical recuperation. On the one hand are efforts to define the object of study – whether the remake or the adaptation – as a genre in its own right and deserving of interpretative frameworks appropriate to its concerns; this strategy attends closely to specificities of production and consumption, and is inclined towards the production of critical and generic taxonomies. On the other hand are efforts to demonstrate the ways in which these cultural forms exemplify key issues in contemporary culture, especially those to do with intertextuality. One implicit, and rather paradoxical, effect of this strategy is to seem to argue for the abolition of adaptation or remake studies as such, but to do so by suggesting that in some fundamental way *all* cultural forms are themselves 'remade' or 'adapted'. For example, in relation to the adaptation, James Naremore argues that

> The study of adaptation needs to be joined with the study of recycling, remaking, and every other form of retelling in the age of mechanical reproduction and electronic communication. By this means, adaptation will become part of a general theory of repetition, and adaptation study will move from the margins to the centre of contemporary media studies. (2000: 15)

Similarly, but in relation to the remake, David Wills argues that 'what distinguishes the remake is not the fact of its being a repetition, rather the fact of its being a precise institutional form of the structure of repetition . . . the "quotation effect" or "citation effect", the citationality or iterability, that exists in and for every film' (1998: 148). Both Naremore and Wills, writing in different contexts, suggest that repetition should not be understood as simply symptomatic of creative bankruptcy or commercial imperative, but rather as revealing a quality integral to every form of cultural production: its intertextual relationship to other texts.

The extent to which a critical framework can be determined by its object is further complicated by the challenges faced in attempting to delimit and categorize the 'remake' or 'adaptation'. Adaptation is a term generally associated with literary 'properties' and more commonly reserved for 'page-to-screen' film or television adaptations, often of canonical or 'classic' texts. Moreover, adaptations are conventionally understood to entail the translation of a source text from one medium to another; Erica Sheen defines adaptation as 'the transfer of an "original" (literary) text from one context of production to an (audio-visual) other' (2000: 2). Where both the source and reworked text occupy the same medium – film – it would seem more appropriate to categorize the resulting film as a remake. Verevis confirms this generic distinction when he writes that a remake 'is generally *a remake of another film*, whereas one of the principal arguments of adaptation theory is concerned with the movement between *different semiotic registers*, most often between literature and film' (2006: 82, emphasis in original). But both are qualified definitions. The parentheses within which Sheen places 'literary' hints at the diverse forms which the source text can take, incorporating classic novels, pulp fictions, graphic novels and cartoons (both print and animated); the emphasis placed on differences in the context of production suggests that literary origin may not be sustainable as a defining feature of this genre. Conversely, differences in the context of production can be as crucial to the remake as the adaptation, whether those differences concern historical context, national provenance, authorship or indeed medium (such as film 'remakes' of television series). The diversity of taxonomies by which critics have attempted to systemize both the adaptation and the remake suggest that its generic identity is far less self-evident than might initially appear; Geoffrey Wagner (1975) identifies 'transposition', 'commentary' and 'analogy' as categories of adaptation, while Dudley Andrew (1984) refers to 'borrowing', 'intersecting' and 'transforming'. Michael Druxman's and Harvey Roy Greenberg's categories of remake are also threefold: for Druxman the 'disguised remake', the 'direct remake' and the 'non-remake' and for Greenberg the 'acknowledged, close remake', the 'acknowledged transformed remark' and the 'unacknowledged disguised remake' (both cited in Verevis 2006). Indeed, *Far From Heaven* might be difficult to place within such taxonomies, given that while the existence of a significant intertextual relationship to *All That Heaven Allows* is not in dispute, it is not directly cited in *Far From Heaven*'s credits, and only indirectly alluded to in the film's title.

Moreover, an understanding of the significance of *Far From Heaven* in the context of film history requires consideration of issues which are also integral to studies of literary adaptations: issues of authorship and canon formation. Both *All That Heaven Allows* and *Far from Heaven* have been emphatically *authored* by their reception. The significance of *All That Heaven Allows* within film history can be attributed to two critical contexts: firstly, its position within the *oeuvre* of Douglas Sirk following the rediscovery of Sirk as an auteur within film theory; secondly, its place within the history of gendered genres of film production, including the melodrama and the 'women's picture', and the reappraisal of these genres by feminist film theory. Indeed, Sharon Willis asserts that '*Far From Heaven* is as much an homage to film theory, and in particular to feminist film theory, as it is to Douglas Sirk. It reads 1950s melodrama (and beyond it, the 1950s in popular memory) through the lens of 1980s and 1990s film theory' (2003: 134). Todd Haynes is a critically acclaimed contemporary director, emerging from the independently produced film sector, whose work is recognized as bearing his authorial signature and has a founding place in the counter-canon of 'new queer cinema' (see de Angelis, 2004). As an 'authored' reinterpretation of a classic source text, Haynes's *Far from Heaven* has a structural resemblance to what Catherine Grant has described as the 'auteurist free adaptation':

> With the vehicle of the free adaptation, contemporary film auteurs can attempt to make aspects of literary classics and other texts their own, over-writing them with their own traceable signatures, perhaps reconfiguring them by incorporating references to other (rewritten) intertexts. (2002: 58)

The free adaptation nevertheless retains its status as an adaptation because of the way in which it foregrounds its relationship to a prior cultural text; I wish to conclude this exploration of the relationship between the remake and the adaptation with reflection on an issue of particular pertinence to *Far From Heaven*: the role of cultural memory.

For all that *Far From Heaven* was a major film production which achieved relative commercial success, it would be difficult to conceive of this project as having the principally commercial motivation often associated with the remake; the Sirkian melodrama does not have the brand identity sufficient to ensure the kind of audience exploitation sought by market-led remakes. As an industrial category of film production, remakes are, as Verevis has put it, '"pre-sold" to their audience' (2006: 3). In this way, the commercial success of the original film or television property is assumed to minimize the financial risk entailed in any major film production; the remake is expected to provide a 'ready-made' audience, reducing the efforts which would otherwise be required to establish and address a market for a new product. Verevis goes on to explain the premise on which the advantages of the 'pre-sold' product relies: 'viewers are assumed to have some prior experience, or at least possess a "narrative image", of the original story – an earlier film, literary or other property – before engaging in its particular retelling' (2006: 3). If Haynes's *Far From Heaven* has been widely identified as a tribute to Sirk's *All That Heaven Allows* this is not necessarily, and certainly not exclusively, due to the capacity of its audience to independently identify its intertextual references to Sirkian melodrama. An appreciation of *Far From Heaven*'s relationship to its cinematic precursors can be gained by an audience without prior knowledge of its source text/s through what Grant calls the 'discourses of publicity, promotion and reception which make known the generic framework within which to comprehend films' (2002: 59). The 'narrative image' to which Verevis refers may be an *effect* of these discourses; in this way such discourses act to confirm or even produce the cultural memory on which the status of the remake and the adaptation relies. Indeed, were either the adaptation or the remake to rely on its audience having a direct and primary 'prior experience' of the source text – whether that be Jane Austen's 1812 novel *Pride and Prejudice* or the popular television series *Starsky and Hutch* (USA, Spelling-Goldberg 1975–79, 'remade' as a film by Todd Phillips in 2004) – its audience would be relatively limited and its commercial success doubtful. Where prior experience is indirect and secondary it must necessarily reside in collective cultural memory; even where this prior experience is direct and primary, it is nevertheless mediated by memory. In both instances the 'narrative image' of the original text will be informed by a host of cultural practices and contexts, both institutional and popular, which act to produce cultural memory as a collective experience; the formation of literary canons and school curricula might serve to ensure an audience for adaptations of Austen's fiction, while nostalgia-based television programming might ensure that *Starsky and Hutch* retains currency, if only as a kitsch signifier of 1970s popular culture. Grant has written that 'the most important act that films and their surrounding discourses need to perform in order to communicate unequivocally their status as adaptations is to [make their audiences] recall the adapted work, *or the cultural memory of it*' (2002: 57, emphasis added). The same is true of the remake. What this means is that the status of the remake or adaptation *as* remake or adaptation is not inherent in the text itself, but is a product of the discourses which surround it: discourses which, as Grant puts it, do not so much 'describe . . . [as] determine'(2002: 69) the knowledge that a film is a remake or adaptation. Hence, *Far From Heaven* is a film whose status as an 'adaptation' of a prior cultural text is deeply implicated in cultural memory.

Haynes's *Far From Heaven* demonstrates an almost excessive fidelity to the cinematic sensibility of Sirk's original: in its rich and dramatic use of heightened colour, its deployment of music to orchestrate audience identifications and its evocation of steeped but contained emotion through the actors' mode of performance, Haynes faithfully recreates a visual and affective experience belonging to film history and memory. In terms of production style and aesthetic it is loyally, almost obsessively, faithful to the original; in a review article aptly and intertextually entitled 'Magnificent obsession', Richard Falcon refers to its 'wholesale appropriation of Sirkian narrative, colour palette, *mise en scène* and acting styles' (2003: 12), and elsewhere Willis offers as evidence an 'obtrusive score, a meticulous attention to colour, strikingly truncated interiors, and a rhythm of hysterical eruptions' (2003: 132). Acclaimed as a 'remarkable tribute' and a 'unique homage' (Falcon 2003: 12) to Sirk's cinema, Haynes's film reaped accolades more commonly associated with 'faithful' literary adaptations of classic texts and yet, in terms of narrative content, it has more in common with the 'free' adaptation in which a film-maker creatively reinterprets the original: that is, it takes liberties which might otherwise announce it as an unfaithful adaptation.

In Sirk's 1955 film Jane Wyman plays a widow, Cary, who is persuaded to renounce her love for another man in the name of fidelity to her husband's memory. In Haynes's film Julianne Moore's Cathy Whitaker is compelled to renounce a romantic friendship with a widowed father. Wyman's Cary defies the disapproval of her adult children, friends and social circle and, a near-fatal accident apart, is able to anticipate a future with her lover, Ron Kirby (Rock Hudson) at the end of the film. In Haynes's version, Cathy's husband Frank (Dennis Quaid) leaves his marriage to live with his male lover. Cathy is not able, however, to anticipate a future with her chosen companion Raymond Deagan (Dennis Haysbert), as not only social ostracism but also racial violence makes a relationship between a white woman and an African-American man unthinkable: in Cathy's words, it is not 'plausible'. As an authentic recreation of a period 1950s genre film, *Far From Heaven*'s representation of homosexuality and inter-racial romance might seem anachronistic; conversely, as an authentic recreation of a historical period, its content might seem apt but its mode of presentation inauthentic to a contemporary audience. What is at stake – and seemingly at odds here – is the film's fidelity *both* to a historical past and to a history of representation. As Richard Dyer has put it, *Far From Heaven* is 'inescapably poised between a sense of telling a 1950s story in a 1950s way and a recognition that a 1950s way could not tell that story and remain a 1950s way' (2007: 177). Significantly, in its fidelity to a gendered genre of popular culture the film refuses the many ironic modes of 'retro' representation which are available for the depiction of 1950s America; moreover, it refuses the corrective imperative often implicit in such retrospective representations. There seems something almost perverse in Haynes's dedication to this aesthetic: perverse, that is, not in the deviant or pathological sense but in the more commonplace sense of being persistent in error – the error here being the apparent mistaking of Sirkian melodramatic modes as authentic; hence the film persists in the possibility that these modes could represent the very hidden cultural narratives which they apparently repress.

By considering *Far From Heaven*'s fidelity in the context of adaptation studies I wish to assess what might be at stake in its renunciation.

As a contested term, 'fidelity' is a key critical concept for adaptation studies. The notion that a film or television adaptation should be judged exclusively on the basis of its fidelity to its source text is one which has been thoroughly problematized within adaptation studies. Not only does the criterion of fidelity fail to acknowledge the inevitably interpretative and transformative quality of adaptation as a process, but fidelity is also implicated, it is argued, in hierarchies which privilege high culture over mass or popular culture, the written word over the visual image, and the 'original' over the 'copy'; in this way fidelity seems structurally determined to find adaptations wanting. As a cultural value fidelity can indeed be reductive; however, I would suggest that fidelity as a mode of cultural practice can be complex and productive. The almost ritual denunciation of fidelity in contemporary adaptation studies has taken on the function of a founding disciplinary gesture; as such it tells us as much about the status of the critic in relation to his/her object of study as it does about the status of adaptation. As a cultural value fidelity arguably reduces the critic to a state of passivity, licensed merely to note and deplore the ways in which the adaptation departs from or distorts the literary original. In this sense, the critic is reduced to the same state of deferential obligation to the original as the 'faithful' adaptation. The critique of fidelity is a claim for a greater degree of critical and interpretative agency; in this way, however, adaptation studies perhaps also seeks to distance itself from the unmediated investments implied in fidelity criticism. The kind of investments to which I am alluding are evoked in Robert Stam's much-quoted critical account of the sentiments of fidelity in his essay 'Beyond fidelity':

> When we say an adaptation has been unfaithful to the original, the term gives expression to the disappointment we feel when a film adaptation fails to capture what we see as the fundamental narrative, thematic and aesthetic features of its literary source . . . Words such as *infidelity* and *betrayal* in this sense translate our feeling, when we have loved a book, that an adaptation has not been worthy of that love. (2000: 54, emphasis in original)

'*When we have loved. . .*' The spectre that is raised here is that of affect: of feeling, emotion, identification. What seems to be improper about fidelity is not merely the critical passivity which it is thought to induce, but also the emotional investments by which it is motivated. What is being renounced here is not simply the sentiment of fidelity, but the impact of affect and its apparently compromising effect on critical judgement.

It is in this context that Haynes's *Far From Heaven* is especially interesting. Haynes's film emulates a Hollywood genre distinguished by its gendered evocation of feeling, emotion and identification: the women's picture. Moreover, the critical fate of the women's picture within the canon of film history is closely intertwined with the fate of affect and its gendered politics in film theory. Until the 1970s the women's picture's critical credentials were seriously compromised by its genre, its audience and its gendering as a melodrama produced for a female audience. Auteur theory enabled the first critical resurrection of these films, the authorial signature of the usually male director effectively countersigning the fact of mass female consumption. Moreover, the interpretation of the women's picture as articulating an auteur's *ironic* comment on bourgeois culture was arguably pivotal in disarming the feminizing effect of sentimental address. Christine Gledhill succinctly captures this implicitly gendered manoeuvre when she states: 'The two audiences for Sirkian irony can further be specified: one which is implicated, identifies and weeps, and one which, seeing through such involvement, distances itself. The fact that, across all classes, the first is likely to be female and the other male was not remarked on' (1990: 12).

Gledhill's work is widely recognized, alongside that of Mary Ann Doane and Laura Mulvey among others, as pivotal in the feminist critical appropriation of the women's picture and its understanding of this genre as giving coded expression to ideological conflict. As Mulvey writes: 'the interest of Hollywood 50s melodramas lies primarily in the way that fissures and contradictions can be shown, by means of textual analysis, to be undermining the films' ideological coherence' (1990: 75). Haynes's indebtedness to this tradition of feminist film theory has been suggested by a number of critics: for example, Verevis proposes that '*All That Heaven Allows* not only remakes film history . . . but . . . recuperates some thirty years of feminist film theory' (2006: 142).

One form that a 'homage to . . . feminist film theory' (Willis 2003: 134) could take might be to initiate a critical intervention in the genre by rewriting its most ideologically compacted premises. However, refusing the kind of retrospective logic which a homage to feminist film theory might offer, *Far From Heaven*'s fidelity to the Sirkian melodrama resides in its fidelity to the affective experience which it evokes; far from offering to resolve the contradictions to which Mulvey refers, it instead elaborates on the gendered and sexual tensions at work within the structures of heterosexual romance. For example, Gledhill has written that feminist interest in the melodrama as a genre can be attributed to the 'large space it opened to female protagonists, the domestic sphere and socially mandated "feminine" concerns' (1990: 10). While this is true of *Far From Heaven* to the extent that its protagonist is a woman whose life is defined by her identity as wife and mother, what is also notable in this film is the space it opens for the consideration of crises of masculinity, particularly in relation to racialized and heterosexual constructions of masculinity. An important effect of this implosion of normative masculinity is the way in which it *amplifies* our dramatic experience of the affective consequences of the conflict between social convention and personal desire. In *Far From Heaven*, Cathy's dilemma is complicated by the conflicted or besieged masculinities of both her husband

and her lover. Cathy's thwarted desires as a heterosexual woman are counterpointed by Frank's socially stigmatized same-sex desire. Cathy's commitments as wife and mother are pitted against Raymond's obligations as a widowed father; her economic and racial privilege cannot protect their relationship from the imperatives which drive Raymond's hard-earned self-sufficiency, and which compel his departure from Baltimore following a racially motivated assault on his daughter.

Far From Heaven recreates the remembered affective and aesthetic experience of the women's picture, but integrates within it the viewer's historical awareness of marginalized sexual and racial realities. Temporal and affective discrepancies are in some sense integral to this mode of representation; in this way it affords both distance and identification, and allows that both are meaningful. In its fidelity, *Far From Heaven* does not merely reproduce but elaborates what Richard Dyer has described as the 'difficulty of emotion in 1950s melodrama' (2007: 178). Our retrospective knowledge of historical realities is not deployed as a pretext to correct the affective structure of 1950s melodrama as inadequately authentic; rather, the affective structure of 1950s melodrama is employed as embodying and expressing the tensions arising out of gendered, sexual and racial inequalities. An appreciation of what a 1950s melodrama could not say is key to an understanding of what 1950s ideologies would not sanction, and in this way the motifs of renunciation in both *All That Heaven Allows* and *Far From Heaven* are testimony to the affective impact of normative violence. Haynes's film in part addresses the desire to revisit and relive a prior cultural experience – as do all remakes and adaptations. While this revisiting evokes the original encounter, it also acts on it; our 'memory' of the 1950s and of its representations through melodrama is both the source and effect of this act of perverse fidelity. I have described *Far From Heaven* as both faithful and free; I would suggest that, paradoxically, it is the film's fidelity to the women's picture as affective experience which informs *Far From Heaven*'s creative departures from its source; in this way, fidelity *acts upon* its object, producing and even transforming the object to which it is nominally devoted.

I wish to conclude by reflecting on a critical framework within which the significance of fidelity, affect and memory in *Far From Heaven* might be theorized. Feminist, lesbian and gay, and queer theories of spectatorship have argued for the active and potentially subversive nature of cinematic consumption; in doing so they have sought to effect a shift in emphasis from the production of meaning by the auteur (and indeed critic) to the appropriation of meaning by the audience, whether intended or unacknowledged. Indeed, it is through the *fidelity* of fans – through the *agency* of their identification – that the work of appropriation occurs. Patricia White's study of lesbian representability in classic Hollywood cinema, *Uninvited*, is exemplary in this sense in the way that it demonstrates the production of unlicensed meanings by unacknowledged audiences. Her concept of 'retrospectatorship' offers a valuable framework within which to conceptualize repetition, as a mode of cultural experience, and its relation to memory and affect; premised on an acknowledgement of affective investment, it might be adapted to contribute to a rethinking of fidelity as something other than a critically suspect sentiment.

White defines 'retrospectatorship' as a form of viewing 'which is transformed by unconscious and conscious past viewing experience' and which, like all forms of spectatorship, 'engages subjective fantasy, revises memory traces and experiences, some of which are memories and experiences of other movies' (1999: 197). Interestingly, the example which White offers from her own childhood memory is itself an adaptation: Fred Zinneman's 1952 adaptation of Carson McCullers's 1946 novel *The Member of the Wedding*. Reconstructing the meaning of the particular charge which this cinematic experience held for her child self, White writes that 'If *The Member of the Wedding* issues an invitation to a queer spectator, it is because at the same time that it expresses the longing to conform, it also enacts a fantasy of difference' (1999: xii). The 'difficulty of emotion' (2007: 178) to which Dyer refers is at work in this remembered experience. In its depiction of an African-American woman (Ethel Waters), a tomboyish white girl (Julie Harris) and a frail and whimsical white male child (Brandon de Wilde) as outsiders, *The Member of the Wedding* reflects dominant racial, gendered and sexual ideologies; in its evocation of the solidarity they share, keeping company in the socially marginalized and feminized space of the kitchen, it imagines some of the compensations of outsiderdom. White recalls how as a child she emphatically '(dis)identified' (1999: xiii) with Julie Harris's Frankie Addams, but as an adult discovered other meanings in her remembered viewing. In the context of his discussion of *Far From Heaven* in *Pastiche*, Dyer suggests:

> What is not imagined in a mode of representation may also have been unimaginable, may have been framed precisely as that which cannot be seen or heard, nor evidently thought and felt. The contours of a structure of feeling are delineated by what is excluded, the emotional pressures at work feel like they do precisely because some of them are implicit. (2007: 177)

A crudely retrospective reading of *The Member of the Wedding* might seek to imagine what seemed 'unimaginable' in the context of its formative viewing: that is, the presence of a queer subtext in the casting and narrative of this film adaptation, and of a nascent sexual identity in its child viewer. Retrospectatorship, by contrast, does not seek to correct the memory of an incompletely understood cinematic experience, but rather to recognize that experience as formative and as meaningful. It is formative in the sense that it becomes the shaping condition for future cinematic engagement; it is meaningful in that the sense of the 'unimaginable' captures the tension between modes of representation and historical realities, and between affective realities and ideological constructions. Similarly, *Far From Heaven* gives expression to a historical sense of the unimaginable in the remembered experience of the Sirkian melodrama but retains, through its fidelity to a mode of representation, its signature 'structure of feeling'.

Retrospectatorship is a cultural practice of subversive consumption whereby a seemingly passive spectatorship actively transforms what it consumes; I have tried to suggest that the 'perverse fidelity' exhibited by Todd Haynes in *Far From Heaven* can similarly be considered as *acting upon* the object which it offers to reproduce, even as it declares its fidelity. In exploring the ways in which the renunciation of fidelity may be implicated in the gendered politics of affect, I have attempted to make explicit the construction of fidelity as a feminized cultural practice; by attributing a certain subversive agency to the practice of fidelity, I wish to suggest that it offers important insights into the dynamic relationship between affect, memory and meaning.

Bibliography

All That Heaven Allows (1955). USA, dir. Douglas Sirk.

Andrew, Andrew (2000), 'Adaptation', in James Naremore (ed.), *Film Adaptation*. London: Athlone Press, pp. 54–76.

Andrew, Dudley (1984), *Concepts in Film Theory*. Oxford: Oxford University Press.

De Angelis, Michele (2004), 'The characteristics of new queer filmmaking: case study – Todd Haynes', in Michele Aaron (ed.), *New Queer Cinema: A Critical Reader*. Edinburgh: Edinburgh University Press, pp. 41–52.

Doane, Mary Ann (1987), *The Desire to Desire: The Woman's Film of the 1940's*. Bloomington, IN: Indiana University Press.

Falcon, Richard (2003), 'Magnificent obsession'. *Sight and Sound*, 13 (3), 12–15.

Far From Heaven (2002). USA, dir. Todd Haynes.

Forrest, Jennifer and Leonard R. Koos (eds) (2002), *Dead Ringers: The Remake in Theory and Practice*. New York: State University of New York Press.

Gledhill, Christine (1990), 'The melodramatic field: an investigation', in Christine Gledhill, *Home is Where the Heart Is: Studies in Melodrama and the Woman's Film*. London: British Film Institute, pp. 5–39.

Grant, Catherine (2002), 'Recognising Billy Budd in *Beau Travail*: epistemology and hermeneutics of an autuerist "free" adaptation', *Screen* 43 (1), 57–73.

Horton, Andrew and Stuart Y. McDougal (eds) (1998), *Play it Again, Sam: Retakes on Remakes*. Berkeley and London: University of California Press.

Mulvey, Laura (1990), 'Notes on Sirk and Melodrama', in Christine Gledhill (ed.), *Home is Where the Heart Is: Studies in Melodrama and the Woman's Film*. London: British Film Institute, pp. 75–79.

Naremore, James (2000), 'Introduction: film and the reign of adaptation', in James Naremore (ed.), *Film Adaptation*. London: Athlone Press, pp. 1–16.

Sheen, Erica (2000), 'Introduction', in Robert Giddings and Erica Sheen (eds), *The Classic Novel: From Page to Screen*. Manchester: Manchester University Press, pp. 1–13.

Stam, Robert (2000), 'Beyond fidelity: the dialogics of adaptation', in James Naremore (ed.), *Film Adaptation*. London: Athlone Press, pp. 54–76.

Verevis, Constantine (2006), *Film Remakes*. Edinburgh: Edinburgh University Press.

Wagner, Geoffrey (1975), *The Novel and the Cinema*. London: Fairleigh Dickinson University Press.

White, Patricia (1999), *Uninvited: Classical Hollywood Cinema and Lesbian Representability*. Bloomington and Indianapolis: Indiana University Press.

Willis, Sharon (2003), 'The politics of disappointment: Todd Haynes rewrites Douglas Sirk', *Camera Obscura* 54, 18 (3), 130–75.

Wills, David (1998), 'The French remark: *Breathless* and cinematic citationality', in Andrew Horton and Stuart Y. McDougal (eds), *Play it Again, Sam: Retakes on Remakes*. Berkeley and London: University of California Press, pp. 147–61.

CHAPTER FIVE

The Folding Text: *Doctor Who*, Adaptation and Fan Fiction

CHRISTOPHER MARLOW

THE DOCTOR: *People assume that time is a strict progression of cause to effect, but actually, from a non-linear, non-subjective viewpoint, it's more like a big ball of wibbly-wobbly, timey-wimey . . . stuff.*

('Blink', *Doctor Who*, 2007)

In 'Blink', writer Steven Moffat's 2007 episode of the long-running British television series *Doctor Who*, problems of chronology play a central role. A key scene shows the episode's heroine Sally Sparrow, in 2007, holding a conversation with a filmed recording of the time-travelling Doctor 'made 38 years earlier'. The Doctor is able to respond to Sally's questions because they are transcribed by her friend Larry as she asks them. The transcript is later given to the Doctor in 2008, and he takes it with him to 1969. Once she understands this process, it occurs to Sally that it puts the origin of the conversation in some doubt. As she says: 'Let me get my head around this: you're reading aloud from a transcript of a conversation you're still having?' The Doctor's reply –'er, wibbly-wobbly, timey-wimey', he says, while waving his hand dismissively – indicates that the subject is closed, and that there are indeed more pressing things on the minds of the characters and their prime-time Saturday night audience, in the shape of the sinister weeping angels. Yet the vexed question of origins posed in 'Blink' is, because of *Doctor Who*'s own complex relationship with alternate and adapted texts, one worth pursuing in the context of the series itself. In this chapter, I will show how *Doctor Who* (2005–) has adapted material *from* its own vast canon in order to adapt *to* current socio-cultural contexts, and I will explore the implications of this process for adaptation studies. 'Blink' itself is an adaptation of Moffat's own 'What I did on my Christmas holidays', a prose story that appeared in the *'Doctor Who' Annual 2006*.[1]

The series, first broadcast in November 1963, was commissioned by Sydney Newman, BBC Head of Drama Group (Television), who explained in an interview that it was his 'admiration for George Pal's 1960 Hollywood adaptation of H. G. Wells's classic science fiction novel, *The Time Machine*, which provided . . . the most immediate inspiration for *Doctor Who*' (Cook 1999: 115). However, James Chapman's work at the BBC Written Archives has revealed the existence of two reports on the possibility of commissioning a science-fiction television series that predate Newman's April 1963 arrival at the Corporation and thus challenge this originary statement. The second of these reports, from July 1962, consists of synopses of five science-fiction novels considered 'potentially suitable for adaptation to television' (Chapman 2006: 17). The report concluded that *Guardians of Time* by Poul Anderson, about a time patrol 'set up to stop anyone from tampering with the past' was 'particularly attractive as a series since individual plots can easily be tackled by a variety of scriptwriters' (Chapman 2006: 17).[2] At the moment of its inception, then, *Doctor Who* was conceived as an adaptation of at least two different source texts. And if the term is given an evolutionary inflection, adaptation has remained part of the DNA of the series ever since, both at a textual and a metatextual level, because its survival has in part depended upon its ability to adapt to its contemporary environment. As John Tulloch and Manuel Alvarado argue in *Doctor Who: The Unfolding Text*, the programme 'draw[s] on a variety of stars and codes of performance, as well as a range of genres' while 'subtly shifting its ground in response to social and professional pressures' (Tulloch and Alvarado 1983: 3). According to this logic, the cancellation of *Doctor Who* in 1989 could be said to have been caused by the series' failure to adapt to the institutional and cultural demands of late-1980s television. On its hugely successful return to the small screen in March 2005, the programme had once again learnt how to adapt to its environment, and it had done so by rediscovering the importance of adapting other fiction. The influence of the US television series *Buffy the Vampire Slayer*, for example, was strongly felt.[3] However, perhaps more interesting is the way that the recent iteration of the series has been influenced by non-televised *Doctor Who* texts such as Virgin's *New Adventures* novels and Big Finish's audio plays. *Doctor Who*'s willingness to adapt its own non-canonical material – its ability to fold and refold its own textual space – is a distinctive attribute of the revived series, and one way in which we might account for its current evolutionary 'fitness'.[4]

In this chapter I will understand 'text' to denote not only the televised adventures of the Doctor, but also the entire corpus of published and non-published fiction dealing with the character. Clearly, the size of this corpus precludes its comprehensive discussion.[5] Instead, this chapter will analyse what occurs when this vast text is folded in upon itself, when, in other words, specific narrative traits or sequences are adapted from one medium to another. My use of the term 'folding' is informed by Jacques Derrida's 'Living on: border lines', an essay that seeks to challenge the integrity of texts themselves. As Derrida argues:

> if we are to approach [*aborder*] a text, for example, it must have a *bord*, an edge ... But when do you start reading it? What if you started reading it after the first sentence (another upper edge), which functions as its first reading head but which itself in turn folds its outer edges back over onto inner edges whose mobility – multilayered, quotational, displaced from meaning to meaning – prohibits you from making out a shoreline? There is a regular *submerging* of the shore. (Bloom *et al.* 1979: 81)

Although Derrida's description of the impossibility of limiting the reference of a text can apply to the whole system of language rather than merely various iterations of one fictive universe, his interest in textual topology – itself a re-articulation of his concept of 'differance' – is a fertile one for *Doctor Who* and the study of adaptation alike. If, for instance, we can reductively understand the 'first sentence' of *Doctor Who* to have been the series' opening episode 'An Unearthly Child', transmitted on 23 November 1963, only those viewers old enough to remember this broadcast, to have sought out one of the few BBC repeats of the episode, or to have purchased a VHS or DVD copy, could be said to have read *Doctor Who* from its first 'reading head' onwards. However, as I have indicated earlier, since this episode was in many ways an adaptation of other material, it is far from clear that it can function as a first reading head at all. Viewers whose initial experience of the programme was the first episode of the 2005 revival have evidently been able to follow the narrative without recourse to its 700 previous episodes: as proof of this, the series is now more popular than at any time in its history.[6] Yet Derrida might argue that the reading experience of these 2005 viewers is materially different from that of their 1963 counterparts because they interpret the text via a separate reading head, a head which, to persist with Derridean terminology, 'folds its outer edges' (its status at time of broadcast as a new episode) 'back over onto inner edges' (the *Doctor Who* corpus in general, and 'An Unearthly Child' in particular). Grounding Derrida's theoretical argument in the material circumstances of the *Doctor Who* text offers a language with which we can describe that text and its relationship to itself. *Doctor Who* continually rejects the notion of linearity across its corpus. Thus when dealing with adaptations within the text of *Doctor Who*, it is no longer feasible to speak of source texts and of fidelity, or otherwise, to them.[7] Instead, attention must be paid to the way in which the text quotes, displaces or folds itself.

Big Finish to BBC One: *Jubilee* to 'Dalek'

The current *Doctor Who* production team have commissioned scripts from a number of writers previously responsible for what are usually considered the Doctor's 'non-canonical' adventures.[8] Indeed, every writer of the first new season of the programme had written *Doctor Who* material before.[9] Show-runner Russell T. Davies justifies this by saying: 'It felt important for the first series to get people who knew the language, the shorthand of the original series' (Russell 2006: 32). Revealingly, rather than use scriptwriters who had contributed to the original run of the programme, only those who had written *Doctor Who* material that most viewers would consider non-canonical were employed. To date, no writer of the 'classic' *Doctor Who* series has contributed to the revival, nor were any commissioned for season four, which began production in July 2007. Davies' interest in securing the services of writers familiar with the programme's heritage thus seems limited only to those whose experience of writing for the character of the Doctor is not tainted by any involvement in the 1989 cancellation of the programme. It is possible to argue, then, that the post-2005 incarnation of *Doctor Who* is an adaptation not of the classic series, but of the version or versions of *Doctor Who* created in alternate media between the years 1989 and 2003, the point at which the series was recommissioned.[10] Since these non-televised versions of *Doctor Who* were themselves recognizable adaptations of elements present in the classic series in the sense that they featured characters, situations and themes that were found in that series, we can speak of a process of adaptation that is twofold, at least: the first (canonical) run of the series was folded into its non-canonical or at least non-televised presence in alternate media, which was itself then re-folded back into the televised canon. Much of the evidence of this folding is invisible, but some can be detected via analysis of the adapted material that has been part of *Doctor Who* since 2005.

The most prominent instance of adaptation in the first season of the revived *Doctor Who* was Robert Shearman's episode, 'Dalek', which he adapted from his own audio drama, *Jubilee*, produced for Big Finish productions in 2003. Set in an alternate version of Britain under the rule of a fascistic dictatorship, *Jubilee* features the Sixth Doctor, his companion, the history professor Evelyn Smythe, and a lone Dalek imprisoned and tortured by human forces in the Tower of London. *Jubilee* itself offers an excellent example of the way that *Doctor Who* has the confidence to fold its effect upon popular culture into its own fictive universe – to fold the extra-textual into the textual. Named in honour of the 40th anniversary of the first episode of *Doctor Who* and itself the fortieth *Doctor Who* CD release from Big Finish, *Jubilee* plays on the huge popularity of the Daleks and Dalek memorabilia in actual 1960s Britain. The drama begins with what appears to be a trailer for a forthcoming *Doctor Who* audio CD featuring the Doctor's long-standing enemy: 'Coming soon . . . *Daleks: The Ultimate Adventure*', intones Nicholas Briggs, the familiar voice of the range's trailers and continuity announcements. It is only when the supposed trailer concludes – after the listener is confronted with sinisterly giggling Dalek voices, a transatlantic-sounding gung-ho Doctor, and the casting of 'Plenty O'Toole [the name of a character in the filmed version of Ian Fleming's *Diamonds are Forever*] as Evelyn "Hot Lips" Smythe' – that its status as part of the text of *Jubilee* is confirmed:

> *Daleks: The Ultimate Adventure.* Coming to a cinema near you, soon. Your supervisor will inform you of the cinema to which you have been assigned. Attendance is compulsory by order of the Historical Instruction Act. All praise the glorious English Empire. (2003: episode 1)

In the England of *Jubilee*, a very real Dalek invasion had been foiled by the Doctor and Evelyn exactly 100 hundred years before the play begins, and the country's victory has given it the confidence and resources to become the world's only superpower. Representations of the humiliated Daleks are used for propaganda purposes, and appear on soft drink cartons, confectionery wrappers, and the silver screen. Ignoring the Doctor's warnings, Evelyn attempts to comfort the last surviving Dalek, which considers her to be its equal. Ultimately, a temporal paradox allows the Daleks to return *en masse*, as a hysterical human crowd baying for the extermination of the last Dalek and the Doctor are themselves transformed into Daleks by the return of the 100-year-old invasion force. This striking metaphor for the inhumanity of humanity – and specifically the inhumanity of Shearman's version of Englishness – is perhaps the most memorable scene in the play.

To fold *Jubilee* back into canonical *Doctor Who*, Shearman's 'Dalek' was first of all situated within the narrative context established for the Ninth Doctor. Episodes of the revived series are set after an unseen Time War that has supposedly eradicated the Daleks along with the Doctor's own race, the Time Lords. Eschewing all references to the real-life cultural impact of the Daleks and the fictional English Empire, and positing that the Dalek which appears in this episode is the only one in the universe, 'Dalek' foregrounds the torture of a Dalek by its human captors. As in *Jubilee*, the fundamental relationship of the episode is that which exists between the nameless Dalek and the Doctor's companion, in this case Rose Tyler. But while they share this almost transgressive central motif of genuine empathy between human and Dalek, the two versions of this encounter reveal the very different fictive and institutional contexts within which the stories are produced. *Jubilee* takes place in an England saturated with Dalek lore and Dalek paraphernalia, while Evelyn is no stranger to the species herself. Similarly, the play was produced by a small independent company for a niche market of dedicated *Doctor Who* fans who might be expected to have a great deal of knowledge about the *Doctor Who* text and the Daleks' place within it. When Evelyn is asked by the Dalek if, despite his current powerlessness, she is afraid of him, what she knows about the Daleks can only lead her to reply: 'Yes, you know I am' (2003: episode 2). By contrast, Rose knows very little about Daleks, and more significantly, neither do many of the millions of prime-time BBC One viewers. Rose's response to the same question, 'Do you fear me?', is simply 'No', and after a touch from Rose that enables the Dalek to regenerate itself and escape its captivity, Shearman devotes the rest of his episode to illustrating exactly why Rose and newcomers to *Doctor Who* should fear Daleks – and why the creatures were successful in the first place. By shifting the context of his narrative from a world where it is impossible to avoid knowledge of the Daleks to one where it is impossible to achieve it, Shearman mimics the movement from Big Finish to BBC One while preserving the emotional core of his story. Assuming no prior knowledge of the Daleks on the part of its audience, 'Dalek' embraces and at the same time seeks to efface not only its status as an adaptation of *Jubilee*, but also as the latest in a long line of adaptations of Terry Nation's original Dalek story of 1963.[11]

The emphasis placed on the emotional connection shared by Dalek and companion in both versions of Shearman's tale is characteristic of the approach taken by writers of the new *Doctor Who*. This sensibility is extended in 'Dalek', where a new sub-plot dramatizes Rose's flirtation with Adam, a young scientist associated with the Dalek's captivity. The episode ends with Adam joining Rose and the Doctor for their next adventure in the future. However, when Adam exploits the future's technological advances for his own benefit, it becomes clear that he is unsuited to a life in the Tardis, and the Doctor angrily returns him to his own time. While an interest in emotions, and in particular emotions prompted by sexual attraction, was not entirely missing from classic *Doctor Who*, it plays a far more important role in the revived programme than it ever did in the past.[12] In particular, the issue of the Doctor's sexuality, almost always a taboo subject in the 1963–89 series, is treated by Davies and his writing team as a legitimate object for dramatization. As Shearman notes with reference to 'Dalek', 'The biggest problem for me was Rose fancying Adam, which I found very hard to do and Russell made it work by making it clear that what Rose fancied in Adam was a Doctorish element' (Russell 2006: 159). As this indicates, one of the key innovations of the 2005 series was its suggestion that Rose and the Doctor were something more than platonic companions, and while there is no definite suggestion that the two have experienced a physical relationship, it is clear that they are in love with one another.[13] When Rose finally confesses to the Doctor in 'Doomsday' that she loves him, his reply, 'Quite right too', reveals that the character's sexuality is still circumscribed by what we might variously interpret as English reserve or alien arrogance. However, at the end of three seasons of the revived programme the viewer has been presented with ample evidence that – at some level – the Doctor is capable of love and affection.[14]

Fan fiction to BBC One and back again

Perhaps the most interesting acknowledgement of the Doctor's emotional life comes in 'School Reunion' (2006) by Toby Whitehouse. The episode strives to fold the classic adventures of the Doctor into the new series by having the Tenth Doctor meet Sarah Jane Smith and K9, companions of his earlier incarnations, and it illustrates the importance of attending to the folding of the text rather than to linear examples of straightforward adaptation. 'School Reunion' is not an adaptation at all in the usual sense of the word, but it taps into a sensibility that most demonstrates the popularity and pleasure of adaptation in contemporary culture: fan fiction. Far from being a simple exercise in nostalgia, the episode, like much fan fiction, reveals a desire to 'rewrite and reinterpret events in the story to suit the desires of the writer' (MacDonald 2006: 28). The episode reveals, in a way that was never made clear during the character's regular travels in the Tardis, that Sarah Jane was – and perhaps still is – in love with the Doctor. When the Doctor discovers in their final scene together that Sarah Jane does not have any children, he remarks:

> THE DOCTOR: Sorry, I didn't get a chance to ask. There hasn't been anyone. . . you know?
> SARAH JANE: Well, there was this one guy. I travelled with him for a while, but he was a tough act to follow. ('School Reunion', *Doctor Who*, 2006)

What the episode does, in a way that will be familiar to any reader of online *Doctor Who* fan fiction, is to recast the canonical relationship of the Doctor and Sarah Jane by introducing a previously unacknowledged romantic or sexual element. Without wishing to suggest that any form of plagiarism has taken place, it is possible to locate numerous similar reinterpretations of the Doctor's relationships in online fan fiction archives.

Of the 5,271 completed *Doctor Who* stories on the website Fanfiction. net in October 2007, 85 were posted before the 2005 series was broadcast, and would therefore not have been influenced by the programme's own increased emotional focus, although they could, of course, have been influenced by non-televised *Doctor Who* material. Ranging from 100 words to the size of a full-length novel, many of these stories are interested in reinterpreting the Doctor's relationships through the lens of sexual desire. Some stories, such as the appropriately titled 'Pygmalion' by Silver Raven, seem to reinforce hegemonic gender stereotypes. In this story Ace, the Seventh Doctor's young female companion, reveals her pleasure at being manipulated by the Doctor:

> [N]ow she will learn the intricacies of both physical and mental intimacy. She thinks he has moulded her into what he needs her to be, which may be the same was [sic] what she was always meant to be. And if it isn't, she doesn't care.[15]

Others treat the Doctor's sexuality in a more interesting manner. In chanformon's 'Younger Women', the Sixth Doctor and Evelyn decide to avoid a long walk back to the Tardis and check into a nearby hotel instead. Despite being more than 600 years old, in this incarnation the Doctor appears to be a man in his early forties; Evelyn is a woman in her late 50s. After they have corrected the hotel receptionist's initial assumption that they are mother and son, the pair find that their relationship has been misinterpreted once again when they discover a double bed in their shared room. The story's punch line, spoken by the Doctor, is: 'Younger women do have their attractions. Maybe we should take advantage of opportunity!', which demonstrates an interest in challenging the dynamics of normative romance fiction and, as the Doctor remarks, 'assumptions based on physical appearance'.[16] 'Old Girlfriends 1: Sarah Jane' by MizJoely takes this impulse further, and bears favourable comparison with 'School Reunion'. While the televised script has the Tenth Doctor tell Sarah Jane that he left her behind because 'I was called back home, and in those days humans weren't allowed', and later suggest to Rose that he sometimes leaves companions because he cannot come to terms with their mortality ('School Reunion', *Doctor Who*, 2006), 'Old Girlfriends 1' offers an explanation that accounts for Sarah Jane's ever-receding agency during the classic series. When challenged by Ace about his fourth incarnation's relationship with Sarah Jane, the Seventh Doctor replies,

> I had to let her go; she'd grown dependent on me. *Too* dependent. When we first met, she was a fiery young thing, filled with passionate convictions and a free-spirited, independent way of looking at life. By the time I received the call to Gallifrey, she'd started . . . regressing. Slowly losing her independence, bit by bit. Relying on me to get her out of scrapes and situations that could probably have been avoided, had she not fallen into the trap of expecting me to come to her rescue all the time. . . . I let her do it, let her get away with it, because I was beginning to enjoy playing White Knight to her Damsel in Distress. When I realized that, I also realized it had to stop.[17]

This version of the story has the advantage of remaining far closer to the events that actually occurred during Sarah Jane's 1970s appearances on the programme, and is thus an interesting example of fan fiction that actually appears more faithful to the televised *Doctor Who* canon than the 'official' post-2005 series, while sharing that series' openness about sexuality. It also recognizes the tendency of some *Doctor Who* writers to relegate the female companion to the status of hysterical victim, and attempts to account for this by emphasizing the Doctor's complicity in Sarah Jane's learned helplessness.

But online fan fiction writers are not content to imagine merely a heterosexual identity for the Doctor. In the genre known as slash (so called because of the '/' symbol used to identify character pairings), writers imagine the Doctor's relationship with his male companions or enemies to be a sexual one. Since the Doctor has often displayed character traits not usually associated with male fictional heroes – intelligence, articu-lacy, asexuality, pacifism, flamboyance – the text is an ideal one in which to explore non-conventional representations of masculinity. As Henry Jenkins argues, 'slash is not so much a genre about sex as it is a genre about the limitations of traditional masculinity and about reconfiguring male identity' (Jenkins 1992: 191). Although the revived *Doctor Who* has strongly implied that the Doctor is heterosexual, it has been careful not to completely close off the possibility that he might in fact be bisexual. Jack Harkness, the openly pansexual companion of the Ninth and Tenth Doctors, offers one avenue through which this idea can be explored by fans; the Doctor's arch enemy, the Master, offers another. Although never as clear about the Doctor's homosexual impulses as it is about his heterosexual ones, the televised text offers fans interested in 'slashing' the Doctor ample evidence upon which to base their stories. For exam-ple, in 'The Parting of the Ways' (2005), Jack kisses the Doctor on the mouth in the same way that he kisses Rose, perhaps suggesting that the three have shared a sexual relationship. Similarly, in 'The Sound of Drums' (2007) the Doctor's first conversation with the Master is charged with emotion, as the Master teasingly points out:

> THE DOCTOR: I've been alone ever since. But not anymore. Don't you see, all we've got is each other.
> THE MASTER: Are you asking me out on a date? ('The Sound of Drums', *Doctor Who*, 2007)

In the following episode, 'Last of the Time Lords', the Doctor cradles the dying Master in his arms and weeps openly when his enemy refuses to regenerate. Once again, moments such as these arise from material pro-duced during the years that the series was off air, and are already being refolded back into the slash genre of fan fiction.[18] As one poster on calap-ine.livejournal.com remarked after the Master's return to the screen in 'Utopia':

> I've gotta say, I never really gave much thought to the Doctor/Master [rela-tion]ship, but after the Master demanded tonight that the Doctor say his name and the Doctor stood outside the locked Tardis and said 'Master' in a pleading voice . . . Oh my god! I'm running to find supporting fanfic![19]

In his work on fan fiction, Jenkins identifies one aspect of the sensibility that underpins its practice: 'unimpressed by institutional authority and expertise, the fans assert their own right to form interpretations, to offer evaluations and to construct cultural canons' (Jenkins 1992: 18). In the revived series of *Doctor Who*, writers like Davies, Shearman and Cornell, whose long-term fan status is made clear by their contribution to *Doctor Who* during its wilderness years, have achieved the very positions of institutional authority and expertise that Jenkins supposes to be beyond the grasp of the disenfranchised fan writer. It is, then, perhaps not the least important achievement of the revived *Doctor Who* that it has managed to preserve the nuanced interest in sexuality displayed in much fan writing even after its practitioners have been welcomed into the institutional fold of the BBC. And the complex internal interrelations of the *Doctor Who* text, that text's willingness to quote, displace and fold itself, also offers the study of adaptation one way in which it can move away from debates grounded in the question of fidelity. If, with Derrida, a text comes to be understood not as a linear model for or adaptation of another text, but as the incalculable sum total of its folded and refolded iterations, we might truly be able to claim that, like the Tardis, the discourse of adaptation is much more sizable than it might at first appear.

Notes

1. Moffat discusses this in an interview published in *Doctor Who Magazine* 384, 25 July 2007.
2. The document is held at BBC Written Archives Centre, Reading: T5/647/1: 'Science Fiction', by John Braybon and Alice Frick, 25 July 1962.
3. Show-runner Russell T. Davies mentions his love for *Buffy*, and lists *Toy Story*, *Shrek* and *The Incredibles* as 'the best template [sic] you could possibly use' in Russell 2006: 35, 37.
4. Notwithstanding the title of their monograph, Tulloch and Alvarado acknowledge that their 'unfolding text' can at times also be a 'folding' one, although they do not use the term itself. See, for example, p. 89.
5. By the time the third season of *Doctor Who* (2005–) had been broadcast in spring 2007 there were 737 televised episodes of the programme, over 100 audio dramas featuring the Doctor, 73 Eighth Doctor BBC novels and 61 Virgin *New Adventures* novels. In addition, on 25 October 2007 the website Fanfiction.net played host to 5,271 completed *Doctor Who* stories. I am unfortunately not able to refer to the 2008 season of the programme, for reasons of time and space.
6. *Doctor Who* is regularly one of the top 20 most-watched programmes broadcast in the UK, and its ratings are often bettered only by those of long-running soap operas and international sporting events.
7. See also Parkin (2007: 248–50), where the author considers the disparate and contradictory nature of the *Doctor Who* canon and notes that the Doctor's televised adventures are not always the origin of the cornerstones of the *Doctor Who* universe.
8. The question of canonicity is an extremely moot one in *Doctor Who*, given its plethora of spin-off material. Some fans insist that all *Doctor Who* material is canonical; others, that only televised stories should be canonized. For a comprehensive overview of the debate, see Parkin.
9. Russell T. Davies, Paul Cornell and Mark Gatiss all wrote novels for Virgin Books' *New Adventures*, with Cornell and Gatiss also scripting CD audio dramas for Big Finish productions, as did Robert Shearman. Cornell also wrote the *Doctor Who* animated webcast 'Scream of the Shalka' (2003). Steven Moffat penned a *Doctor Who* short story for Virgin Books and a parody, *Doctor Who and The Curse of Fatal Death*, for BBC One's Comic Relief 1999.
10. In an interview with Dale Smith, Paul Cornell revealed that during the writing of his 2005 episode, 'Father's Day', he was specifically asked by Davies to adopt the emotionally inflected voice he used when writing for the *New Adventures*. He adds: 'that wasn't on the to-do list of the old show. The *NAs* put human drama high on the list.' See Smith 2007: 269.

11. Although there is not the space to discuss it here, a similar 'blank-slate' technique was used to reintroduce the Cybermen to the programme in 2006. Again loosely adapted from a Big Finish audio play, in this case Marc Platt's *Spare Parts*, the televised episodes 'Rise of the Cybermen' and 'The Age of Steel' by Tom MacRae transfer the creation of the Cyber race to a parallel Earth and thus avoid contradicting established *Doctor Who* continuity or alienating viewers unfamiliar with it.

12. Although Barry Letts, producer and scriptwriter of classic *Doctor Who*, emphasized the programme's interest in emotion in a 1981 interview, John Tulloch and Henry Jenkins note that the pre-2005 series did not dramatize 'love/sexual relationships'. See Tulloch and Jenkins 1995: 92.

13. The first indication that the Doctor possesses romantic feelings occurred in *Doctor Who* (1996), when Paul McGann's Eighth Doctor kissed Grace Holloway.

14. Moffat's 'The Girl in the Fireplace' (2006), which owes much to Audrey Niffenegger's novel *The Time Traveller's Wife*, clearly shows the Doctor falling in love with Jeanne-Antoinette Poisson. In 2007, Paul Cornell's two-part adventure 'Human Nature'/'The Family of Blood', adapted from his own *NA* novel *Human Nature*, sees the Doctor become human and fall in love with a woman he meets in 1913 England. Keen to reveal the series' ability to enfold spin-off material within itself, the BBC made Cornell's out-of-print *Human Nature* available online, with additional notes from the author describing the adaptation process.

15. www.fanfiction.net/s/35926/1/Pygmalion, posted 21 June 2000. [Accessed 25 October 2007.]

16. www.fanfiction.net/s/16994/1/Younger_Women, posted 30 March 2000. [Accessed 25 October 2007.]

17. www.fanfiction.net/s/2129283/1/Old_Girlfriends_1_Sarah_Jane, posted 10 November 2004. [Accessed 25 October 2007.]

18. The relationship between the Doctor and the Master, often represented as one of friendly rivalry in the televised series, is fraught with sexual tension in, for instance, Cornell's 'Scream of the Shalka' webcast.

19. See http://calapine.livejournal.com/392680.html, posted by shadowturqouise on 17 June 2007. [Accessed 30 October 2007.]

Bibliography

Anderson, Poul (1999), *The Guardians of Time*. London: Pan.

Buffy the Vampire Slayer (1997–2003). Mutant Enemy Productions.

Calapine.livejournal.com.

Chapman, James (2006), *Inside the Tardis: The Worlds of Doctor Who – A Cultural History*. London: I. B. Tauris.

Cook, John R. (1999), 'Adapting telefantasy: the *Doctor Who and the Daleks* films', in I. Q. Hunter (ed.), *British Science Fiction Cinema*. London: Routledge, pp. 113–27.

Cornell, Paul (1995), *Human Nature*. London: Virgin.

Derrida, Jacques (1979), 'Living on: border lines', in Harold Bloom, Paul De Man, Jacques Derrida, Geoffrey H. Hartman and J. Hillis Miller, *Deconstruction and Criticism*. London: Routledge & Kegan Paul, pp. 75–176.

Doctor Who (1963–89). BBC Television.

Doctor Who (1996). BBC Television, Universal Television.

Doctor Who (2005–). BBC Television.

Doctor Who and the Curse of Fatal Death (1999). BBC Television.

Doctor Who Magazine 384, 25 July 2007.

Hickman, Clayton (ed.) (2005), *'Doctor Who' Annual 2006*. London: Panini.

The Incredibles (2004). USA, dir. Brad Bird.

Jenkins, Henry (1992), *Textual Poachers: Television Fans and Participatory Culture*. New York and London: Routledge.

Jubilee (2003). Big Finish Productions.

MacDonald, Marianne (2006), 'Harry Potter and the fan fiction phenom', *Gay and Lesbian Review Worldwide*, 13, 28–30.

Niffenegger, Audrey (1994), *The Time Traveller's Wife*. London: Jonathan Cape.

Parkin, Lance (2007), 'Canonicity matters: defining the *Doctor Who* canon', in David Butler (ed.), *Time and Relative Dissertations in Space: Critical Perspectives on 'Doctor Who'*. Manchester: Manchester University Press, pp. 246–62.

Russell, Gary, (2006), *Doctor Who: The Inside Story*. London: BBC.

Shrek (2001). USA, dir. Andrew Adamson and Vicky Jenson.

Smith, Dale (2007), 'Broader and deeper: the lineage and impact of the Timewyrm series', in David Butler (ed.), *Time and Relative Dissertations in Space: Critical Perspectives on 'Doctor Who'*. Manchester: Manchester University Press, pp. 263–79.

Spare Parts (2002). Big Finish Productions.

The Time Machine (1960). USA, dir. George Pal.

Toy Story (1996). USA, dir. John Lasseter.

Tulloch, John and Manuel Alvarado (1983), *Doctor Who: The Unfolding Text*. New York: St Martin's Press.

— and Henry Jenkins (1995), *Science Fiction Audiences: Watching 'Doctor Who' and 'Star Trek'*. London: Routledge.

www.bbc.co.uk/doctorwho/classic/webcasts/shalka

www.fanfiction.net

Part II

After-images

CHAPTER SIX

3:10 Again: A Remade Western and the Problem of Authenticity

PETE FALCONER

Any responsible critic looking at adaptation must address the effects of historical change. The perspective from which earlier versions are viewed and the contexts in which newer ones are produced and understood can be important in explaining their priorities and points of emphasis. One type of adaptation, the movie remake, is particularly useful in bringing these issues into focus. Since differences in medium are (usually, although not always, especially given the increased prevalence of digital technologies) a much less central concern with remakes, historical changes between different versions of a film can be identified more clearly.

Particularly relevant to an understanding of the two versions of *3:10 to Yuma* (Delmer Daves, 1957 and James Mangold, 2007) are historical changes relating to genre. Both are Westerns, but in the fifty years between them the implications of making and watching a Western have drastically altered. As a consequence, we can see different, even incompatible, standards of authenticity operating in the two movies.

The earlier film is itself an adaptation, of the Elmore Leonard story 'Three-ten to Yuma', first published in *Dime Western Magazine* in 1953. The story establishes the basic situation: an outlaw is apprehended in the town of Bisbee in the Arizona Territory and taken to nearby Contention, where he is held in a hotel room awaiting the 3:10 train to Yuma Territorial Prison. It is told primarily from the point of view of deputy marshal Paul Scallen, who is responsible for holding and transporting the outlaw, Jim Kidd. It begins with the men arriving in Contention, placing Kidd's arrest in the backstory. The first film version expands on this, showing the earlier action in Bisbee, and alters the two central characters. Professional lawman Scallen becomes Dan Evans (Van Heflin), a homesteader who has volunteered because he needs money to buy water rights for his drought-stricken ranch. Cocky young outlaw Kidd becomes Ben Wade (Glenn Ford), an older man with greater charm and authority. The 2007 film retains and develops these changes, making it more an adaptation of the first movie than the story. I would also argue, however, that the newer *3:10* is as much an adaptation of the Western genre as it is of any specific predecessor. Many aspects of the 2007 movie can be attributed to its having to address the peculiar status of Hollywood Westerns in the early twenty-first century.

Although several critics, such as Jim Kitses (1998: 15) have rightly disputed claims that the genre is dead, it is clear that Westerns are no longer a prominent part of popular filmmaking. While this statement might seem like a platitude, its implications for the contemporary Westerns that *are* made have not been fully examined. Some of these implications can be seen in the introduction to an *American Cinematographer* article on the 2007 *3:10*:

> The 'horse opera' was once a staple of Hollywood and the stock in trade of dozens of great ASC cinematographers, but today the Western remains a rare treat. This autumn promises to end the drought with *3:10 to Yuma*, *The Assassination of Jesse James by the Coward Robert Ford* and *No Country for Old Men*. (Donovan, 2007: 72)

Here, we have a contemporary moment in which filmmakers are unaccustomed to making Westerns and, importantly, audiences are unaccustomed to watching them. Given these circumstances, and the relative isolation of twenty-first-century Westerns – each 'a rare treat,' with no current generic mainstream to be judged against – definitions of what the genre is understood to include are likely to vary considerably from film to film. This is reflected in the three movies offered as a Western revival in 2007. One is a Western action-adventure, one a somewhat ponderous art-house movie, and one a border thriller set in 1980. Without a continuing tradition, it falls to the individual film to define and explain the genre for itself.

This burden of explanation (and, implicitly, justification) weighs heavily on the 2007 *3:10*. The film works hard to establish its version of what a Western is and means. Much of the new material it introduces can be understood in these terms. Consider its deployment of three key iconographic elements: hats, horses and guns. As we might expect, these are all present in the 1957 movie. However, they are not given the self-conscious emphasis that they receive in 2007. The later film's handling of these generic features centres on Ben Wade (Russell Crowe). Wade is an ambiguous character in both films, but is treated more sympathetically in the second, as something approaching an anti-hero. This portrayal is reinforced by the ways in which our attention is drawn to his hat, horse and gun.

All three are marked as somehow special and unique, all three are mentioned in the dialogue, and all three are lost and regained by Wade in the course of his captivity. His hat is black with a patterned band, and distinctive in outline – narrower in the brim and squarer in the crown than a conventional stetson. The importance of its colour is underlined during the film's climactic scenes when Wade's henchman, Charlie Prince (Ben Foster) orders some local gunmen, whom he has enlisted to help rescue his boss, not to shoot at 'the black hat'. To use this as shorthand for the outlaw seems a conscious allusion to the popular myth about older Westerns – that the hero wears a white hat and the villain a black one. While the film does not endorse this fallacy, it still serves to remind us that the hat is a specifically Western element.

Wade's hat is also given greater narrative significance in the recent *3:10*. It is worn by a deputy who replaces Wade on the stagecoach that had been transporting him, acting as a decoy to draw his gang in the wrong direction. This episode is also in the earlier film, and is similarly staged: the driver intentionally gets a wheel stuck in a ditch as a pretext for stopping outside Dan Evans's house. There, the switch is made, using the coach to conceal it from Wade's men, who are watching from up on a rise overlooking Dan's spread. In the 1957 version, it is assumed that Wade's outline (hat included) is sufficiently generic for a similarly-built man to pass for him at a distance. In the 2007 version, his silhouette is distinctive enough to make the hat vital to a successful impersonation. Again, the film is drawing attention to its iconography – Westerns, like gangster films, obsessively reproduce the same basic physical outline – but here its role in the presentation of Wade is more evident. He is both connected to the iconic outlines of classic Western characters and distinguished from them. He is the only character in the recent *3:10* who is permitted to be mythic, and given heroic status.

Wade's horse and gun perform similar functions. They are unique and distinctive – while the other characters ride any old horse and fire any old gun, Wade's are identifiably his. He takes their theft by the thuggish Tucker (Kevin Durand) as a personal affront, and later justifies his stabbing of Tucker as revenge. Both horse and gun also contribute to the mysticism that the 2007 film adds to Wade's character. His control over his horse is unusually strong – it comes when he whistles, even galloping after the Yuma-bound train at the end. His gun, black and decorated with a crucifix, is called 'The Hand of God'. Wade alleges that the gun is cursed, and indeed, the two characters who steal it are killed.

In both films, implausible claims like this are made by characters and borne out by the subsequent action. The shift in perspective between the two versions is visible in the differences between these claims. In the 1957 film, Dan Evans asserts, despite three years of drought, that it is 'bound to rain' within six months. His fragile, uncertain optimism is vindicated at the end of the movie. Besides showing the contrasting sympathies of the two films, this comparison underlines how localized the mythic content of the later version is. While the coming of rain, implicitly triggered by Dan's heroism – his 'action ends the drought as the quester's can in legend' (Pye 1975: 43) – transforms the whole world of the movie, the cursed-gun motif is limited in scope by its connection to Wade.

The Mangold movie concludes with the restoration of Wade to full power. He regains his hat, his gun, and finally his horse. Although he does board the 3:10 train (and hand his gun to the guard) in tribute to the fallen Evans (Christian Bale), this gesture only indicates his complete control over the situation. The last thing we see Wade do is whistle for his horse, which follows the train, implying that escape is imminent. Throughout the film, our attention is drawn to these pieces of iconography, which are significant exclusively in relation to Wade. Their restoration to him becomes as important a narrative resolution as any achievement on the part of Dan Evans. Retrospectively, this makes the entire narrative seem like just another exciting episode in the life of Ben Wade.

That the 2007 film is so emphatic about both highlighting iconographic elements, and delimiting their significance, can be related to the conditions in which twenty-first-century Westerns have to operate. Western imagery is still pervasive enough in popular culture – in cartoons, advertising, fashion and elsewhere – to be recognizable to a contemporary audience, but expectations concerning its function and significance in a Western movie are likely to be much more vague. In 1957, the first *3:10* had an audience with the cultural capital to understand it in relation to other films in a genre still current and proliferating. In 2007, the impulse to fix the significance of generic iconography comes from the knowledge that this significance cannot be taken for granted.

An interesting parallel can be drawn with some of the problems confronting film adaptations of older literary works. As Brian McFarlane reminds us:

> In 'period' films, one often senses exhaustive attempts to create an impression of fidelity to, say, Dickens' London or to Jane Austen's village life, the result of which, so far from ensuring fidelity to the text, is to produce a distracting quaintness. What was a contemporary work for the author, who could take a good deal relating to time and place for granted, as requiring little or no scene-setting for his readers, has become a period piece for the filmmaker. (1996: 9)

The 'period' in the 2007 *3:10* is less nineteenth-century Arizona than 1950s Hollywood Cinema. Its contexts and conventions are those that must be reconstructed, made obvious and explained.

While adapting historical details is different from adapting aesthetic conventions, it is still clear that Westerns now require considerably more 'scene-setting' than they once did. Compare McFarlane's remarks to Robin Wood's, concerning two different approaches to the genre, typified by Ford and Hawks:

> The term 'traditional', applied to the Western, can mean two things, and two very different kinds of Western. The genre gives great scope for a director

with a feeling for America's past, for the borderline of history and myth, the early stages of civilization, primitive, precarious and touching. But the genre also offers a collection of convenient conventions which allow the director to escape from the trammels of contemporary surface reality and the demand for verisimilitude, and express certain fundamental human urges or explore themes personal to him. If the classic Westerns of John Ford, with their loving and nostalgic evocation of the past, are the supreme examples of the first kind, *Rio Bravo* is the supreme example of the second. (1968: 37)

Despite the frequent tendency of critical accounts to privilege Ford and the first approach, most Westerns made during the genre's popular heyday fall into the second category (see Pye 1996: 10). However, as I have already argued, this is no longer a convenience that filmmakers can exploit. Fidelity to familiar conventions will no longer be understood as substituting for a kind of realism. For newer Westerns, this means the return of what Wood calls 'the demand for verisimilitude', that is, the necessity to provide a backdrop to the action that the audience will consider plausible.

As Douglas Pye observes, the 1957 *3:10* has often been valued for its 'realism' (1975: 42). Michael Walker takes this position, praising Daves for 'showing the harsh conditions under which men and women lived and worked' (1996: 146). I do not wish to dispute this, but it is equally important to acknowledge (as both Pye and Walker do in different ways) that these conditions are presented in an often quite stylized fashion. An example of this is the strange emptiness of the towns of Bisbee and Contention. Although there is vestigial evidence of social life in the latter, both are characterized by an extreme sparseness of population. Walker observes an alien quality, calling the siesta that keeps the citizens of Bisbee out of sight 'a very un-American activity' (145). This eerie feeling is present in the short story: 'It was almost noon, yet there were few people about. He wondered about this and asked himself if it was unnaturally quiet for a Saturday noon in Contention. . .' (Leonard 2007: 185) but is more fully elaborated in the 1957 film, where the emptiness indoors and outdoors is an important and reasserted context. In contrast, the towns in the newer movie are positively bustling. The streets are full of extras engaged in various forms of labour and commerce. In the Daves film, Bisbee's drinking, banking and law all apparently take place (when they do) under one roof. In the Mangold version, they are given separate premises, implying a broader social and commercial scope.

It is as if the 2007 movie cannot risk provoking the question 'where is everybody?' This is something that a 1957 audience, more accustomed to variations on the 'traditional one-street Western town' (Walker 1996: 160), would be less likely to ask. This is not to say that the empty spaces in the earlier film are not noteworthy (I have already argued that they are), but that they would be more readily understood in relation to established generic possibilities, on a familiar continuum from boom town to ghost town. With no such frame of reference to rely on, the 2007 version is compelled to demonstrate the everyday workings of its locations, in order to give them the necessary background credibility.

This impulse to *show more* can also be seen to account for the greater length and altered structure of the newer *3:10*. It is an understandable temptation for contemporary film-makers, who cannot be sure where their audience's next Western is coming from, to cram as many different aspects of the genre as possible into one film. The journey to Contention is shown only briefly in the 1957 version. In 2007, it becomes a much larger section, taking Wade and his captors through 'renegade' Apache country and bringing them into contact with a Chinese work crew tunnelling through the mountains. As well as these additional historical/generic elements, this section also introduces a narrative situation reminiscent of several classic Westerns, including *The Naked Spur* (Anthony Mann, 1953) and *Ride Lonesome* (Budd Boetticher, 1959), in which an unstable group escorts a captive through the wilderness. The cumulative impression is of an attempt to present the genre's 'greatest hits'. This can also be seen in *Appaloosa* (Ed Harris, 2008), the episodic sprawl of its plot incorporating situations recalling Westerns from *Rio Bravo* (Howard Hawks, 1959) to *Butch Cassidy and the Sundance Kid* (George Roy Hill, 1969).

The impulse to show in the 2007 *3:10* is combined with an impulse to explain. Some of the most significant additions to the dialogue involve adding details to characters' backstories. Ben Wade became a Scripture-quoting criminal, we learn, because he was abandoned as a child with only the Bible to read. Dan Evans has a wooden leg, having been wounded by friendly fire during an ignominious retreat in the Civil War. Dan needs money not just because of the drought, but because he is in debt to Hollander (Lennie Loftin) and has spent money treating his son's tuberculosis.

These somewhat overdetermined revelations tell us less about the characters than they do about the 2007 filmmakers' attitude to the 1957 movie. Mangold describes Dan Evans, as incarnated by Van Heflin, as 'a coward' who is 'innately hesitant or nervous' in contrast to the Evans in his own film, who 'has been wounded' and whose actions we consequently 'understand' (Esther 2007: 30). Accusing the 1957 Evans of ingrained cowardice is a gross misrepresentation of the movie, in which his character and circumstances are placed in conflict. By the end, he has managed to overcome his more pragmatic motives (i.e. money) for taking Wade to the station. Thus, his actions come to seem more selfless and heroic. Throughout the 2007 version, Evans is inextricably defined by his circumstances. The final journey from the hotel to the station contains much new and recapitulated backstory. One particularly significant moment is when Evans reveals the less than heroic fashion in which he lost his leg. Wade has overpowered Evans at this point, but the information causes him to take pity and relent. Evans's achievement in getting Wade to the train is undercut because he does so only with the outlaw's permission. It should be noted that Wade also intervenes on Evans's behalf in the 1957 film, but this takes place at the very last moment and is motivated by respect, not pity. In the 2007 movie Charlie Prince, having shot Evans down, remarks that 'For a one-legged rancher, he's one tough son-of-a-bitch.' Prince speaks for the film, which consistently defines Evans in terms of its limited sense of what a 'one-legged rancher' can achieve.

Reflecting on critical tendencies to characterize the history of the genre as an 'evolution' from simplicity to sophistication, Tag Gallagher comments that:

> Perhaps older westerns, like olden times, will always strike the modern mind as less complex, less amoral, and above all less vivid – particularly when the modern mind feels it unnecessary to examine the past in any detail. (2003: 263)

The view that Gallagher describes clearly informs the ways in which the newer *3:10* adapts its genre. Its insistence on presenting its characters as produced and confined by 'real' circumstances implies that this is a dimension its predecessor lacks. As Richard Dyer observes:

> . . .very often what is involved in pastiche, as well as other kinds of revisionist and self-aware Westerns, is the construction of an implicit model of the Western that turns out on inspection to be at the least questionable. (2007: 117)

Just as the 2007 *3:10* labours to compartmentalize its iconography, it also represses the realist side to the 1957 movie, representing it as unreconstructed myth, ripe for debunking. When Mangold says of his version that 'In a sense, I don't view it as repudiation. I view it as an embracement' (Esther, 2007: 28), it is significant that he treats 'repudiation' as the obvious place to start. The Mangold film embraces the Daves with the assumed caveat that it will have to be made acceptable to contemporary sensibilities. The most obvious examples of this are the moments where the 2007 Ben Wade is portrayed as exposing hypocrisy, especially his speech describing the atrocities committed against Apache women and children by Byron McElroy (Peter Fonda). The introduction of this material makes it clear that it is not just the earlier movie (which contains no representations of Native Americans, problematic or otherwise) that is being accused of naïve mythologizing, but older Westerns in general.

The 1957 film is in fact neither entirely mythic nor entirely realist. Rather, it relies on a tension between the two modes. Pye sets up these terms for understanding the movie, but characterizes it as 'a *collision* of mode and manner' (1975: 43). For Pye, who uses categories derived from Northrop Frye, the dominant mode of the film is 'low mimetic', that of 'most realist fiction' (1975: 33). The collision comes with the rain at the end, which introduces 'unprepared dimensions (the solemn sympathy of men and nature characteristic of Romance) in a way that seems to threaten the film's unity' (Pye 1975: 43). I would argue that these dimensions are prepared for in the various ways in which the film resembles a fable. This is established in the title sequence. Visually, it is much starker than what will follow, with the slow tilt across the arid plains revealing the stagecoach silhouetted on the horizon, and the subsequent shot of the horses' shadows on the ground. The theme song, performed by Frankie Laine, with its references to 'ghosts' and 'fate', adds to the sense that we are being told a tale, the kind that might involve mythic juxtapositions and supernatural possibilities.

While it is true that the rest of the film uses a fuller, more prosaic landscape, the potential for fantastic occurrences is maintained by the insistent and ambiguous presence of the title song. Its melody recurs frequently in the score, often on guitar, played slowly and loosely as if being idly strummed by a character just out of sight. It is also whistled by Wade and performed by an unseen female singer. In this last instance, we cannot be sure whether the characters can hear it. Evans seems unmoved, but Wade makes a vague, wistful remark about how he likes to hear 'a girl singing'. This sustained diegetic ambiguity preserves our sense of something beyond the immediate world of drought, poverty and toil. That this is connected to the special actions and perceptions of the characters is evident in the parallel between the 'girl singing' and the later moment when Dan Evans, his heroic resolve becoming more evident, hears thunder and his wife Alice (Leora Dana) does not. When the rain comes at the end, the song returns in its original arrangement (with Laine), and the diegetic sound disappears, signalling a resolution of the film's structuring tensions in favour of the mythic.

The other continuing reminder that the world of the 1957 movie might not be entirely naturalistic is its use of names. Simon Petch (who also calls the film a 'fable') identifies this element (2007: 48–50) but does not develop it, preferring to pursue a psychoanalytic reading. Petch points out the similarities between the names Dan and Ben, Alice and Alex (the Bisbee 'town drunk' and fellow volunteer, played by Henry Jones), but fails to indicate the significance of the latter pairing (they are both catalysts for Dan's action). These names actually form part of a larger series of correspondences. Dan and Ben are indeed similar, but are more meaningful in relation to the actors who play them (Dan and Ben/Van and Glenn). The film also contains two sets of alliteratively named brothers: Bill and Bob Moons (Boyd Stockman and Sheridan Comerate) and Dan's sons, Matthew and Mark Evans (Barry Curtis and Jerry Hartleben). Tellingly, the 2007 version removes this, omitting Bob Moons and calling Dan's elder son William (Logan Lerman).

The subtle interplay of realism and myth in the older *3:10* is only possible with an audience who have well-developed generic expectations.

Only in comparison to other 1950s Westerns can the film's unusual interest in a poor sodbuster, and its forestalling of heroic action, be considered realistic. Walker (1996: 123) remarks that the movie's plot combines aspects of *Shane* (George Stevens 1953) and *High Noon* (Fred Zinnemann 1952). Indeed, it can be seen as responding to these movies, which juxtapose myth and realism more schematically. In both earlier films, the innately superior hero is contrasted with the common people, who are noble but ineffectual (*Shane*) or cowardly and venal (*High Noon*). In the 1957 *3:10*, the hero is an ordinary man, the significance of this difference underlined by the casting of Van Heflin, who played homesteader Joe Starrett in *Shane*. It is not unduly speculative to suggest that this would be apparent to much of the 1957 audience, since *Shane* was the third-highest grossing film of 1953 (Krämer 2005: 112). While both *Shane* and *High Noon*, as popular landmarks of the genre, are still available reference points for contemporary film-makers, they cannot presume the same levels of recognition. This is evident in the way that the 2007 *3:10* references *High Noon*. In the new movie, the deputy marshals in Contention (Girard Swan and Christopher Berry) are named after characters in *High Noon*, and the marshal (Sean Hennigan) is given a name that was considered for the movie but not used. The relative obscurity of this allusion recalls Noël Carroll's concept of a dual register in Hollywood movies since the 1970s:

> It seems that popular cinema wants to remain popular by developing a two-tiered system of communication which sends an action/drama/fantasy-packed message to one segment of the audience and an additional hermetic, camouflaged, and recondite one to another. (1998: 244)

Because only a minority of the audience will understand the reference, it cannot be given an important function. Thus, it seems isolated and incidental. The Mangold film cannot enter into sustained dialogue with its intertexts because of the likelihood of incomprehension.

The one intertext that the newer film is compelled to substantially engage with is, of course, the older film. Enough of the 1957 screenplay is retained to earn its writer, Halsted Welles, a joint credit in 2007. Given the shifts in emphasis and tone between the two movies, it seems strange that so much material is reused. Much of what remains feels incongruous and contradictory. The lingering references to the drought seem particularly out of place. It is given passing mention early in the film, but only as one of several reasons why Dan Evans is in debt. It is given no special emphasis. The Arizona that we see does not look as though it has gone without rain for very long: the sky is often grey, the ground is not particularly dry, and there is even some snow. And yet, references to the drought are persistent enough that the newer film eventually has to remind us that it is not Dan's major motivation. When the characters arrive at the hotel room in Contention, Dan looks out of the window

and sees clouds on the horizon. Wade notices them too and asks Dan
if he still needs money. The question seems strange, since we know
that the money in this version is to repay Hollander, not to buy water. In
the next hotel scene, Wade asks Evans how he will spend the money
now he no longer needs it for irrigation. Dan replies, 'I owe people
money, Wade. That drought left me in the hole.' This explanation is
redundant – we already know about his debts. It only makes sense in
relation to the earlier film. It is as if Evans is telling the small segment of
the audience who have seen the 1957 movie that the drought is less
important *this time*, and they should forget about it.

Thus, we have another example of the 2007 *3:10* adapting its source
material by containing potentially confusing elements. This strategy can
be connected to Vera Dika's notion of 'simulated genres' (2003: 207),
revisited forms which reproduce generic conventions out of context.
In simulated Westerns, Dika observes a number of instances where
'the surface elements returned while their deeper structures seemed to
have been left behind' (215). It is important to remember, however, that
the 'deeper structures' of older Westerns are not constructed from
scratch each time, and that their depth is the result of many repetitions
and accumulations. The 2007 *3:10* faces the unenviable task of making
its generic elements significant in themselves, without a tradition to
depend on.

Attentive readers will notice that I have indulged my compulsion, as
a fan of the genre, to critique the recent movie's lack of richness as a
Western. It behoves me to admit that my model of generic authenticity
is also problematic. Jim Kitses has attacked 'the persistent and narrow
identification of the Western with its traditional model', arguing that
'there have always been dissents, deviations, aberrations, revisions'
(1998: 17). I maintain that tradition and dissent are not mutually exclu-
sive, and that the better a genre's conventions are understood by its
audience, the more scope there is for variations, whether critical or
merely novel. Kitses claims that 'even as the exceptions have begun to
outnumber the rule, the idea that these films now constitute the creative
mainstream of the genre has not truly registered' (1998: 19). The 'rule',
however, is a retrospective construction, and if we are to avoid charac-
terizing the history of Westerns as a teleological progression towards
revisionist enlightenment, we would do well to remember the versatil-
ity of older forms. By relating adaptation to genre, the importance of the
contexts in which different adaptations are produced and consumed
become clearer. Having examined a relatively extreme case of a film's
need to adapt generic conventions for its audience, it would be interesting to see if similar considerations apply in more favourable conditions.
Perhaps all genre movies are adaptations.

Bibliography

3:10 to Yuma (1957). USA, dir. Delmer Daves.

3:10 to Yuma (2007). USA, dir. James Mangold.

Appaloosa (2008). USA, dir. Ed Harris.

The Assassination of Jesse James by the Coward Robert Ford (2007). USA, dir. Andrew Dominik.

Butch Cassidy and the Sundance Kid (1969). USA, dir. George Roy Hill.

Carroll, N. (1998), 'The future of allusion: Hollywood in the seventies (and beyond)', in N. Carroll, *Interpreting the Moving Image*. Cambridge: Cambridge University Press, pp. 240–64.

Dika, V. (2003), *Recycled Culture in Contemporary Art and Film: The Uses of Nostalgia*. Cambridge: Cambridge University Press.

Donovan, J. (2007), 'Unsafe passage', *American Cinematographer* 88, 10, 72–9.

Dyer, R. (2007), *Pastiche*. London: Routledge.

Esther, J. (2007), 'Avoiding labels and lullabies: an interview with James Mangold', *Cineaste* 33, 1, 28–30.

Gallagher, T. (2003), 'Shoot-out at the genre corral: problems in the "evolution" of the Western', in B. K. Grant (ed.) *Film Genre Reader III*. Austin: University of Texas Press, pp. 262–76.

High Noon (1952). USA, dir. Fred Zinnemann.

Kitses, J. (1998), 'Introduction: post-modernism and the Western', in J. Kitses and G. Rickman (eds), *The Western Reader*. New York: Limelight Editions, pp. 15–31.

Krämer, P. (2005), *The New Hollywood: From 'Bonnie and Clyde' to 'Star Wars'*. London: Wallflower.

Leonard, E. (2007), 'Three-ten to Yuma', in *The Complete Western Stories of Elmore Leonard*. London: Phoenix, pp. 179–93. First published in *Dime Western Magazine*, March 1953.

McFarlane, B. (1996), *Novel to Film: An Introduction to the Theory of Adaptation*. Oxford: Oxford University Press.

The Naked Spur (1953). USA, dir. Anthony Mann.

No Country for Old Men (2007). USA, dir. Joel and Ethan Coen.

Petch, S. (2007–8), 'Return to Yuma', *Film Criticism* 32, 2, 48–69.

Pye, D. (1975), 'Genre and movies', *Movie* 20, 29–43.

— (1996), 'Introduction: criticism and the Western', in I. Cameron and D. Pye (eds), *The Movie Book of the Western*. London: Phoenix, pp. 9–21.

Ride Lonesome (1959). USA, dir. Budd Boetticher.

Rio Bravo (1959). USA, dir. Howard Hawks.

Shane (1953). USA, dir. George Stevens.

Walker, M. (1996), 'The Westerns of Delmer Daves', in I. Cameron and D. Pye (eds), *The Movie Book of the Western*. London: Studio Vista, pp. 123–60.

Wood, R. (1958), *Howard Hawks*. London: BFI/Secker and Warburg.

CHAPTER SEVEN

Child's Play: Participation in Urban Space in Weegee's, Dassin's, and Debord's Versions of *Naked City*

JOE KEMBER

Among Weegee's most celebrated photographs of New York City is his *Summer, The Lower East Side, 1937*, an image which depicts a group of children playing in a jet of water from a water hydrant. Though this photograph did not subsequently appear in his remarkably popular 1945 collection of photographs, *Naked City*, as with many of this book's most memorable images it depicts a moment pregnant with half-finished actions and half-realized glances. Some of the children receive their drenching, mouths open in shock or rapture or just plain fun; others head out of frame; a few adults gather to watch; meanwhile the regular commerce of the street continues, paying passing attention to the action that occupies the camera. In the book itself, two similar images appear in a chapter entitled 'The Escapists', which is otherwise largely dedicated to images of popular shows and their audiences. In the first, Weegee depicts a great many of what he calls the 'tenement people' as they 'got cooled off'. In the second, this brief narrative comes to a close: 'But a cop came around and shut the hydrant off . . . As soon as the cop leaves . . . the hydrant will be opened up again' (1973: 110–11). The book's hydrant images suggest that though the cop is able to abruptly transform the street back into a thoroughfare, its inhabitants will just as surely reappropriate its architecture as an apparatus for play.

These images follow chapters concerning fires, murders, sudden deaths and funerals, but are among a number in *Naked City* that claim an affinity with more obviously legitimate works of American photo-graphic realism in the tradition of Jacob Riis or Alfred Steiglitz (Weegee 1973: 233–5; Higashi 2007: 358–62). As such they can be read as setting themselves against the prevailing tabloid aesthetics of the book, becoming linked to exploratory or observational evocations of working-class identity. But it would be a mistake to separate altogether the spectacle of street-level everydayness presented by these images from the more obviously sensational aspects of the book: they too are part of what V. Penelope Pelizzon and Nancy M. West have described as the 'picaresque' structure of news photographers' autobiographies such as Weegee's (2004: 32). Though the images do not draw extensively upon Weegee's reputation as an accomplished gatherer of newsworthy images, they certainly do dramatize an entrepreneurial scenario in which 'the photographer's insight and sheer physical presence enable him to procure what he wants' (2004: 32). Coupled throughout the book with casually hard-boiled reminiscences concerning New York life, they serve both to legitimize Weegee's self-identification with the streets of New York and to corroborate his confessed playfulness in relation to his subject matter. Like the children in *Summer, the Lower East Side, 1937*, Weegee reinterprets the thoroughfare and its infrastructure as a space of play as well as spectacle, experiencing this space with a different sense of attachment, purpose and duration than do the adult passers-by, or those who observe from the tenements and sidewalk. The camera's act of laying bare is not, therefore, so much a matter of exposing the city's *penetralia*, as of participating differently in the street's experiential surface. Like the disembodied arm emerging from left frame to rig the fire hydrant, the camera is an agent within the scene, setting the various children and adults into their discrete, but interlinked, orbits of action.

In this chapter, I will argue that a series of texts which shared the title *Naked City* through the 1940s and 1950s also shared this interest in bringing to attention – and playing with – the multiple and intersecting rhythms of urban experience. Indeed, the staging of urban drama as a process in which contrasting modes of experience are led to interact is precisely what is revealing about the scenarios of exposure these texts openly proposed. As in the water hydrant images in Weegee's *Naked City*, urban space is represented as constantly subject to the multiple interests of its varied users, always shifting from one rhythmic configuration to another depending on the balance of agents in play. And because the structures of everyday life represented by these texts are always in the midst of change, they also appear as prominent features of the viewing or reading experience. From Weegee's collection of photographs, to Jules Dassin's 1948 police procedural-cum-film noir, to Guy Debord and Asger Jorn's psychogeographic map, which appeared first in 1957, to the ABC television series which ran from 1958 to 1963 (but whose many, complex episodes are beyond the scope of this chapter), each of the *Naked City* texts developed formal mechanisms that enabled it to map the material qualities of the medium on to multiple, subjective orientations of urban space.

This is where the question of adaptation becomes interesting in relation to these texts: though the narrative and style of each is greatly at variance, and though questions of fidelity or transcription as usually posed are largely beside the point, they initiate and adapt methods of representing the criss-crossing rhythms and varied textural surfaces associated with urban experience. Importantly, because they are also open and direct about this, they often appear, quite knowingly, as prime movers within the action. The result is a series of texts, each of which pursues similar representational goals in relation to the use of city space, and each of which is obliged, because it appears in a different medium, to adopt formal strategies that announce themselves as playful, experimental or even transgressive in relation to other, implicitly normalized, texts within the same medium. Such continuities are neatly preserved by the title – one which has remained pervasive in popular representations of the city – which does not work to identify a textual tradition so much as a persistent *attitude* to the city and to the process of its representation.

Urban harmonies

Henri Lefebvre's late work concerning 'rhythmanalysis', published posthumously in 1992, offers a useful starting point for my analysis, in part because it is informed by a critical self-consciousness concerning everyday urban experience not so different from that exhibited by the *Naked City* texts. For the 'rhythmanalyst', according to Lefebvre, the apparently chaotic traffic of the street could be interpreted as a series of interlocking rhythmic relationships whose complexity was best identified from a space, such as the window of an apartment, that is 'simultaneously inside and outside' (2004: 27). Looking down from his open window, Lefebvre identifies the miraculous cooperation of the multiple uses made of the busy Parisian street:

> The harmony between what one sees and what one hears (from the window) is remarkable. Strict concordance. Perhaps because the other side of the road is taken up by the immense shopping centre, nicknamed Beaubourg after the name that immortalised a president. On this side, people walking back and forth, numerous and in silence, tourists and those from the outskirts, a mix of young and old, alone and in couples, but no cars alongside culture. After the red light, all of a sudden it's the bellowing charge of wild cats, big or small, monstrous lorries turning towards Bastille, the majority of small vehicles hurtling towards the *Hôtel de Ville*. The noise grows, grows in intensity and strength, at its peak becomes unbearable, though quite well borne by the stench of fumes. Then stop . . . Hard rhythms: alternations of silence and outburst, time both broken and accentuated, striking he who takes to listening from his window, which astonishes him more than the disparate movements of the crowds. (2004: 28–9)

Though the rhythms played out below him are both intense and varied, Lefebvre's prose in such moments is dedicated to exposing the harmonies that pertain between them. The citizens on the street may not often know that they are part of an ordered network of rhythms (that kind of principled, heightened sensitivity belonging, presumably, to the rhythmanalyst), but their manner of going on in the world continually enacts their participation in this network.

This work of citizens in coordinating the multiple rhythms to which they are subjected, and hence in making the question of rhythm retreat from conscious consideration, is not accomplished without training and effort. Within what Lefebvre calls 'eurythmic' systems, all proceeds in a harmonious and practised manner – and this is not accidental:

> One can and one must distinguish between education, learning and dressage or training [*le dressage*]. Knowing how to live, knowing how to do something and just plain knowing do not coincide. Not that one can separate them. Not to forget that they go together. To enter into a society, group or nationality is to accept values (that are taught), to learn a trade by the right channels, but also to bend oneself (to be bent) to its ways. Which means to say: dressage. Humans break themselves in [*se dressent*] like animals. (2004: 39)

Dressage tends to stand in for our initiative, since it makes each unique moment in our lives appear to be the repetition of another, and enables us to respond to these in an equally repetitive, socially sanctioned manner. At the same time it gives us a use value coordinated with that of other individuals, one that is today most often tied to capital. It becomes most evident on social occasions, when it emerges in the form of relatively explicit sanctions and prohibitions on action. But it can also be seen, more positively, as the factor that enables such complex events to take place in a formally coherent manner. In this sense, dressage is a shared but implicit understanding of what is appropriate, or what 'works' at any given moment. It suggests that it is necessary to continually adapt your perspective on the scene before you, or to occupy several positions at once, and that these transitions are not necessarily experienced in terms of conflict or dislocation. Thus, for Lefebvre, there is no particular reason, even in the apparently chaotic scene of a busy city street, for different and even opposed rhythms to contribute to an arrhythmic experience. Most of the time, individuals fulfil their own objectives in a manner that does not conflict with others because all activities are syncopated by the rhythmic conventions of street-use.

Texts such as the water hydrant images in Weegee's *Naked City* also dramatize this type of harmony. Although the nature of the street changes radically depending on those making use of it, its dynamism remains, for the most part, eurythmic. Equally, Lefebvre's complex prose, which permits him to immerse himself in the street scene while maintaining an aspect of critical detachment, is not dissimilar from the mixture of participation and voyeurism enacted by Weegee's camera. Indeed, I am suggesting that it is exactly this intricate formal balance between engagement and detachment that the *Naked City* texts delivered to popular audiences.

Weegee's and Dassin's *Naked City* texts

Probably it is this tendency towards self-reflexivity that has made three out of the four *Naked City* texts and series such good objects for criticism in the past 15 years (and the TV series is surely soon to follow).[1] Some of these accounts have traced cultural continuities between Weegee's book and Dassin's film, especially insofar as they have offered their audiences models for a kind of utilitarian habituation to an uncontrollable, overwhelming environment (Orvell 1992; Dimendberg 2004: 57). However, an approach focused on these texts' formal mechanisms for representing the city's rhythms suggests that they drew quite knowingly and openly on patterns of urban dressage that audiences already understood. Rather than being simply a reaction to popular fears concerning urban chaos, these texts therefore formalized, and made open play with, their audiences' existing expertise in the practice of everyday life.

Most obviously, in the case of Weegee's book, the 18 thematic chapters each emphasize different areas of the city or distinct modalities of urban experience which, according to Weegee's brief prelude, 'seemed to form a pattern' (1973: 11). In the opening chapter, 'Sunday Morning in Manhattan', the streets are depicted at night with those who choose, or are obliged, to sleep on it captured unawares. Most of the other chapters depict the city in motion, but they do not follow the progress of a day in chronological order. Rather, the pattern emerges cumulatively throughout the book, which gradually establishes a loose typology of urban experience. For example, those chapters dealing with specified areas of the city, the Bowery, Coney Island and Harlem, tend to isolate individuals, groups and actions that come to typify these locations: in the Bowery it is Sammy's Club and the El; in Harlem there is the Savoy Club, a riot, and Easter Sunday morning at the church. But the typages of class and race that lend these chapters their coherence also insinuate themselves into others. Class in particular is a dominant theme within the book, and Weegee especially seems to delight in juxtaposing absurd images of wealth with poverty: the pampered poodle set against the abandoned baby; the society folk going to the opera in pearls and galoshes while others wait in the rain.

Similarly, thematic chapters such as 'The Escapists' also tend to define specific modes of urban experience that reappear throughout the book. For example, the second chapter, 'The Curious Ones', represents a wide variety of walkers on New York's sidewalks, but its principal interest is in their propensity to stop and stare at disruptions to the customary business of the street. As such, it thematizes not only curiosity – this, after all, is enacted principally by a confessedly voyeuristic camera – but also an interest in the nature of curiosity, especially as this is registered by the faces of urban protagonists. Such faces are caught frozen in open-eyed attention, an effect which is especially striking when replicated by numerous individuals within a crowd. Though Weegee's prose often provides motivation for these glances out of frame, sometimes it does not, leaving the faces especially exposed to the equally inquisitive gaze of the viewer of these images. On pages 38 and 39, for example, we are presented with a series of eight portrait-style photographs, each depicting an individual staring out of frame. On this occasion no caption serves to anchor these images into an identifiable narrative, and there are only sparse emotional cues to suggest the nature of the spectacles being witnessed. The background of most of the images is also difficult to discern, but the variations in what we can see makes it seem likely to the reader that the images have been assembled from numerous events. What remains to connect the images is the gesture itself, and in this respect they have been arranged with great precision. All eight photographs depict individuals staring out of frame at something that seems to be just above them; all of them have one hand raised towards their mouths in a gesture suggesting interest or contemplation; each stare possesses a quality of intensity, implying that they are attending to an event, action or conversation of some significance. The general implication is that, though these individuals have been photographed in the course of separate lives, they share in certain unities of mood and attention that the city has fleetingly provided for them. Or we might say, borrowing Lefebvre's terms, that they participate in a particular eurhythmic configuration of the street, one in which commerce, mobility and dialogue have momentarily paused in favour of an equally dynamic exchange of gazes.

It is tempting to read such connections as articulations of a form of dressage associated with the quiet, thoughtful processing of urban spectacle. In this light, the images of corpses, criminals and celebrities which follow can be read, with critical self-consciousness tolerably intact, as objects of a similarly contemplative gaze. But if the thematizing of curiosity serves a function of reassurance for readers of *Naked City*, it is also the primary means for Weegee to poke fun at them, and at the subjects of his photographs. Of the eight portraits of New York citizens, the four on the left page are young men, each of whom stares out of frame to the right, and the four on the right are well-dressed women looking to the left, generating a half-realized impression that the men and women are, in fact, gazing at each other. But this sight gag, which jumps out at the reader on first viewing these pages, certainly exists in tension with the mood of contemplation that characterizes each face, and the contrast points purposefully to Weegee's playful manipulation of his protagonists. Like the commentary which frames each of the chapters and the captions that accompany many of the images, the arrangement of these pages therefore couples the close engagement with textures of urban experience to a degree of critical detachment. The complex relationships between image and image and between text and image within the book therefore lead its readers, following – but also critiquing – Weegee's interests, to enact a comparable experience of self-conscious immersion in the street, as Lefebvre practised from his apartment window in Paris.

The formal arrangement of narration and image within Jules Dassin's *The Naked City* also creates a degree of self-consciousness concerning the representation of urban space. In this film, the voice-over is performed by the movie's producer, Mark Hellinger, an individual whose New York newspaperman credentials were even better established than those of Weegee (Kozloff 1988: 84–5). In the film's opening sequence, for example, Hellinger's narration connects the opening aerial shot of the city with the lives of several of its citizens and spaces at night: an empty theatre, a luncheonette, a late-night DJ at work, a cleaning woman, and the murder of Jean Dexter which sets the plot in motion. Such moments are intended to imitate a sense of mundanity and routine which will come to pervade the criminal investigation about to take place, but they also represent another instance of self-conscious immersion into city space. They seem uneasily poised between the casual omniscience promised by the camera's mobility within the city and a pithy, if somewhat hackneyed, evocation of urban subjectivity. The same kind of uneasy transition is also accomplished by Hellinger's narration, which routinely invades the experiences of city dwellers as the film progresses, recalling in turn Weegee's playful manipulation of his subjects.

Although, as Edward Dimendberg clarifies, Weegee's vigorous self-promotion as a form of hard-boiled urban hero actually resulted in very little direct creative impact upon this film, the adaptation nonetheless maintains the highly structured and self-conscious mode of observation practised by the book (2004: 56). As in the book, the film surveys a surprisingly wide typology of different urban environments and models of individual experience, with the nature of the realist spectacle presented therefore changing from scene to scene. Moving between spaces that include the suburban family life of the novice detective, Jim Halloran, to the relatively static spaces of the police headquarters, to the opaque, chaotic spaces of the Lower East Side, the film seems most interested in the articulation of urban discontinuities, expressed partly through typage similar to that within the book. Equally, much of the voyeuristic charge associated with the camera's penetration into such spaces is again displaced on to the curiosity of the urban crowds, who are routinely depicted in the act of gawking: consuming news of the murder in newspapers; gathering outside Jean Dexter's apartment following her death; running to the noise of a gunshot; and, in the final moments of the film, staring at the spectacle of the murderer, Willie Garzah, fleeing from the police across Brooklyn Bridge. Moreover, because the film maintains the fourth-wall principle of classical narrative, concealing the cinematic apparatus from the viewer, it develops a series of other formal methods that imitate Weegee's direct involvement in the city scene. Most obviously, some of Weegee's scenes are staged for the film, including the spectacle of children playing in a water hydrant. Seemingly disconnected from the narrative, these moments are among a number that privilege the spectacle of street life as worthy of attention in itself.

In one such scene, the senior police figure, Lieutenant Muldoon, looks out from his office window on to the street below, where children are singing and playing jump rope, while adults pass by on the sidewalk. This is presented as an over-the-shoulder shot, with the voyeuristic interests of the camera openly motivated by Muldoon, whose mode of observation therefore seems closely related to a Weegeeian (as well as a Lefebvrian) analysis of the space. Though the shot lasts only a few seconds, it is among a number without apparent narrative significance that emphasize the capacity of individuals, and especially children, to reinvent the rhythmic configuration of the street. Muldoon's distant participation in the street scene is also marked when he smilingly joins in with their song, before shutting the window so that the differently rhythmed action of the scene can commence. The act of gazing that is so significant in Weegee's book reappears in the film in a number of such narratively static moments, wherein the observation of everyday life briefly predominates. Moreover, even in scenes that are principally dedicated to narrative action, the city is often presented as an alternative focus within the shot. In part, such shots deliver familiar images of New York as a touristic spectacle, as in the dialogue with Jean Dexter's mourning parents, which takes place in front of Brooklyn Bridge at sunset and not simply on a dead-end street beside the river, at night, as the screenplay more solemnly suggests (Wald and Maltz 1979: 68). Equally, though much of the film takes place within interior spaces – Halloran's house, the offices at police headquarters, the various houses, apartments, offices and shops that the police encounter in their investigations – busy streets frequently appear through windows in these spaces, where they serve less as a background than as an alternative, neatly framed, spectacle within the scene. Elsewhere, the teeming city streets are surveyed through the windscreens of police cars, again suggesting an enframing of city space associated directly, here, with the invasive mobility of New York's cops.

However, the film does not only represent the city as the object of variously configured gazes from viewers and characters. It also elaborates, in a way Weegee's camera can only imply, on different modes of movement through the city, distinguishing, in particular, between the uses made of city streets by several of its key protagonists. For example, Halloran is introduced as Muldoon's 'legs' on the case, and he is regularly depicted walking from site to site in the city as he and other officers conduct the investigation. Smart, upright and composed even on hot summer days, Halloran has a gait which is purposeful and regular, carrying the institutional ambience of police headquarters to all areas of the city. As the narrator clarifies, the act of walking is part of a quasi-military professional praxis that connects the movements of cops on the street: 'Jimmy Halloran's an expert with his feet. He pounded a beat in the Bronx for a year as a cop . . . during the war he walked half-way across Europe with a rifle in his hand.' However, though logical and programmatic, it is the institutional rhythm of Halloran's movements that make Garzah so difficult to trace during the bulk of the movie. Though the cops are predominantly associated with the spectacle of children playing (and Garzah is prepared to mow down one child in his juggernaut-like progress across the bridge), it is Garzah who adopts the childlike ability to transform the city for his own purposes. Creative and improvisatory, he has a slouching gait that allows him to blend into the crowd, while his strength and agility allow him a miraculous freedom to negotiate windows, fire escapes, walls and other urban boundaries.

Certainly, the highly physical performances associated with Halloran and Garzah strongly embody the oppositions between authority and criminality on which police procedural movies, such as *The Naked City*, focused. But the relatively clear distinctions between these two also underpin a series of more subtle rhythmic discriminations between the experiences of urban citizens. These are carried by the wide range of incidental and supporting characters that populate the film, many of whom are linked by Halloran's perambulations through the city: from those engaged in the mundane business of the working day, to the girls staring into shop windows, to the children on the street. Dwelling for a few moments on these characters, just as it does on the protracted movement through the city performed by Halloran, Garzah, and others, the film implies a multiplicity of urban practices, whose interplay generates the rhythmic configuration of the street. Though only a few of these renditions of urban experience will have a direct impact on the film's principal narrative action, the open implication is that the street also represents the intersection of countless possible narratives. Furthermore, each practice implies a form of dressage that is specifically tailored to an effective use of city space, from Halloran's method of interpreting the streets by exhaustively walking them to Garzah's intuitive mastery of opaque spaces. But while the film strives to deliver an impression of participation in the experiential surface of the street, its selective narrative interests also imply a degree of distance from the urban arena. Again, it is this tension between immersion and reflective observation of city space that proves so productive, providing for viewers a kind of analogue, but one staged in a spectacular urban arena, for their own, everyday, practices of critical self-consciousness.

Metropolitan expertise

This process of mapping selected models of everyday experience on to highly coded textual conventions is well described by Martin Lister in his work on digital photography, which identifies a mirroring effect between forms of attention and media as a fundamental property of modern life:

> On the one hand, many, often stressful, forms of contemporary wage labour demand single-minded attention to a range of information relayed through various levels of technology . . . On the other hand, much of leisure time involves similar, if differently paced, forms of multiple simultaneous concentration, the pleasure of conversing with a friend, registering the ambient music, in a pub or on a picnic, where attention shifts back and forth from what is said and what is seen. Our point is that developed social forms of complex stimulus and attention come to be reflected in the cultural forms of media we develop. (1995: 151)

This suggests that the attempt made by the *Naked City* texts to find some formal mechanism for representing the varied rhythms of everyday life is not, in some way, a special case of 'multiple simultaneous concentration'. Indeed, as Mikko Lehtonen has also argued in extending Lister's argument, this kind of multimodality is one of the primary characteristics of modern popular media in general (2000: 74–5). However, both book and film do embody a set of formal principles openly dedicated to the representation of metropolitan forms of 'complex stimulus and attention', and in doing so they frequently exhibit an unusually marked self-consciousness in their articulation of these principles.

In this light, Debord and Jorn's map, *The Naked City*, reportedly named by Debord after the film, is only the most direct and purposeful transcription of a motive that had also informed both of the earlier texts: it openly sought to represent a critical but immersive attitude to the city. As Simon Sadler explains, the map, one of several produced by the Situationist International during the late fifties and early sixties, described an 'urban navigational system that operated independently of Paris's dominant patterns of circulation' (1998: 88). Calling on the walker to adopt a kind of critical playfulness in relation to city space, Debord and Jorn intended *The Naked City* to identify certain 'unities of ambiance': connections marked by arrows between certain sections of the city that had been established 'without regard for practical considerations', but which might helpfully coordinate the constructive/transgressive practice of drifting that was endorsed (1998: 88). Of course, for Debord, such experiments in cartography were intended to do much more than stimulate and satisfy curiosity, or foster reflection on the nature of urban experience. The map was a playful and premonitory means of critiquing the power of spectacle within the urban arena, and a precursor to the radical architectural solutions that the SI proposed for a post-spectacular city. But the establishment of an attitude to city space that allied participation with critical distance remained fundamental to this version of *The Naked City*, and was a cornerstone of Situationist thinking in this period.

It was equally significant within Lefebvre's expansive work concerning everyday life in the same period. Though Lefebvre's relationship to Debord and the SI, which was an important influence on the development of both during the 1950s, had by the early 1960s degenerated into mutual recrimination, the similarities between their positions would remain at least as significant as the differences. The differences would be starkly expressed in the final part of Lefebvre's work on everyday life, his essays on rhythmanalysis, where the mode of critical engagement with urban space associated with Lefebvre's view from a window is self-evidently to be distinguished from that of Debord's walker on the city streets. But for both writers, the construction of a perspective on the city that allied participation with critical distance was extremely productive. Debord was able to imagine the formulation of a new and dominant mode of urban consciousness that would lead to 'unitary urbanism', in which the circulatory patterns of the city were no longer driven by capital; Lefebvre's project during the 1980s proposed nothing less than a new science concerning the multiple, complex interactions of bodily, social and institutional rhythms that took place in everyday life. For both writers, the project began with a minute analysis of existing experiential patterns in the city, an analysis only made possible once a marginal position, neither inside nor outside of action taking place, had been adopted.

Within their mainstream cultural contexts, Weegee's and Dassin's *Naked City* texts also adopted formal mechanisms which enabled critical observation to take place in relation to an experience of participation. For Weegee, the productivity of this approach was channelled by means of his own persistent self-publicity and physical presence behind the camera into a kind of identification with New York itself. His book adapted and developed a consumable typology of urban experience for a national and international audience, and fostered faith in his near-mystical attachment to the varied rhythms of the city streets. In the film, the street remains the focus of this kind of typology, but the interests of camera and voice-over suggest an overview of such experiential patterns that allied the spectatorial expertise routinely practised by individuals in the theatre to their everyday mastery in the practice of everyday life. By way of conclusion, I would also note that this kind of formal logic also provides us with a powerful rationale for beginning to consider the remarkable scale and variety of urban representations on offer in the 99 episodes of the *Naked City* television series. Indeed, the preoccupation of this show with filling in the back-stories of assorted urban protagonists, from Robert Duvall's troubled criminal in 'A Hole in the City' (1 February 1961) to Gene Hackman's philosophical cop in 'Prime of Life' (13 February 1963), perhaps demonstrates most clearly the narrative productivity of Lister's contention concerning the relationship between multimodal structures of everyday life and modern media. Like the book and the film, the television show offered expansive opportunities for reflection on the multiple forms of specialized attention that had come to typify modern everyday life. In doing so, all of the *Naked City* texts imitated a kind of casual knowingness concerning structures of everyday life: an attitude that had long been prevalent not only within texts about the city, but also within the city itself.

Notes

1. On Weegee, see especially Orvell 1992; Serlin and Lerner 1997; Barth 2000; Pelizzon and West 2004. On Dassin's film, see McNamara 1996: 174–208; Dimendberg 2004: 21–85; and Higashi 2007. On Debord and Jorn's map, see McDonough 1994; Sadler 1998: 82–90; Andreotti 2000.

Bibliography

Andreotti, L. (2000), 'Play-tactics of the "Internationale Situationiste"'. *October*, 91, 36–58.

Barth, M. (2000), *Weegee's World*. London: Bullfinch.

Dimendberg, E. (2004), *Film Noir and the Spaces of Modernity*. Cambridge, MA: Harvard University Press.

Higashi, S. (2007), 'The American origins of film noir: realism in urban art and the Naked City', in J. Lewis and E. Smoodin (eds), *Looking Past the Screen: Case Studies in American Film History and Method*. Durham, NC: Duke University Press, pp. 353–79.

Knabb, K. (1989), *Situationist International Anthology*. Berkeley, CA: The Bureau of Public Secrets.

Kozloff, S. (1988), *Invisible Storytellers: Voice-over Narration in American Fiction Film*. Berkeley, CA: University of California Press.

Lefebvre, H. (2004), *Rhythmanalysis: Space, Time, and Everyday Life*. London: Continuum.

Lehtonen, M. (2000), 'On no man's land: theses on intermediality'. *Nordicom Information*, 3–4, 71–84.

Lister, M. (1995), *The Photographic Image in Digital Culture*. London: Routledge.

McDonough, T. F. (1994), 'Situationist space'. *October*, 67, 58–77.

McNamara, K. (1996), *Urban Verbs: Arts and Discourses of American Cities*. Stanford, CA: Stanford University Press.

The Naked City (1948). USA, dir. Jules Dassin.

Naked City (1958–63). USA, ABC Television.

Orvell, M. (1992), 'Weegee's voyeurism and the mastery of urban disorder'. *American Art*, 6:1, 18–41.

Pelizzon, V. P. and N. M. West (2004), '"Good stories" from the mean streets: Weegee and hard-boiled autobiography'. *The Yale Journal of Criticism*, 17:1, 20–50.

Sadler, S. (1998), *The Situationist City.* Cambridge, MA: MIT Press.

Serlin, D. and J. Lerner (1997), 'Weegee and the Jewish question'. *Wide Angle*, 19:4, 95–108.

Wald, M. and A. Maltz (1979), *The Naked City.* London: Feffer and Simons, Inc.

Weegee (1973), *Naked City.* New York: Da Capo.

CHAPTER EIGHT

Charlotte's Website: Media Transformation and the Intertextual Web of Children's Culture

CATHLENA MARTIN

Children's literature provides a rich heritage of stories from which to draw material for twenty-first-century media. Adapted texts saturate children's culture – lining toy stores, pervading bookshelves, filling television time slots, and permeating internet websites. Media theorists Marsha Kinder (1999) and Henry Jenkins (2006), among others, examine transmedia intertextuality and transmedia storytelling by focusing on a narrative arc that transitions across multiple media. Postmodern literary critic N. Katherine Hayles (2005) explores a similar strain of a print text transformed into an electronic text, but refers to the process as media translation. Media transformations are inundating current children's culture, and this chapter will examine the transitions and convergences between old and new media. In particular, I will provide connections between children's print media and digital media using multiple versions of *Charlotte's Web* as a way to approach questions of fidelity/infidelity within adaptation. Additionally, given the primary theme of death in E. B. White's *Charlotte's Web* (1952), the video game version presents a case study for textual infidelity because of its lack of violence or player death. The game thus contradicts the normative stereotype of video games as being equated with violence, and denies a major theme from the original print text in doing so.

Adaptation usually places texts in a hierarchy of source text as original and adaptation as derivative. This common strain of adaptation theory largely focuses on the fidelity of the adaptation to the original, with most media adaptation studies spotlighting literature and film. But film adaptation studies have increasingly approached film as a series of intertexts, thus opening up adaptation to the notion of intertextuality, following James Naremore's assertion that 'The study of adaptation needs to be joined with the study of recycling, remaking, and every other form of retelling in the age of mechanical reproduction and electronic communication' (2000: 15). Intertextuality broadens the scope of adaptation, placing the derivative text within its cultural moment and linking it to a web of other texts and influences.

Intertextuality can come from anywhere and everywhere, referencing, alluding to and transforming texts from any medium, but what mass culture is currently experiencing in its reanimation of classical and established texts is not merely intertextuality. Authors, producers and directors are not simply making reference to other cultural works, be they movies, video games or print texts, but through intertextuality, transmedia crossing and convergence, they are redefining those cultural works. This is particularly true among children's texts, a complex area of textual transformation across media.

Because of the expanded media used by children, children's texts have increased and become an area of boundary crossing and blurred divisions. In the introduction to their edited collection *Toys, Games and Media* (2004), Jeffrey Goldstein, David Buckingham and Gilles Brougere state:

> Children's culture is now highly intertextual: Every 'text' (including commodities such as toys) effectively draws upon and feeds into every other text. When children play with Pokemon cards or toys, for example, they draw on knowledge and expertise they have derived from watching the TV shows and movies, or from playing the computer games. Each play event is a broader flow of events that crosses from one medium or 'platform' to another. This is play that involves . . . flexibility across different media and modes of communication. (2004: 2–3)

This overlapping, intertextual nature of children's culture has happened in the past, but its mass prevalence is part of the larger scope of today's digital era. In *Remediation: Understanding New Media* (2000), Jay Bolter and Richard Grusin posit that all media forms draw on their predecessors for remediation design options, and that old media can be hypermediated through new media. More specifically, comparative media theorist Jenkins explores old and new media convergence in *Convergence Culture* (2006). He explains convergence as:

> A word that describes technological, industrial, cultural, and social changes in the ways media circulates within our culture. . . . Perhaps most broadly, media convergence refers to a situation in which multiple media systems coexist and where media content flows fluidly across them. Convergence is understood here as an ongoing process or series of intersections between different media systems, not a fixed relationship. (2006: 282)

Convergence is important for the study of children's literature and adaptation, because it exemplifies the current moment in popular children's culture and allows scholarship of children's literature to grow with the expanding digital era. With the increased accessibility of print and digital media, children's texts are transforming in terms of transmedia storytelling, participatory culture, and marketing. In tandem with adaptation and intertextuality, convergence provides another avenue into discussing children's texts that have been transformed across media.

The transmedia effect in children's texts can be seen in multiple dimensions. Yet children's texts are becoming a franchise: these texts refuse to be confined to one medium, and need to be examined across a range of media for their cultural significance. The child consumer is probably largely unaware of this media convergence as a new occurrence because computers, video games and the internet have always been an everyday part of his/her life. These are the children of the digital age, or the 'net generation' as Don Tapscott describes them in *Growing Up Digital* (1998). *Charlotte's Web* serves as an example of adaptation where a children's text is being transferred or converted from one medium to another. Specifically, the transformation of *Charlotte's Web* as a text/artifact in American culture, since its original publication in the 1950s, both reflects moments of past American media culture, and encapsulates the present digital age.

In 1952, more than a decade and a half before the internet started brewing in the labs of the Pentagon's Defense Advanced Research Projects Agency (DARPA), a little spider communicated through the simple lines of a web thread. E. B. White's *Charlotte's Web* (1952) was published in the second golden age of children's literature. The book won White a Newbery Honor in 1953.

For many years, the original 1952 novel by White comprised the entirety of the story of *Charlotte's Web*. Today, however, stories do not stay confined to one medium. The Hanna-Barbera animated film was released in 1973, with a sequel in 2003: *Charlotte's Web 2: Wilbur's Great Adventure*. Finally, in 2006 the live action film was released, along with a video game. These print and media versions converge to create a larger ur-text. In the mind of the consumer there may not be a clear division between original and adaptation, depending on which version the consumer was exposed to first. With the creation of film and video game versions of the story, modern audiences can now experience the narrative of 'Charlotte's Web' as a broader and more inclusive text than just the original printed novel. 'Charlotte's Web', the story, now consists of an amalgam of print, film and digital sources, which combine to create what the reader interprets and assimilates as 'Charlotte's Web'. Each of the media versions of 'Charlotte's web' *is Charlotte's Web*, yet each of them is also distinct and unique. The novel's account of Charlotte and Wilbur's friendship is different from that of the animated film, through the basic change in form and narrative, yet they are both 'Charlotte's Web'. In this instance the print version came first chronologically, and therefore most other versions look back to it as the original. But these additional texts can also be studied independently. Instead of being simply an adaptation or a rewriting of an original, a new media version of a text expands the text's boundaries, generating an additional primary text within that story's scope. A new media version of the text creates a type of convergence – transmedia storytelling – that expands the text's scope, generating an additional primary text and expanding the boundaries of what we perceive as the narrative, while adding the assets of its own medium.

Peter Neumeyer, in annotating *Charlotte's Web*, notes:

> This great American children's novel has stood by itself without the aid of notes for over forty years. Certainly, it could continue to be read without. But if selected insights into the workshop of a thoroughly self-aware author enrich the reading for some . . . then this edition justifies its existence. (1994: xviii)

This great work can also continue to be read without any awareness or recognition of the other media texts associated by name, but additional texts could also enrich the reading for some, and may be the only engagement with 'Charlotte's Web' that some children experience. This begins to fulfil André Bazin's prophetic statement that the 'critic of the year 2050 would find not a novel out of which a play and a film had been "made", but rather a single work reflected through three art forms, an artistic pyramid with three sides, all equal in the eyes of the critic' (2000: 26). We are at the forefront of that movement now, but Bazin omitted one art form – the video game. Adult readers may resist multimedia adaptation, relying on the supremacy of print text as 'high art' compared to 'lowbrow' video games, but consumer children experience transmedia stories on a regular basis; they no longer view the printed text as the only way to experience 'Charlotte's Web' because multimedia adaptations of texts have been the normal publishing practice in their lifetime.

Immediately after the book's publication in 1952, various people tried to secure the rights to handle the adaptation, including Disney Studios, but White was concerned about his work being adapted and 'was skeptical of and cautious about film versions of *Charlotte's Web*' (Apseloff 1983: 174). He wrote in his letters that he did not want an adaptation to violate 'the spirit and meaning of the story', and he wanted 'the chance to edit the script' (quoted in Apseloff 1983: 172). According to Marilyn Apseloff, 'many of White's fears came to pass' (1983: 175) when the animated film was released 21 years after the book had been first published. She describes how the animated version of *Charlotte's Web* 'captures the spirit in part, but too often the cartoon intrudes' (Apseloff 1983: 180), and she ultimately concludes that:

> the film *Charlotte's Web* can stand on its own as an entertaining, rather skillfully animated musical for children and adults, well voiced, with distinctive

characters and some memorable songs and visual effects. It is when the adaptation is compared with the book and the book's *intent* that its divergence from White's work is realized. (1983: 181)

Her sentiments embody much of what is insufficient about the fidelity approach to adaptation, with the secondary text paling in comparison to the original.

But this type of fidelity analysis in adaptation is quickly losing ground with critics such as Linda Hutcheon, who believes that 'an adaptation is a derivation that is not derivative – a work that is second without being secondary' (2006: 9). Reference books on children's media such as *From Page to Screen* (1992), edited by Joyce Moss and George Wilson, show the changing thoughts on fidelity by providing both an adaptation rating to 'indicate how closely the film adaptation reflects its literary source', and a cinematic rating to 'indicate the film's strength independent of the book' (1992: xiv). Adaptations can be looked at in addition to the original to comprehend the entirety of what *Charlotte's Web* has become as it is constructed across media, and not solely to judge how faithful the adaptations are to the original text.

Also, the notion of interpretation and the degree of adaptation become questionable. 'White wrote to one entrepreneur hoping to film the barnyard saga, "I saw a spider spin the egg sac described in the story, and I wouldn't trade the sight for all the animated chimpmunks in filmland"' (quoted in Neumeyer 1994: xxix). Here, White is describing a first-hand visual account that he experienced and subsequently penned into the story through a textual rendering in descriptive narrative form, thus providing one level of transformation. White's text then proceeds to incorporate another level of transformation by illustrating the text with pictures by Garth Williams. Williams's illustrations do more than just add pictures: they enhance the meaning of the story and work cooperatively with the written text to create an interplay of image and text that becomes the novel. For example, after the line 'When she was finished ripping things out, her web looked something like this:' there is a line drawing of a web (White, 1952: 92). This displays a visual interpretation of the intended meaning of White's words in a similar way to how a film version would, but with one image instead of 24 frames per second. Similarly, Neumeyer annotates another picture of Charlotte's web, now complete with the word 'Terrific' in the centre and Wilbur positioned underneath: 'since White doesn't describe the expression on Wilbur's face, this illustration is testimonial to Williams's own creative bent' (1994: 95). White approves the illustrations, yet he is opposed to revisualizing his retelling of the event on film. His opposition may have been due to White's need for control over his story, but in the end adaptations were made.

The film and media transformations of *Charlotte's Web* exemplify the larger movements in American culture through the various technological shifts in available film techniques, from animated cells to computer-generated imagery (CGI). The animated feature film by Hanna-Barbera added a musical twist which was also popular with the other cartoon powerhouse, Disney. The 1970s were a unique time because a legacy had died with Walt Disney in 1966, but other cartoon production companies became more active. Film historian Leonard Maltin speculated that the 70s witnessed a 'cartoon renaissance' that 'saw a remarkable proliferation of feature cartoons, from here and abroad, for every possible type of audience' (1980: 342). The closest Disney release to Hanna-Barbera's *Charlotte's Web* (1973) was also a children's book adaptation, *Winnie the Pooh and Tigger Too* (1974), though this was an animated short.

The animated feature contributes to the overall story of *Charlotte's Web*, just as the live action film (made with the aid of live animals and computer animation) brought *Charlotte's Web* to life and also reintroduced the story to a new generation. In 2006, with CGI graphics becoming more and more realistic and feasible, the cultural moment called for a live action remake. The year before, Hutch Parker, president of production at 20th Century Fox Film, claimed: 'Even five years ago, we shot one or two movies a year with a significant number of effects. Today, 50 per cent have significant effects. They're a character in the movie' (quoted in Thompson, 2005: np). *Charlotte's Web* had behind it the legacy of another live action hit, with a talking pig – *Babe* (directed by Chris Noonan, 1995). Winning the 1996 Oscar for Best Effects, Visual Effects, *Babe* paved the way for a live action, barnyard family movie.

A video game, marketed as based on the 2006 film version of *Charlotte's Web*, was released in November 2006 on several platforms including PC, GameBoyAdvance, PlayStation2, and Nintendo DS, illustrating the typical progression of children's classic texts from print to film to video game. Since the original children's book was written well before today's millennial generation was born, the release of a lone video game of *Charlotte's Web* may not have had its name recognized by the child purchaser. Since the text's original audience was not the video game's target audience, the game needed first to be presented through a movie in order to introduce children to the characters their parents were already familiar with. Each new text links to the previous one, but also remains its own text. In *Intertextuality* (2000), Graham Allen posits: 'The idea of the text, and thus of intertextuality, depends, as Barthes argues, on the figure of the web, the weave, the garment (text) woven from the threads of the "already written and the already read"' (2000: 6). *Charlotte's Web* is no different. Each text builds on the central radial hub but adds additional threads, part and parcel of creating the larger web, or ur-text.

Most video games that accompany the release of a live action film are largely dependent on that film because of shared graphics and a similar marketing plan; however, the *Charlotte's Web* video game is not simply a playable version of the film or the novel. The game reverted back to animated visuals; it was distinct from both the film and the book's narrative, but freely drew source material from both. The DS game returns to a first draft of Charlotte's Web where, according to White, 'the story did not contain Fern' since he added her character at the last minute before sending the manuscript to the publisher (*Letters of E. B. White*, 1976: 648). The game does not use Fern as the primary playable character. Using her may have exacerbated the gender divide, whereas playing as Wilbur is gender-neutral and opens the game up to a wider audience. Fern as the avatar might promote the game's classification as a girl's game, thus limiting its selling range. Instead Fern is displayed occasionally, primarily in the role of healer to pet Wilbur to preserve his health, thus increasing the longevity of his game life.

In place of Fern, Wilbur is the main playable character. Again, the game has reverted to a pre-publication version of *Charlotte's Web*. Neumeyer writes that White intended 'that chapter in praise of the barn [Chapter Three] to open the book' (1994: xxix). The adventure portion of the video game begins in 'Level 1: Zuckerman's Barn'. Stills from the live action movie accompany the game's narration: 'I was born in a barn . . . just a plain old barn. But every barn needs a pig!' After this short-cut scene the game begins by waking Wilbur up in the barn, where the player then controls Wilbur and learns his actions through a short tutorial. The player guides Wilbur, and occasionally Templeton, through 16 levels from the barn to the state fair, collecting letters along the way. Just as the beginning of the game skips a section of the novel, it also ends before the novel concludes. 'Level 16: Say Uncle' concludes the game at the state fair after Wilbur and Templeton find Charlotte's egg sac.

The game consists of three modes: adventure, mini-games and storybook. The storybook mode displays stills from the live action movie with an abbreviated and adapted version of the novel. The story in the storybook mode begins:

> Wilbur was born the runt of the litter. Since Wilbur is not able to fend for himself, Mr Arable decides to give him to his daughter, Fern. Fern loves Wilbur, and tends to his every need, including long walks. When Wilbur grows too old to stay in the Arable house, Fern give him to her Uncle Zuckerman to take care of, on a great, big farm. (2006)

The story continues with a still picture from the movie in the upper screen and a short text in the bottom screen, presenting the entire story, or rather the video game version of the story, in 16 sentences.

Even though the game presents its own interpretation of the story in the various modes, being able to play *Charlotte's Web* adds a new level of interaction with the story. The adventure mode is the most obvious form, but the mini-games creatively adapt the story into short, active games, pushing the boundaries of the story. The mini-games sometimes take themes or instances from the story and rework them into short games that can be played in one sitting. Pulling from the gathering of words for Charlotte's web, one mini-game gives the player a jumble of letters and s/he has to create words of three letters or more. In another game the player helps Templeton catch food droppings to eat at the fair. Some games are based on those that Fern, Henry and Avery may have played at the fair, such as bumper cars and ring toss. Some are thematically linked to a barn – as in 'Bale Out', where the player manoeuvres Wilbur through a hay-bale maze. The PC version of the game added a special game not found on the DS, 'Petting Pen', where players can care for Wilbur. In this instance there is no need for a visual avatar of Fern because the player literally becomes the Fern character by taking care of Wilbur.

While the current strain of adaptation theory is pushing against the established debate about fidelity to the original text, instances of infidelity still prove noteworthy. Critics are largely concerned with how faithful a film or video game is to the original work, but breaches of fidelity prove interesting – particularly with the video game *Charlotte's Web*, which chooses to delete a central theme in the novel: death.

Charlotte's Web is, according to children's literature pioneer Francelia Butler, 'One of the most notable treatments of death in children's literature' (1984: 85). Neumeyer claims the work as 'one of the first children's books to deal seriously, without sentimentality or condescension, with death' (1994: xix). Animal death was part of White's everyday life on his Maine farm from 1938 to 1944. He loved being in the barn and around animals, and death on a farm is inevitable. But this sort of raw reality is foreign to mainstream American children today. For them, images of death are usually mediated through television, movies and video games. The *Charlotte's Web* video game chose to preserve the innocence of a childhood unmarred by thoughts or images of death: death, as well as violence, are completely removed from both the narrative and the game play, reflecting a backlash of political and parental activism against media violence. Instead of remaining faithful to a key theme of the novel, the video game distances itself from both the novel and any potential controversy, presenting a sanitized version of *Charlotte's Web*. This may be an attempt by SEGA, the game's publisher, to address current concerns about video game violence.

Because children are largely removed from natural death, educators and others connected with children are concerned by the type of death and violence that children are now experiencing vicariously, particularly through various media. But the novel *Charlotte's Web* is a story whose themes include life, death, salvation and rebirth. In particular, the opening includes a strong presentation of killing and death.

'Where's Papa going with that ax?' opens the text (White, 1952: 1). Fern, because she 'was only eight' (White, 1952: 1), does not link her father or the axe with danger, violence or death, and thus asks her question in a very casual way – that of someone who sees her father with an axe regularly. It is not until her mother gently breaks the news to Fern that her father is going to 'do away' with a runt pig that Fern becomes agitated. Because she has grown up on a farm, Fern understands the euphemism and translates it into the harsh reality that her father is going to '*kill*' the runt [emphasis in original]. As Mr Arable's intentions are disclosed, White uses the tension created by death and killing as a plot device to both hook the reader and drive the action forward.

Potential violence is again implied with the introduction of Fern's ten-year-old brother Avery: 'He was heavily armed – an air rifle in one hand, a wooden dagger in the other' (White, 1952: 4). But then tension subsides as the possible death is averted. Of course the tension associated with impending death recurs throughout the entire novel, propelling the action and keeping Wilbur and readers wondering if he is going to be slaughtered. Only when Wilbur is finally safe does Charlotte die. Hers is a peaceful, yet heartbreaking, death not associated with any violence, but presented as the natural conclusion to life. Yet this conclusion is not the end. There is renewal in the spring as Charlotte's children are born and three decide to stay with Wilbur, providing a happy ending to the cyclical tale of life, death and rebirth.

Not only does the text of the novel present a violent tension, but the first two illustrations also visually increase the tone of violence. The escalation of emotions during the conversation between Fern and her mother is heightened by Garth Williams' drawing of Fern struggling with the axe in her father's hands (White 1952: 2). In the next illustration, the reader is visually introduced to a boy holding a rifle and clutching a knife (White 1952: 5). In the third illustration peace resumes, illustrated by a maternal scene of Fern cradling Wilbur in her arms and feeding him from a bottle. He has become 'her infant' and through her motherly love peace is restored, and violence and death diverted (White 1952: 6). No other illustration in the text contains man-made weapons. The most violent scene portrayed after the first chapter's pictures is Avery trying to capture Charlotte by knocking her into a box with a stick, but that image carries a comedic tone by showing Avery landing on his head with his feet in the air (White 1952: 73). The violence is also neutralized by the stench of a rotten goose egg that Avery breaks open when he falls.

Compared to the opening chapter in the novel, the video game version of *Charlotte's Web* (2006) contains no killing, violence, or death. Something so central to the novel – death – is completely removed from the video game. In the adventure mode, Wilbur is never in fear of dying at the hands of either Fern's father or Mr Zuckerman. Wilbur does have to evade Lurvy in one chapter of the game but, as in the book chapter 'Escape', there is no immediate threat. Even if a player tries to kill Wilbur by letting him drown in a water obstacle, he cannot really die. He squirms comically, his health bar drops to zero, and the game restarts at the most recent checkpoint to give the player yet another chance. No matter how many times Wilbur runs out of health, the game always restarts with new lives for Wilbur. Violence in video games is a politically charged topic, but the video game *Charlotte's Web* deflates the notion in its adventure mode, which purposefully avoids death and violence, thus remaining unfaithful to a key theme presented in the novel.

The storybook mode does not delete every instance of potential death in the novel, but glosses over Wilbur's potential fate by euphemistically stating: 'Learning that Wilbur is destined to become a holiday ham, Charlotte tries to save his life by letting everyone know, he's "Some Pig."' But Wilbur's fate is never mentioned again. Also, his first brush with death is removed so that the humane Mr Arable 'decides to give him to his daughter, Fern' instead of Fern having to plead for Wilbur's life.

As well as avoiding death, the video game also leaves out the cycle of life and rebirth. The adventure mode ends at the fair, and does not continue back to the barn. The storybook mode goes one episode further: 'When Wilbur comes home, he watches Charlotte's babies hatch and fly away.' Both modes, in sanitizing the story by removing the cycle of life, death and rebirth, provide a cultural commentary on the sanctioned avoidance of such topics for today's children, regardless of their inclusion in the original text.

As is the case with *Charlotte's Web*, where a book has become a revered 'classic' most readers will evaluate its film, and especially video game, adaptations on the basis of fidelity. Throughout the history of adaptation studies, questions of fidelity to the source have dominated theoretical discussion by questioning whether (for example) the movie faithfully represents the text, leading to a strong critique on points of departure from the original. With the current trend for releasing movies and games based on popular children's books, the fidelity question is at its nadir. However, sometimes points of infidelity prove the most interesting, especially in the convergent web of intertexts.

Bibliography

Allen, Graham (2000), *Intertextuality*. London: Routledge.

Apseloff, Marilyn (1983), '*Charlotte's Web*: flaws in the weaving', in Douglas Street (ed.), *Children's Novels and the Movies*. New York: Frederick Ungar Publishing, pp. 171–81.

Babe (1995). USA, dir. Chris Noonan.

Bazin, Andre (2000), 'Adaptation, or the cinema as digest', in James Naremore (ed.), *Film Adaptation*. New Brunswick, NJ: Rutgers University Press, pp. 19–27.

Bolter, Jay David and Richard Grusin (2000), *Remediation: Understanding New Media*. Cambridge, MA: MIT.

Butler, Francelia (1984), 'Death in children's literature', in Francelia Butler and Richard Rotert (eds), *Reflections on Literature for Children*. Connecticut, USA: Library Professional Publications, pp. 72–90.

Cartmell, Deborah and Imelda Whelehan (2005), 'Harry Potter and the fidelity debate', in Mireia Aragay (ed.), *Books in Motion: Adaptation, Intertextuality, Authorship*. New York: Rodopi, pp. 37–49.

Charlotte's Web (1973). USA, dir. Charles A. Nichols and Iwao Takamoto.

Charlotte's Web (2006). USA, dir. Gary Winick.

Charlotte's Web (2006) (electronic video game). USA, Sega.

Cook, David A. (2000), *Lost Illusions: American Cinema in the Shadow of Watergate and Vietnam, 1970–1979*. History of the American Cinema vol. 9. New York: Charles Scribner's Sons.

Goldstein, Jeffrey, David Buckingham and Gilles Brougere (eds) (2004), *Toys, Games, and Media*. Mahwah, NJ: Lawrence Erlbaum Associates.

Hayles, N. Katherine (2005), *My Mother Was a Computer: Digital Subjects and Literary Texts*. Chicago: Chicago University Press.

Hutcheon, Linda (2006), *A Theory of Adaptation*. New York: Routledge.

Jenkins, Henry (2006), *Convergence Culture: Where Old and New Media Collide*. New York: New York University Press.

Kinder, Marsha (1999), *Kid's Media Culture*. Durham, NC: Duke University Press.

Maltin, Leonard. (1980), *Of Mice and Magic: A History of American Animated Cartoons*. New York: McGraw-Hill.

Moss, Joyce and George Wilson (eds) (1992), *From Page to Screen: Children's and Young Adult Books on Film and Video*. Detroit, MI: Gale Research.

Naremore, James (ed.) (2000), *Film Adaptation*. New Brunswick, NJ: Rutgers University Press.

Neumeyer, Peter F. (1994), *The Annotated Charlotte's Web*. New York: HarperCollins.

Sutherland, Zena (1997), *Children and Books*. 9th edn. New York: Longman.

Tapscott, Don (1998), *Growing Up Digital*. New York : McGraw-Hill.

Thompson, Anne (2005), 'F/X gods: the 10 visual effects wizards who rule Hollywood'. *Wired*, 13 February. <http://www.wired.com/wired/archive/13.02/fxgods.html?pg=1&topic=fxgods&topic_set=>.

White, E. B. (1952), *Charlotte's Web*. New York: HarperCollins.

— (1976), *Letters of E. B. White*, ed. Dorothy Lobrano Guth. New York: Harper & Row.

CHAPTER NINE

'Stop Writing or Write Like a Rat': Becoming Animal in Animated Literary Adaptations

PAUL WELLS

In Michel Ocelot's original animated fairytale *Azur and Asmar; The Prince's Quest* (2006, Fra, dir. Michel Ocelot) the blonde, angelic hero, Azur, must confront a crimson lion on his way to rescuing the Jihn Fairy. Previous suitors have found that the lion has embraced their visits as an opportunity for lunch, but Azur is far too prepared to become the next victim of the lion's voracious appetite. He carries with him large pieces of meat to feed the lion, but more importantly, a potion which empowers him with a lion's roar, and the intrinsic ability to communicate with the lion, and to solicit his help in the next stage of the journey. So far, so fairytale, but an incident which nevertheless raises key questions about the status of the animal in animated film. In this comparatively unusual case, the lion – though mythic – is treated purely as an animal, and is allowed no anthropomorphic characteristics. Indeed, he is even allowed the primacy of his own language as the method by which his innate 'animalness' might be reached and negotiated with. This is not the funny talking animal of the Disney and Warner Brothers cartoons of the 'golden era', but a creature understood to be intrinsically 'different' from humans, yet somehow powerfully related to a natural order which includes both humans and animals. Ironically, even though such animals have populated the animated form since its earliest development, and become the lingua franca of the cartoon, comparatively little attention has been given to their presence, identity or meaning.

Animated film has often drawn from literary sources and, unsurprisingly, any number of works written for children, and featuring animals, have been adapted in animation. There is often an assumed relationship between children's illustrated books and animations, since the former are already visualized and might immediately translate to the animated form, and in my discussion here I wish to address this by looking at particular examples of animated literary adaptations: Maurice Sendak's *Where the Wild Things Are* as a short animation, P. L. Travers's *Mary Poppins* as a part-live-action, part-animated film, and George Orwell's

Animal Farm as a full-length feature – an adult fable but one that has been absorbed into the children's literary canon, having often been set as a school examination text. These films represent different approaches to storytelling using animation, and employ animals to suggest specific features of being human, and to comment on the relationship between humankind and animals. All feature creatures who embody particular meanings, and achieve particular emotional affects in their animated 'animal' guise; an issue I wish to pursue throughout the rest of my discussion.

I have written extensively elsewhere about strategies to address these ideas, placing the analysis of animals in animation within a structure called 'bestial ambivalence'.[1] This paradigm allows for an assessment of the animal as it exists in an animated sequence or narrative, to operate as a flux of meanings. There are four core aspects to the paradigm that suggest these meanings, often overlapping and oscillating, and calling particular concepts into tension or conflict. The first aspect is the 'pure animal' (animals demonstrating exclusively animal characteristics), the second is the 'humanimal' (comparing parallel and existing metaphors about animal and social culture), the third is the 'aspirational human' (when the animal is used to advance positive views of human behaviour and conduct) and, finally, the fourth is 'the critical human' (when the animal is used to critique human activity and culture). This model itself exists within a broader template of the 'naturalcultural', which I define as a set of complex conditions and contexts which delineate the relationship between contested views of 'nature' and 'culture'. In this instance, then, I will be exploring how the animal functions in animated literary adaptations, using this model to some extent, but more specifically, employing the work of Gilles Deleuze and Felix Guattari, to suggest some points of connection between the animal and the animator; the literary animal and its animated form; and the political and social conditions which underpin using animals as key narrative characters and symbols.

At a very simple level, animation has always used animal characters to avoid, comment on, or subvert the human social, political and religious taboo which would otherwise be self-evident in the depiction of humankind. For the most part, ironically, this has served to make 'the animal' invisible, essentially promoting meaning and affect through the 'phenomena' of animated characters and forms. The animal, in this model, becomes a filter by which sub-textual ideas about human conduct are explored, insisting that issues are addressed discursively rather than explicitly – in Michel Ocelot's words, 'making the audience intelligent'.[2] It is the presence of 'the animal', then, which problematizes form, and prompts discourse. In essence, this has liberated animators and given them a particular empathy with the animal that may be immediately evidenced through the profound attention to detail that animators have paid in reproducing animal anatomy and motion, characterized by their sensitivity in producing quasi-anthropomorphic or natural 'performances' in animal representation.

Less acknowledged are the number of occasions in which animators also have to be responsive to literary sources, and the way in which narrative functions to define animal traits and tropes. Given animation's unfair but enduring status as 'children's entertainment', it is perhaps inevitable that animated adaptations emerge from children's literature, where the nature and identity of the animal may already be established in the child's mind, or may end up being defined by the animation a child sees. It is easy to forget that Walt Disney's *Bambi* (1941, USA, dir. David Hand), for example, is based on Felix Salten's romantic tale, *Bambi: A Forest Life* (1934). Such literary and animated texts in some senses represent the struggle to know the animal, and this has been a long-held and demanding task for humankind. It has not merely gone through a variety of historical phases, but has also been played out through the shifting dynamics of the nature and growth of human beings from childhood to mature adulthood, as well as through changes in social and cultural orders across nation and time. The human preoccupation with the animal has been literally from cradle to grave, and truly a matter of cross-disciplinary and inter-disciplinary enquiry.

The psychoanalytic critic Bruno Bettelheim notes of fairytales, for example, 'An animal is either all devouring or all helpful. Every figure is essentially one-dimensional, enabling a child to comprehend its actions and reactions easily' (Bettelheim 1978: 74). This observation merely tells us that humankind has sometimes constructed the animal as a one-dimensional figure in order to clarify the identity of the animal in the child's experience or imaginary. It is ultimately a highly reductive statement, but one which Bettelheim believes accords with the ways in which humankind must *necessarily* seek to assimilate the animal, as 'Only when animal nature has been befriended, recognised as important, and brought into accord with ego and superego does it lend its power to the total personality' (Bettelheim 1978: 78). Bettelheim is actually suggesting, then, that the animal is an inherent part of the human sensibility, and part of its intrinsic 'wholeness'; that psychologically and emotionally, right from the earliest years, humankind uses a 'creative' interpretation of the animal to clarify something in itself, and achieve an embeddedness of the animal within the human personality. It is useful, then to initially explore how a model of children's literature has been adapted into an animated film. The clear visual relationship between models of illustration and animation sometimes prompts animated versions of established illustration styles and approaches.

The issues I have raised so far, therefore, find ready purchase in a consideration of the animated version of Maurice Sendak's classic, *Where the Wild Things Are*, first published in 1963, and adapted by veteran animator Gene Deitch for Scholastic Education, in 1988, at the Weston Woods studio in the USA.[3] Such was the iconic nature of Sendak's work that it was necessary to maintain complete fidelity to his style, while finding the most pertinent ways in which animation could add to the resonance of his text and imagery. In some ways this was straightforward. Sendak's work is a sustained engagement with methods of 'telling' and 'showing', and finds ready correspondence with the ways in which animation condenses material to determine the maximum degree of suggestion with the minimum of imagery. More significantly, here, *Where the Wild Things Are* is also an interrogation of the relationship between child and creature; 'animals' and 'animality' as 'same' and 'other'; and the reconciliation of psychological, material and social worlds. It is important, for instance, to notice that Deitch's film uses the credit sequence to anticipate the dream-like world of the 'wild things', and the voiceover, read by Peter Schickele, to suggest the threat of the creatures. Further, in a short sequence which precedes Sendak's opening image of Max, in his bedroom, nailing a blanket rope to the wall in anticipation of creating 'a den', Max is seen not only in his 'wolf suit', but pretending to be an animal, flexing his claws.

This immediately draws Sendak's story into one of the most interesting aspects of the graphic representation of animals. As Steve Baker has pointed out,

> 'A theriomorphic image would be one in which someone or something (in the words of the OED definition) was presented as 'having the form of a beast'. Therianthropic images, in contrast, would be those 'combining the form of a beast with that of a man' . . . Where animal imagery is used to make statements about human identity, metonymic representations of selfhood will typically take theriomorphic form, whereas metaphoric representations of otherness will typically take therianthropic form' (Baker 2001: 108).

Though these aspects of representation are quite common, they are not entirely proven in the case of animated film, as the theriomorphic can wholly preserve the nature of the beast in animation, while still invoking the human, and the therianthropic can often be represented as a convention of design and the execution of a character. The 'therianthropic', though, can be highly persuasive when used as a conscious device, and a deliberate strategy in calling attention to the 'relatedness' of seemingly separate social, cultural, personal or phenomenological aspects of existence. Max's 'wolf' persona suggests his compatibility with, yet difference from, 'the animal', and the transposition he makes as his bedroom metamorphoses into the jungles of the land of the 'wild things' (surely influenced by similar transitions in Winsor McKay's comic strip, *Little Nemo in Slumberland*), becomes an empathetic rite of passage in which he explores his unconscious motivations and actions.

Animation is especially capable of illustrating interior states – psycho-somatic, mechanistic, organic – and here, Deitch takes Sendak's compression of space and time as the specific transition in its visual narrative. Metamorphosis – the literal act of seamlessly moving between images without edit, exposing the nature of the de-stabilization and re-stabilization of the form – is fundamental to the elemental nature of animation, and significantly services the translation of Max's anger with his mother, for sending him to bed without supper, into the less definable and complex feelings of confronting the 'wild things'. Crucially, both Sendak's imagery, and Deitch's empathy with it – a point I will return to later – seeks to move into an arena in which the suggestion is that there are many kinds of experience which cannot be 'told' but can only reach consciousness by being 'shown'. In this way animation services a pre-linguistic model of engagement and understanding, using the non-linguistic idea of animal consciousness as the mediator both of the concept and its representation. When Sendak abandons text in his story to spreads of 'wild rumpus', Deitch's animation plays out a carnivalesque revelry in motion, not merely revealing Sendak's deliberate incongruity between the 'terrible roars', 'terrible teeth', 'terrible eyes' and 'terrible claws' of the creatures and what Jonathan Jones has described as 'hilarious beasts, massive and toothy and hairy, but drawn with warmth that makes them lovable' (Jones 2008: 35), but also revealing how the notion of 'the animal' works outside easy moral codings or known social infrastructures. There are echoes of Pablo Picasso and Henri Rousseau in Sendak's art, and of the modernist imperatives that informed their work, but ultimately it is the animated form which translates Sendak's suggestion of a psychological and emotional space parallel *to* the material world, into one with the same conviction and pertinence *as* the material world.

Max, dubbed by the creatures the most wild thing of all, seems to reconcile his more aggressive, sensual and creative imperatives, as he commands the wild things to be still; a moment of contemplation in which his stare frightens his adversaries, and wins their respect. This turning point demonstrates how Max begins to define and refine his emotional intelligence, enjoying its uncertainty and owning its consequences, before returning to the everyday world of his bedroom, and a hot supper self-evidently provided by a forgiving mother. Sendak's approach in *Where the Wild Things Are* points to his desire to have 'a vision difficult to verbalise. I no longer want simply to illustrate – or for that matter simply to write. I am now in search of a form more purely and essentially my own' (Quoted in Meglin 2001: 158). Arguably, here, animation functions as that very form between visualization and text, and the animal becomes both the mediator of the animator, and the liberator of alternative codes which speak to Bettelheim's model of assimilation. I wish to suggest, then, that the animated film, in all its flux and openness, across its styles and techniques, through its phases and developments, constitutes the most significant modern interrogator of the meaning of the animal through its intrinsically metaphorical and metaphysical status as an expressive language – and, in consequence, helps to reveal an intrinsic sense of humanity. Further, in order to substantiate this claim, I look to the work of Deleuze and Guattari in relating animal culture to literary texts, and their subsequent animation.

Deleuze and Guattari define the animal as follows:

> First, individuated animals, family pets, sentimental oedipal animals each with its own petty history, 'my' cat, 'my' dog. These animals invite us to regress, draw us in to narcissistic contemplation, and they are the only kind of animal psychoanalysis understands, the better to discover a daddy, a mommy, a little brother behind them (when psychoanalysis talks about animals, animals learn to laugh): *anyone who likes cats or dogs is a fool.* And then there is a second kind: animals with characteristics or attributes; genus, classification, or State animals; animals as they are treated in the great divine myths, in such a way as to extract them from series or structures, archetypes or models (Jung is in any event profounder than Freud). Finally, there are more demonic animals, pack or affect animals that form a multiplicity, a becoming, a population, a tale . . . Or once again, cannot any animal be treated in all three ways? (Deleuze and Guattari 2004: 265, emphasis in original)

These definitions seek to advance a view of 'the animal', which places it within the context of anthropomorphized domestication, further, as part of a mythic or totemic construct (see Wells 2009: 41–7), and finally, as an abstract model, more specifically understood through its intrinsic animality as a totality rather than through easily anthropomorphized or individualized examples. In seeking out something of the 'pure animal' in these definitions, Deleuze and Guattari are looking to a particular kind of essence or essentialism which might then become part of the creative process which, in itself, seeks to express it. Their concept of 'becoming animal' (Deleuze and Guattari 2004: 256–351), a treatise aligning the animal with the process of creativity, effectively defining the artist engaging with, or depicting, the animal as subject to a transcendent empathy, enables the essence of the animal to find representation outside orthodox social categories or literal artistic models. As Steve Baker has pertinently remarked of this perspective, 'The artist and the animal are, it seems, intimately bound up with each other in the unthinking or undoing of the conventionally human' (Baker in Rothfels 2002: 80). It is this central premise that I wish to apply to animators – and by extension, animation writers and directors – who are seeking to adapt literary sources into animated 'phenomena'. This will be specifically addressed when we look at the ways in which practitioners facilitate their work through the use and deployment of animal imagery, and take into account more of Deleuze and Guattari's definitions of animal culture. At a basic level, though, this 'unthinking' or 'undoing' of convention calls particular discourses about animals into narratives which can provoke significant difficulties.

P. L. Travers's dissatisfaction with Walt Disney's film adaptation of her *Mary Poppins* stories is well documented (see Lawson 2005), for example, though this becomes more ambivalent following the immense popularity of the part-live-action, part-animated *Mary Poppins* (1964, USA, dir. Robert Stevenson). Travers was particularly critical of the animated sequences in what is essentially a live action musical, but ironically it is these aspects of the film, featuring an intrinsic 'animality', which actually revise and recast the stories in ways which best reveal the essence of the stories' moral outlook and purpose. Based on six core chapters from *Mary Poppins* (1934), and elements of *Mary Poppins Comes Back* (1935), the film seeks to make Travers's heroine less prickly and defensive, less scornful and frightening, while preserving her disciplinary zeal and magical shape-shifting qualities. Douglas Brode has argued that this transformation is fundamentally concerned with making Mary a 'hippyesque' figure, appealing to the mid-1960s zeitgeist (Brode 2004: 25–6, 93–6), but more significantly, this may be concerned with reconciling Disney's (and indeed, Travers's) constant pre-occupation with the fear of actually losing a parent and the general sense that it is harder to represent an effective model of parenting in an increasingly secular world. Mary is essentially the agent by which she makes herself obsolescent; by enabling Mr and Mrs Banks to see that despite their significant social roles as respectively a bank clerk and a women's rights campaigner, their first duty is to achieve an openly loving relationship with their children.[4] In doing so, her role as 'nanny' – embodying a short-lived English institution which existed between the early Victorian era and the closure of the Second World War – is made unnecessary, and her mythic identity as the facilitator of significant rites of passage and metamorphoses becomes more pronounced. The Sherman brothers, adaptors of the Mary Poppins stories and masters of developing narrative through songs, at first had no idea what a 'nanny' was, believing it to be a goat, and it is this playful 'mistake' which prompts the following analysis (see Lawson 2005).

The books themselves toy with the question of just what Mary is – a fairy, a witch, an earth mother, a free spirit, or a supernatural force – but it is Disney that locates her powers directly in relation to animals. This is unsurprising for several reasons. Walt Disney himself asks:

[H]ow does a human being react to stimulus ? He's lost the sense of play he once had and he inhibits physical expression. He is a victim of a civilisation whose ideal is the unbotherable, poker-faced man, and the attractive, unruffled woman. Even the gestures get to be calculated. They call it poise. The spontaneity of animals – you find it in small children, but it's gradually trained out of them. Then there's the matter of plastic masses, as our animators put it – mass of face, of torso, and so on. Animation needs these masses. They're the things that can be exaggerated a little and whirled about in such a way as to contribute the illusion of movement, you see, like a bloodhound's droopy ears and floppy gums or the puffy little cheeks and fat little torsos of chipmunks and squirrels . . . For contrast, think of the human being as the animator sees him . . . The typical man of today has a slim face, torso and legs. No scope for animation, too stiff, too limited. (Quoted in Schickel 1968/1986: 180–81)

Disney, in a surprising critique of human conduct and behaviour, seeks to recover the sense of humanity through the spontaneity and uninhibitedness of animal movement, and its expression through the apparent spontaneity and uninhibitedness of the animated form. The animator becomes Deleuze and Guattari's 'sorceror', not playing or imitating the animal but realizing a 'becoming':

> . . .the 'becoming-animal of the human being is real even if the animal the human being becomes is not; and the becoming-other of the animal is real, even if that something other it becomes is not. This is the point to clarify: that a becoming lacks a subject distinct from itself, but also that it has no term, since its term in turn exists only as taken up in another becoming of which it is the subject, and which co-exists, forms a block, with the first. (Deleuze and Guattari 2004: 262–3)

Though initially difficult to fully comprehend, this model offers a metaphysical definition of both the literal process of creating animation (one image becoming another, effacing itself as it does), and of its (animal) characters as phenomena. Mary's uncertain status as a 'magical' figure in the film is readily aligned with the 'becoming animal' of the animation, and the animal-populated narrative sequences with which she becomes associated. Interestingly, the animals in these sequences – the farmyard chorus; the penguin waiter dancers; the horses at the fairground and racetrack; the horses, dogs and fox in the hunt – recall Deleuze and Guattari's 'pack', and through their actions 'affect' a bond with Mary which reinforces and naturalizes her magical powers. Discussing Hugo Von Hofmannsthal's fictional 'Lord Chandos', a writer increasingly frustrated by the ineffectuality of language in describing his moods and feelings, Deleuze and Guattari reiterate his imperative that he should 'either stop writing, or write like a rat', noting that 'If the writer is a sorcerer, it is because writing is a becoming, writing is traversed by strange becomings that are not becomings-writer, but becomings-rat, becomings-insect, becomings-wolf etc' (Deleuze and Guattari 2004: 265). Crucially here, I wish to argue that given the scale of 'animal-becoming' in animation, literally and metaphorically, and through visual codes, this is where the 'sorceror' truly dwells, and in the case of *Mary Poppins* makes the unnameable parallel universe of the animated animal/natural world a 'genuine' context in which Mary's affective otherness is legitimized and proven. Let us not forget either that Mary's 'supercalifragilisticexpealidocious' is the word that is conjured when it is not possible to say anything else, or there is nothing else to say.

Arguably, Mary (or indeed 'The Birdwoman', selling birdseed for tuppence a bag) is therefore also a version of Deleuze and Guattari's 'anomalous' figure, which they define through the example of Herman Melville's *Moby Dick*. They argue that:

> *Moby Dick* in its entirety is one of the great masterpieces of becoming; Captain Ahab has an irresistible becoming-whale, but one that bypasses the pack or the school, operating with a monstrous alliance with the Unique, the Leviathan, Moby Dick . . . the exceptional individual has many possible positions . . . In short, every Animal has its Anomalous. Let us clarify that: every animal swept up in its pack or multiplicity has its anomalous . . . the anomalous is a position or a set of positions in relation to a multiplicity. Sorcerors therefore use the old adjective 'anomalous' to situate the positions of the exceptional individual in the pack'. (Deleuze and Guattari 2004: 268–9)

The animated sequences reveal Mary's irresistible 'becoming-animal' (she can talk with animals, and in the books conjures many connections with animals), and it is this which empowers her influence on the latter narratives, in which adults and children realize their intrinsic humanity.

Animals are often used in stories like this, but in works from Edgar Allan Poe's *Murders at the Rue Morgue* (1841), with its animal sound as an alternative notion of 'language', Anna Sewell's *Black Beauty* (1877), with its narrative told from a horse's 'point of view', through to Will Self's *Great Apes* (1997), in which ape culture is established as a social orthodoxy, it is the voice of the animal itself which has simultaneously proved most elusive, yet most persuasive when defining alternative perspectives. Interestingly, these literary examples mark out a distinctive terrain in text-based storytelling, but ones which are actually largely conventional orthodoxies in animal animation. Animal 'sound', animal point of view and animal 'worlds' are established as the core means by which literate and metaphorical perspectives are engaged with. In animation, this has been at the heart of the 'flux' of representational models of animals – 'bestial ambivalence' – which allows the animator to speak in a range of discourses that most readily define the animal, the human, and the 'becoming-animal' as they reveal complex and contradictory issues. The conventions marked out in 'Murders in the Rue Morgue', 'Black Beauty' and 'Great Apes', then, are common to many animated films, and it remains to demonstrate their presence in a key example. To conclude, therefore, I will comment on Halas and Batchelor's 1954 adaptation of George Orwell's 'Animal Farm' (1945), his satirical novella engaging with post-revolutionary Stalinism in the former Soviet Union, and issues of animal welfare. 'Animal Farm' is a convenient demonstration of both animated bestial ambivalence and conventional literary adaptation.

Almost certainly covertly funded by the CIA as part of a Cold War propaganda strategy (see Halas and Wells 2006), *Animal Farm* (1954, UK, dir. John Halas and Joy Batchelor) represents an important landmark not only because it was the first British fully animated feature, but also because it had to resist a long-established tradition of 'funny' animals in animated cartoons. Though animation in Russia, China, or Japan drew on complex fairytale or folk-tale conventions, and inevitably had more amoral and adult-orientated themes, it was Hollywood cartoons, and especially the long shadow of Disney, that dominated the form in the global marketplace, thus establishing 'the animal' in animation as intrinsically amusing. In order to recover the seriousness at the heart of Orwell's fable, animals in *Animal Farm* had to be serious characters, and defy expectations of the animated cartoon as a vehicle for comedy. Halas and Batchelor had already established their credentials in creating such material through their films for the Ministry of Information during the Second World War; and for the Central Office of Information during post-war reconstruction and the rolling out of the Beveridge Plan to make Britain into a Welfare State. The thematic seriousness of *Animal Farm* was therefore not a challenge to the studio because they had already employed the idioms of modern art to revise the aesthetics of the studio's output, and saw the functionalism of the Bauhaus as an ideological as well as an artistic inspiration in using animation as a socially relevant educational tool.

A cursory examination of the 'bestial ambivalence' model reveals how the film eventually embraced Halas' own utopian convictions, the covert and implicit needs of the American backers, and Orwell's own didactic perspectives. The 'aspirational human' reading of the animal implicitly extols the benefits of democracy, notions of dignity and mutual respect, the value of hard work and intellectual endeavour and, ultimately, the sense of an English pastoral idyll, a highly specific and quasi-mythic version of the resolution of 'nature' and 'culture'. The 'critical human' perspective, at the political level, is particularly concerned with a rejection of the brutalities and exploitation of totalitarian regimes, and in raising issues and debates about the treatment of animals, and animal welfare. The 'humanimality' in the film finds a direct parallel between the hierarchical construction of animals in the domesticated farmyard context, and implicit notions of 'great chains of being' and 'the circle of life' (made explicit for example in Disney's *The Lion King*, 1994, USA, dir. Roger Allers and Rob Minkoff) and the political hierarchies inherent in the forms of government in revolutionary Russia which informed Orwell's original metaphor. The most controversial aspect was the change from Orwell's original ending – the film merely showing the continuing corruption of the pigs, and the resolution of the animals in mounting another revolt. Though Halas always claimed that this was to create a more universal, humanitarian fable, with an anti-totalitarian position, enabling the audience to take some degree of relief and reassurance from the film, such an ending did, of course, suit CIA anti-communist objectives.

The most important aspect of the film, though, which enabled the creation of these discourses and promoted resistance to the idea of animated animals as comic figures, was the recall of the 'pure animal'. This was achieved in a number of ways and predominantly involved long non-dialogue sequences which merely privileged animal movement, using the kind of empathetic anthropomorphism – the 'becoming-animal' in Deleuze and Guattari's 'sorcerors' – that revealed the 'parallel' point of view of the animal. An animal 'anthem' was constructed only from animal sounds. Scenes of brutality where animals kill other animals were included, along with others in which primal expression by animals – most notably, Benjamin the Donkey's painful bray at the death of Boxer the horse – were played out as the purest expression of 'emotion'. It should be stressed, too, that when Napoleon asks the animals to consider their future, they only have visions of a hurtling butcher's block and hanging carcasses in an abattoir; an image far from the Disney vocabulary.

Halas and Batchelor's recall of the 'pure animal' reanimated traditional animation. As the form entered the mid-1950s, its 'golden era' was coming to an end with the closure of many of the leading studios' theatre cartoon divisions, and the rise of television was imposing a different economic model on production, requiring 'reduced' or 'limited' animation in the Hanna Barbera style. *Animal Farm* therefore provides evidence of 'the anomalous': this animated literary adaptation proves that just as an industry had nearly stopped 'writing', it was possible again to 'write like a rat'. The film inspired many of the animal narratives that followed it – *Where the Wild Things Are* and *Mary Poppins* among them – to trust the animal, and consequently, to better reveal the human.

Notes

1. See Wells, Paul, 2009. *The Animated Bestiary : Animals, Cartoons, Culture*. New Brunswick, NJ: Rutgers University Press.
2. Personal interview with the author, July 2008.
3. Prague-based American animator and illustrator Gene Deitch worked for United Productions of America in the mid-1950s, when the studio produced cartoons resistant to the dominant Disney style, embracing the idioms of modern art and contemporary graphic design. He made 'Tom Terrific' cartoons for Terrytoons and revisionist, Eastern European-inflected 'Tom and Jerry' shorts; and he revived 'Krazy Kat' in the early 1960s for a short-lived King Features TV series.
4. In correspondence with writer and critic Brian Sibley during the 1980s, Travers could not accept key narrative conceits in the Disney version – Mr Banks' elevation from bank clerk to board member; his cruelty in tearing up the children's poem delineating their preferences for a new nanny; Mrs Banks re-cast as a suffragette; and most importantly, Mary's transition from a plain, morally incorruptible, if slightly vain, professional figure into a coquettish heroine. (Personal interview with the author, May 1987).

Bibliography

Baker, Steve (2001), *Picturing the Beast: Animals, Identity and Representation.* Urbana, IL: University of Illinois Press.

— (2002), 'What does becoming animal look like?', in Nigel Rothfels (ed.), *Representing Animals.* Bloomington, IN: Indiana University Press, pp. 67–98.

Bettelheim, Bruno (1978), *The Uses of Enchantment: The Meanings and Importance of Fairytales.* London: Peregrine Books.

Brode, Douglas (2004), *From Walt to Woodstock: How Disney Created the Counter-culture.* Austin, TX: University of Texas Press.

Deleuze, Giles and Felix Guattari (2004), *A Thousand Plateaus.* London: Continuum.

Halas, Vivien and Paul Wells (2006), *Halas and Batchelor Cartoons: An Animated History.* London: Southbank Publishing.

Jones, Jonathan (2008), 'Wild things, I think I love you', *The Guardian Weekend*, 12 April, 35–9.

Lawson, Valerie (2005), *Mary Poppins She Wrote: The Life of P. L. Travers.* London: Aurum Press.

Meglin, Nick (2003), *Humorous Illustration.* New York: Watson Guptil Publications.

Schickel, Richard (1968/1986), *The Disney Version.* London: Michael Joseph.

Wells, Paul (2009), *The Animated Bestiary: Animals, Cartoons, Culture.* New Brunswick, NJ: Rutgers University Press.

Part III

Reproducing the Past

CHAPTER TEN

Historicizing the Classic Novel Adaptation: *Bleak House* (2005) and British Television Contexts

IRIS KLEINECKE-BATES

Dickens has always been a popular choice for adaptation, both for the big screen and for television. From early on in cinematic history there have been landmark adaptations that have paid homage to Dickens but have also become cinematic masterpieces in their own right and have often become associated with the work of particular directors, such as David Lean's famous adaptations of *Great Expectations* (UK, 1946) and *Oliver Twist* (UK, 1948).

On British television the classic novel adaptation, from the earliest days of British television onwards, has occupied an important role in public service broadcasting, with educational aspirations leading to a strong tradition of adaptations that are often noted for their faithfulness to the literary source (see Giddings and Selby, 2001). Dickens' cultural significance has made the author attractive in a public service context, a combination of entertainment and educational values being closely linked to the adaptation of classic literature. In this context, the well-known nature of an established literary classic and the classic author has very specific implications for the classic novel adaptation: there are often pre-existing expectations and knowledge which need to be negotiated, while at the same time the continuous reworking of familiar stories serves to keep the material fresh and meaningful. Thus, although classic novel adaptations, through their explicit referencing of an often very well-known original, offer a sense of stability and durability, the existence of multiple versions also makes it possible to trace changes and transformations over time. As Geraghty notes, 'in this way, while repetition marks such adaptations, they also allow for a more open narrative process in which it is possible to see variations in how particular incidents or characters are handled and how the familiar is updated' (2008: 15).

The close link between the classic novel adaptation and the notion of quality has meant that, in the case of Dickens, popularity within the medium has exceeded the adaptation of the literary text and led to a number of programmes that not only explore aspects of Dickens's life, such as the drama-documentary *Dickens* (BBC, 2002) but also stretch into non-adapted drama with series such as *Micawber* (Carlton, 2001) and even a 'guest appearance' of Dickens in episode 3, 'The Unquiet Dead' of the second season of *Dr Who* (BBC, 2005–). Utilization of Dickens as an author and as a cultural signifier highlights not only the way this significance is used in the television context to foster notions of quality, but also his place in the national consciousness (see Clayton, 2003).

In response to the popularity of Dickens as a source for adaptation, there is a wide range of critical work on adaptation which often focuses on the cinematic qualities of Dickens's prose, his use of the grotesque and the ridiculous, and the affinity of his literary work with the theatre and film (see Poole, 1983; Eisenstein, 1999; Altman, 1999; Glavin, 2003; Geraghty, 2008). However, despite isolated exceptions, there is still a shortage of work on Dickens and television – which is all the more notable given the dominant role that television plays, not only in the construction of our understanding of the literary classic, but also more generally in the formation of our relationship with the past. Thus, as Connerton points out, 'The practice of historical reconstruction can in important ways receive a guiding impetus from, and can in turn give significant shape to the memory of social groups' (1989: 14). Television's representation of the past in history programming, and also in the classic novel adaptation, is both a reflection of, and an active tool for the shaping of attitudes to the past and the way history is understood; if adaptations are part of their own particular space and time, their representations of the past are also reflections of particular socio-cultural contexts.[1]

Representations of Dickens' Victorian England have shaped our ideas of the Victorian age as much as those ideas have been shaped by cultural and historical influences. This is perhaps even more the case in relation to an author such as Dickens, where the status of the author exceeds our familiarity with most of his prose. Thus, novels such as *Bleak House* and *Our Mutual Friend*, and their television counterparts, may be less well known than other classic texts, but Dickens as an author triggers specific narrative and visual expectations in the audience. Dickens and our understanding of the Victorian age seem intermeshed, even if representations of, and interest in, Dickens' particular imagination changes, going in and out of fashion. Moreover, Dickens' place in the canon of classic literature has not only ensured his place in a public service broadcasting context but also, because of his cultural weight, allowed the medium of television to grow and transform around him, to evolve while relying on the cultural significance and assumption of quality associated with his work.

Accordingly I am interested here in the medium-specific manifestation of Dickens on British television and the way in which Dickens as a cultural phenomenon not only impacts on adaptation, but also how this phenomenon reflects and impacts on the medium's promotion of itself. This chapter will, through an analysis of the 2005 BBC adaptation of *Bleak House*, explore the connections between Dickens and the medium of television in the British context, and suggest ways in which an adaptation like *Bleak House* is part of a shift in our understanding of the past, as well as highlighting changes in television at a particular point in time.

The 2005 BBC adaptation of *Bleak House* is one in a long line of Dickens adaptations for British television.[2] Scripted by Andrew Davies, and shown on BBC TV in December 2005 in 15 half-hour episodes, screened twice weekly, this adaptation was highly acclaimed and noted for its unusual format and style:

> It has always been recognized as one of Charles Dickens' literary masterworks, but this *Bleak House* is now fast-moving, daring, gripping television. Here is the murder mystery, the love story, the comic genius and the tantalizing scandal of the novel, but, stripped of its sentimentality, we find ourselves swept along by a pulsating and edgy drama. (DVD, *Bleak House*, 2005)

Promotional material such as the slogan above serves to emphasize the series' particular aims, and also the importance of Dickens as a classic author in the adaptation context. Thus the advertising on the DVD cover highlights the cultural significance of Dickens's prose and the expectations that his name conjures and also suggests a medium-specificity that refers both to television and the television text, and to a shift in representational emphasis away from the literary towards the marketing of 'a good story' – described by Jane Tranter, Head of Drama (2005), as 'Bold. Fresh. Imaginative'. Although the statement itself would apply to much landmark period drama, it also indicates a shift in emphasis from adaptation to television drama; *Bleak House*, or so we are to believe, is more than an adaptation, more than a literary masterpiece – it is now on television, an edgy, modern drama that sweeps the viewer along at a fast pace.

This shift in emphasis can be seen as a result of pressures in the current television environment, including competition and the struggle for ratings. Successful adaptations, such as ITV's *Forsyte Saga* (Granada, 2002–3) which, with its seven episodes in the first season was longer than the average classic serial of recent years, influence the handling of successive adaptations. The success of *Bleak House* has since in turn influenced the adaptation of *Little Dorrit* in 2008, also adapted by Andrew Davies, which follows a similar format of half-hour episodes. At the same time the combination of classic author and innovative style is pervasive in a television environment in which the role of public service broadcasting is increasingly questioned and under threat, making it necessary to use innovative stylistic elements and structure to showcase quality and sophistication. Thus, the imminent licence fee renewal in December 2006 prompted the presentation of the adaptation as fresh and imaginative and, through its novel high definition production format, state of the art – but at the same time also associated with notions of quality provided by the high-culture status of Dickens, as well as by the use of well-known actors and scriptwriter Andrew Davies.

While the publicity attached to *Bleak House* often emphasized innovation, it is worth noting that innovative aspects of the drama are also a return to medium-specific traditions previously displaced by channel competition, and the pressures on the medium in a multi-channel digital environment. Thus, although the twice-weekly schedule of short episodes was an unusual format for an adaptation in the current television context, it also represented a return to an earlier style of adaptation marked by series such as *Upstairs Downstairs* (LWT, 1971–75). At the same time, in a move that approaches differently notions of faithfulness and authenticity in the television adaptation, the format is also a return to Dickens as an author, and mimics the instalment format in which *Bleak House* was originally published.

The parallel is embraced in the official publicity material for the series. Thus, as producer Stafford-Clark (2005), points out in the BBC press pack, '[Dickens] was unashamedly writing for a mainstream audience and that tends to get . . . forgotten today because his books have become classics.' Dickens's work, Stafford-Clark notes, was published in a serialized form and structured to keep readers interested, in ways not dissimilar to modern television series. This approach was used to justify the emphasis of publicity on the drama's popular aspects, which were further underlined by the scheduling of the series in an earlier viewing spot, directly after *EastEnders* (BBC, 1985–). This scheduling decision, it was hoped, would increase audience figures by capturing soap viewers as previously untapped audiences for classic novel adaptations.[3] The utilization of Dickens as a household name to instil notions of quality and high culture was matched by an equal desire to highlight the 'low-culture', popular approach to literary material. The conscious design was to bring Dickens back to the audience for which he was writing, to make adaptation popular rather than highbrow in a way that, rather than 'tarnishing' Dickens's reputation as a classic author, instead aimed to make what is deemed high-culture accessible and popular.

In terms of the narrative and visual adaptation of Dickens's novel, this utilization of Dickens as a classic author, and simultaneous reaching out to popular audiences, results in an emphasis on drama and a foregrounding of the medium which plays with representation and viewer expectation, and mixes traditional tropes and – for period drama in this medium – unusual visual styles. This play with classic serial convention and medium transparency is already apparent in the opening of the first episode of *Bleak House*. The drama starts with a credit sequence that highlights the complexity of the multi-stranded narrative about to commence, and also showcases a visuality that, through collage, draws attention to its constructedness. There is a subtle shift away from a traditional credit sequence towards an emphasis on the main elements of the drama; a complex, 'soap-like' narrative, represented by the array of characters and objects, seemingly unconnected yet narratively linked; and a visual style which combines a period-style look with an editing style that serves to distance the viewer and make them aware of the 'visual fabric' of the drama. This is a move away from traditional television aesthetics which, in the case of the classic novel adaptation, have often been indebted to information and education, thereby facilitating a particular style and a propensity to respect and emphasize the written word. As Kerr suggests:

> The very desire to adapt classic novels for British television stems at least partly from the degree to which television is still seen as a transparent medium and, in Britain, as a transparent technology whose function quite simply is to facilitate the 'transmission' of the writer's work. (1982: 12)

The association with public service, in particular in the context of the television adaptation, usually creates a transparency and a realism which contrasts with the often more self-conscious nature of cinematic adaptations of the same texts, making this emphasis on style and the fabric of representation in the opening of *Bleak House* unusual.

The episode opens with Esther Summerson's (Anna Maxwell Martin) journey to London. Here again, the editing and framing draw attention in an unusual way. The carriages, wet cobble-stones and costume are recognizable as the visual tropes of the classic serial and in particular the Dickens adaptation, but these familiar sights are undercut by fast and self-conscious editing which draws attention to itself through odd camera angles, extreme close-ups, and sudden cuts which give the impression of hurry and confusion and frustrate the viewer's desire to linger and see. This again sets the opening apart from a more traditional period drama style, characterized by slow editing and often long takes which allow the viewer to take in and admire locations and detail. The new approach suggests the influence of contemporary television drama, such as the previous work of director Justin Chadwick on the BBC spy drama *Spooks* (BBC, 2002–).

This sequence culminates in a sudden cut to the High Court of Chancery, the heart of the intrigues which surround the many narrative strands of *Bleak House*. Notably, although the style of the adaptation here again self-consciously draws attention to its fabric, this visual trope is supported by Dickens's prose. Thus, *Bleak House* starts with a description of the High Court of Chancery that is, in its effect, not unlike the introduction of the Court achieved in the adaptation:

> Fog everywhere. Fog up the river, where it flows among green aits and meadows; fog down the river, where it rolls defiled among the tiers of shipping, and the waterside pollutions of a great (and dirty) city. . . . The raw afternoon is rawest, and the dense fog is densest, and the muddy streets are muddiest, near that leaden-headed old obstruction, appropriate ornament of the threshold of a leaden-headed old corporation: Temple Bar. And hard by Temple Bar, in Lincoln's Inn Hall, at the very heart of the fog, sits the Lord High Chancellor in his High Court of Chancery. (1996: 13–14)

The adaptation responds to Dickens's prose in a visual way. This is also particularly pronounced in the adaptation's 'transformation' of the London fog which, in *Bleak House*, serves as a metaphor for the stifling legal process of Chancery, but which, in the context of Dickens on screen, has also become an often over-used stereotype. Again, the adaptation uses camera work and editing to convey the visual obstruction of the fog without having to resort to a more familiar visual vocabulary. Dan Hill describes the function of editing and camera in this context as follows:

> The camera obscures; . . . characters were pushed to sides of the screen; filmed through doorways; shot over the shoulder of other characters; seen obscured through blurred whiskers. Candlelight and dark wood interiors, . . . as well as the abundantly fertile paper undergrowth of legal chambers, provided numerous opportunities to crowd the actors – such that the overall effect was as oppressive as the absent fog, everyone hemmed in by circumstance and their surroundings, conveying a sense of gnawing claustrophobia. (2006: np)

While there is a deliberate response to and undercutting of audience expectations, the adaptation still responds to notions of faithfulness to the literary source which have traditionally been so pronounced in the context of the television adaptation. At the same time the fast pace and extreme close-ups shift audience focus. If, to refer to Caughie's argument (2000), one pleasure of the classic serial is the enjoyment of detail, of profusion and the ornamental, the fast pace and rapid editing of this adaptation force viewer attention away from these traditional pleasures and towards a focus on narrative and action which is all the more pronounced because of the less well-known nature of the source text. At the same time, the drama still engages the viewer in an appreciation of what Caughie identifies as a pleasure in performance and ornament. However, unlike in many recent television adaptations, this pleasure is derived not only from the ornamental nature of an elaborate period style and character acting, but from a showcasing of individual well-known actors, and at times a performance style that emphasizes the element of caricature in Dickens's prose – as with Guppy and Smallweed, for example, characters who were noted by Andrew Davies as his favourites (Cartmell and Whelehan 2007: 240); other sources of pleasure include an appreciation of the break with tradition and expectation, and of the innovative technical effects.

The move away from familiar visual vocabulary and realism, and towards an appreciation of style, is also significant in the context of period representation, in particular in light of the close link between Dickens and the way in which the Victorian age is imagined. 'The past,' as Raphael Samuel has expressed it, 'can never be transcribed, but has always to be re-invented' (1994: 411), and period representation has changed over time both as a result of, and as an active driver in, changes in the appreciation and imagination of specific periods in history. From early on, adaptations of Dickens's novels and their depiction of the Victorian age, in particular of Victorian London, have been influential in shaping how the period is imagined, and in fixing a notion of the Victorian age as a time of repression, anxiety and hypocrisy, though the period is also seen as one of groundbreaking changes, and great scientific and technological advancement.

This kind of ambiguity in the understanding of, and emotional response to, the period has often been noted. Michael Mason addresses this tension as follows:

> More than any other era [the Victorian age] awakens in us our capacities to feel hostile towards a past way of life, to perceive the past as alien, unenlightened, and silly. This is by no means the only feeling we have about the Victorians, but in attracting certain other feelings – including the positive ones of nostalgia, sense of affinity, and even admiration – the Victorian period is like any historical era. What makes it distinctive is the hostility in the mix of attitudes we have about it. . . . We can have a variety of feelings about . . . Jane Austen, Thomas Paine, . . . and William Blake, but there is not mixed up in them that curiously personal disapproval which we tend to feel for any comparable group of Victorians. (1994: 1–2)

The reasons for this conflicted attitude can be found in the role which the period plays in relation to the present. Through the society-shaping events of the time and the changes they caused to the fabric of society, the Victorian age has been the birthplace of modernity. This is often reflected in the period's visual representation. Thus, Garrett Stewart (1995) argues that there is a noticeable 'push' and 'pull' in the representation of the Victorian period: it is seen as 'anti-romantic', a period associated with prudery and 'buttoned-up' attitudes, known for its industriousness rather than its romanticism, against which the present can define itself as modern, and there is a simultaneous sentiment of nostalgia, a yearning for origin.

At the same time however, though not in as linear a way as it may appear here, attitudes have shifted over time, being subject to cultural, social and political forces. Thus, even while classic novel adaptations for British television share a concern for faithfulness to the literary source, and authenticity, different periods have produced stylistically very different adaptations. Accordingly, while the heritage movement of the 1980s and early 1990s celebrated the period for its values and especially its work ethic, representations in the mid- and late-1990s focus more heavily on period authenticity, than even on faithfulness to the literary source. One such example is the acclaimed BBC adaptation of *Our Mutual Friend* (1998), which emphasizes realism at the expense of the more carnivalesque aspects of Dickens's prose.

This shift can be understood in part as a reaction to the stylistic trends of the earlier decade which, in parallel with the growing heritage industry, favoured a style which has since been criticized for its nostalgia and idealization of the past, its narrowing down of difference to a representation of an often pastoral Englishness (see Higson 1993, 2003 and Wollen 1991). Moving away from an overused visual and narrative style, a noticeable trend developed in the mid-1990s towards a re-discovery of the period as less simplistic and more diverse and complex than its stereotype, and towards a depiction of hidden aspects of the Victorian age. Interestingly, adaptations of Dickens were not dominant during this decade, and I suspect that the more carnivalesque qualities of Dickens' writing jarred with the concern for realism and period authenticity that was at the heart of the struggle to re-discover the period as a complex and real past. It is fitting, then, that the few Dickens adaptations that stand out include *Our Mutual Friend* and *Great Expectations* (1999), both of which present a darker, more realist Dickens, focusing on the gloomier aspects of Dickens' world and forgoing the wildly caricatured characters and absurdity of Dickens's imagination for a bleaker, more naturalistic representation of the period.

At the same time, the shift can perhaps also be understood in the context of wider trends in television programming and scheduling. Thus, the 1990s were marked by an interest in the detail of ordinary life which was displayed not only in the abundance of history programming and its specific pitch during that period, but also more widely in the explosion of lifestyle programming and reality television. These programmes shared an aim to show the extraordinary nature of ordinary life, the magical and individual in the familiar and everyday. While this trend was manifest in the transformations at the heart of many lifestyle programmes, it also impacted strongly on trends in both factual history programming, with programmes such as *1900 House* (Wall to Wall, 1999) investing in the experience of an authenticity of everyday life, and also on period drama's emphasis on the extraordinary nature of the re-discovered life of ordinary people.

Currently, representations of the Victorian period seem to be slightly less popular. Attention has shifted to other periods in history, suggesting that this particular representation of the Victorian age has played itself out. It is, then, perhaps fitting that Dickens can be reconsidered with a fresh eye, with an adaptation that seems wise to the pitfalls of stereotypes, an approach that is rediscovering an emphasis on story over history. At the same time, the shift towards a more carnivalesque and 'playful', riotous and exaggerated Dickens is perhaps only another manifestation of television's struggle for faithfulness and authenticity; after all, the carnivalesque and vividly visual qualities of Dickens' prose help to explain this author's enduring status, and authenticity and realism in representation are shifting and fugitive concepts, subject to transformations as hitherto new representational styles become familiar and stereotypical. As Jacobson points out in his essay on realism in art, the definition of what is perceived as realist, and thus an accurate representation of reality, is marked by a tendency and drive towards ever new and different versions of what can be regarded as authentic. Thus, as Jacobson puts it: 'The words of yesterday's narrative grow stale; now the item is described by features that were yesterday held to be the least descriptive, the least worth representing, features which were scarcely noticed'(2002: 41). Thus, the rediscovery of Dickens in this context is again part of a wider shift in the British television environment.

Competition has always been one of television's driving forces, and repeated questioning over the BBC licence fee has increased pressures on the medium, especially on its ability to reinvent itself in a way that satisfies both popular and public service demands. Recent years have seen further shifts in television programming that suggest a celebration of television's nature as a popular mass medium, and if British television is turning towards the popular as a way to rejuvenate itself it is perhaps not surprising that the medium uses Dickens as a way to engage with these trends, while at the same time maintaining a foothold in the struggle to present both the popular and the highbrow, to provide both entertainment and quality. Television remains concerned with the elusive goal of authenticity, but authenticity as a representational style is shifting sand, and the return to the popular as a site of authenticity, in the case of Dickens, is also a return to the traditional, to Dickens' prose as popular serialized narrative.

The popularity of Dickens adaptations has survived numerous revisions of the classic serial, and the choice of text and format of this adaptation of *Bleak House* suggests that in some ways we may have come full circle even while moving into the next manifestation of Dickens. If the classic novel adaptation reflects one of the ways in which culture speaks to itself, then perhaps the return to Dickens as the site of a reinvention of the classic novel adaptation is also an indication of a different kind of nostalgia and longing. The return to a format of instalments is at once faithful to the literary source, an instance of nostalgia for television's own history, and a celebration of both the format of the series and the medium of television. The links between Dickens and modern popular culture continually affirm the value of television as the medium that is most influential on modern life, and a justification for the merging of high and popular culture.

Notes

1. This neglect of Dickens on television can be understood as part of a wider neglect of television's role in the construction of memory and history, an area that, as work by for example Ann Gray and Erin Bell, Amy Holdsworth and Iris Kleinecke shows, has recently started to attract more academic interest.
2. Previous BBC adaptations of *Bleak House* are by Cox (1959) and Hopcraft (1985).
3. At the same time, however, this move again represents the simultaneous coexistence of innovative approaches and a return to tradition – thus, the earlier viewing slot also reflects a return to a more traditional viewing time for the classic serial which started out as a Sunday tea-time treat for the entire family.

Bibliography

1900 House (1999), Channel 4 Television/WNET Channel 13 New York/Wall to Wall.

Altman, R. (1999), 'Dickens, Griffith, and film theory today', in R. Abel (ed.), *Silent Film*. London: Athlone, pp. 145–62.

Bleak House (2005). BBC, Deep Indigo Productions.

Bleak House (1985). BBC.

Bleak House (1959). BBC.

Brown, M. (2005), 'A defining moment for television: BBC1's soap-style adaptation of *Bleak House* is the first major British drama to be shot in high-definition format'. *The Guardian*, 7 November. Available at: http://media.guardian.co.uk/print/0,3858,5327222-105559,00.html. [Accessed 21 December 2005].

Cartmell, D. and I. Whelehan (2007), 'A practical understanding of literature on screen: two conversations with Andrew Davies', in D. Cartmell and I. Whelehan (eds), *The Cambridge Companion to Literature on Screen*. Cambridge: Cambridge University Press, pp. 239–51.

Caughie, J. (2000), *Television Drama: Realism, Modernism, and British Culture*. Oxford: Oxford University Press.

Clayton, J. (2003), *Charles Dickens in Cyberspace: The Afterlife of the Nineteenth Century in Postmodern Culture*. Oxford: Oxford University Press.

Connerton, P. (1989), *How Societies Remember*. Cambridge: Cambridge University Press.

Dickens, C. (1996), *Bleak House*. London: Penguin Classics.

Dickens (2002). BBC/Opus Arte.

EastEnders (1985–). BBC.

Eisenstein, S. (1999), 'Dickens, Griffith and ourselves [Dickens, Griffith and Film Today]', in L. Braudy and M. Cohen (eds), *Film Theory and Criticism: Introductory Readings*. Oxford: Oxford University Press, pp. 426–34.

Geraghty, C. (2008), *Now a Major Motion Picture: Film Adaptations of Literature and Drama*. New York: Rowman & Littlefield.

Glavin, J. (ed.) (2003), *Dickens on Screen*. Cambridge: Cambridge University Press.

Giddings, R. and K. Selby (2001), *The Classic Serial on Television and Radio*. London: Palgrave.

Great Expectations (1946). UK, dir. David Lean.

Great Expectations (1999). BBC/WGBH Boston.

Grey, A. and E. Bell (2007), 'History on television: charisma, narrative and knowledge', *European Journal of Cultural Studies*, 10, 113–33.

Higson, A. (1993), 'Re-presenting the national past: nostalgia and pastiche in the heritage film', in L. Friedman (ed.), *Fires Were Started: British Cinema and Thatcherism*. Minneapolis, MN: University of Minnesota Press, pp. 109–29.

— (2003), *English Heritage, English Cinema: Costume Drama Since 1980*. Oxford: Oxford University Press.

Hill, D. (2006), '*Bleak House* without a foggy day in London town'. *City of Sound*, 7 January. Available at: http://www.cityofsound.com/blog/2006/01/bleak_house_wit.html. [Accessed 6 September 2007].

Holdsworth, A. (2006), '"Slow television" and Stephen Poliakoff's *Shooting the Past*', *Journal of British Film and Television* 3, 1, 128–33.

— (2008), '"Television resurrections": television and memory', *Cinema Journal*, 47, 3, 137–44.

Jacobson, R. (2002), 'On realism in art', in L. Matejka and K. Pomorska (eds), *Readings in Russian Poetics: Formalist and Structuralist Views*. Chicago: Dalkey Archive, pp. 38–46.

Kerr, P. (1982), 'Classic serials – to be continued'. *Screen* 23, 1, 6–19.

Kleinecke, I. (2006), 'Representations of the Victorian age: interior spaces and the detail of domestic life in two adaptations of Galsworthy's *The Forsyte Saga*', *Screen*, 47:2, 139–62.

— 'Victorian realities: representations of the Victorian Age on 1990s British television', unpublished doctoral thesis, 2006.

Little Dorrit (2008). BBC.

Mason, M. (1994), *The Making of Victorian Sexuality*. Oxford: Oxford University Press.

Micawber (2001), Carlton/LWT/Yorkshire Television.

Our Mutual Friend (1998), BBC.

Oliver Twist (1948), UK, dir. David Lean.

Poole, M. (1983), 'Dickens and films: 101 uses of a dead author', in R. Giddings (ed.), *The Changing World of Charles Dickens*. London: Vision and Barnes & Noble, pp. 148–62.

Samuel, R. (1994), *Theatres of Memory: Volume 1: Past and Present in Contemporary Culture*. London: Verso.

Spooks (2002), BBC.

Stafford-Clark, N. (2005), BBC press pack for *Bleak House*. Available at: http://www.bbc.co.uk/pressoffice/pressreleases/stories/2005/10_october/04/bleak.shtml. [Accessed 25 August 2008].

Stewart, G. (1995), 'Film's Victorian retrofit'. *Victorian Studies* 38, 2, 153–98.

The Forsyte Saga (2002/3), Granada Television/WGBH Boston.

Tranter, J. (2005), '*Bleak House* production diary', BBC website. Available at: http://www.bbc.co.uk/drama/bleakhouse/behindthescenes/production_diary_paginated_feature.shtml. [Accessed 25 August 2008].

Upstairs Downstairs (1971–75), LWT.

Wollen, T. (1991), 'Over our shoulders: nostalgic screen fictions for the 1980s', in J. Corner and S. Harvey (eds), *Enterprise and Heritage: Crosscurrents of National Culture*. London: Routledge, pp. 178–93.

CHAPTER ELEVEN

Embodying Englishness: Representations of Whiteness, Class and Empire in *The Secret Garden*

KAREN WELLS

The Secret Garden (UK, 1993, dir. Agnieskza Holland) is emblematic of a contemporary genre of children's films that engage in the nostalgic representation of a particular kind of English identity and landscape. *The Railway Children* (UK, 2000, dir. Catherine Morshead) or *A Little Princess* (USA, 1995, Alfonso Cuarón) would be similar examples. This genre is not of course limited to children's films; the adaptation to film and television of the novels of Jane Austen, George Eliot and E. M. Forster display a similar nostalgia for imperial Englishness. Films like these, typically thought of as 'costume dramas' or 'heritage films', 'depict a landscape that is saturated with the desire for social whole-ness' (North 1999: 38; see also Hill 1999: 73–91). They 'signify English national heritage and all that implies of the past as an idyll of village life in a pre-industrial society, of traditional class and gender hierarchies, sexual propriety and Christian values' (North, 1999: 38). These nostalgic depictions of a mythical England depend on the representation of a sense of belonging to the English landscape that is ultimately rooted in whiteness. In this kind of film the fault-lines of class and 'race' that complicate the presumed simplicity of Englishness before post-colonialism are either ignored or rendered as personal/psychological problems.

Heritage films for children are a minor genre in a market dominated by animation, and teen melodrama from the USA. Nonetheless, these films deserve critical attention for several reasons: firstly, adaptations of books that have been given the status of 'children's classics' for their depiction of Edwardian England as a place uncomplicated by the fault-lines of class and race deploy a myth of nationhood that elides the multicultural histories of England and the English (Nayak 1999). Secondly, the importance of the figure of the child in both Romantic discourse and popular nostalgia makes children's heritage films a particularly effective vehicle for the deployment of Romantic nationalism and national nostalgia. Finally, the continued circulation of films in which a longing for social wholeness and personal redemption is collapsed into nostalgia for a colonial England before 'the Empire strikes back' contracts the discursive resources available to children for the construction of a multicultural English identity.

Frances Hodgson Burnett's novel *The Secret Garden* (first published in 1911) opens with a description of the central character's life before she comes to England. The opening paragraph establishes one of the book's central themes, the impossibility of Mary, a European girl, being at home in India:

> When Mary Lennox was sent to Misselthwaite Manor to live with her uncle, everybody said she was the most disagreeable-looking child ever seen. It was true, too. She had a little thin face and a little thin body, thin light hair and a sour expression. Her hair was yellow, and her face was yellow because she had been born in India and had always been ill in one way or another . . . when Mary was born she handed her over to the care of an Ayah, who was made to understand that if she wished to please the Memsahib she must keep the child out of sight as much as possible . . . She never remembered seeing familiarly anything but the dark faces of her Ayah and the other native servants. (1951: 1).

Her parents have died in a cholera outbreak and Mary is sent to Yorkshire, England. The housekeeper of the manor, Mrs Medlock, meets her at the railway station and takes her by train and carriage from London to her uncle's manor house on the Yorkshire moors. On her first day at the manor Mary walks through the kitchen gardens where she sees a robin, and this 'bright-breasted little bird brought a look into her sour little face which was almost a smile . . . He was not like an Indian bird, and she liked him and wondered if she should ever see him again' (1951: 36). It is this bird who shows her the way to the secret garden. She meets Dickon, the brother of her servant, and he teaches her to cultivate the garden. One night she hears someone crying and following the sound she comes upon a boy, Colin, the sickly son of her uncle. Through her cultivation of the garden Mary has become healthier, physically and emotionally. She brings Colin to the garden in the belief that this healing space will also restore him to health. With the support of Dickon and Mary, Colin learns to walk. Under Colin's direction the children perform a magic ceremony to bring his father back to him. When his father returns to the manor he goes to the garden to find Colin. The boy, who is racing against Mary and Dickon, bursts out of the door of the secret garden at the same moment that his father arrives there. His father saves him 'from falling as a result of his unseeing dash against him' (1951: 250).

The film adaptation is largely faithful to the text, as these kinds of heritage films tend to be (North 1999: 38). In adaptations of

Jane Austen and E. M. Forster the literary merit of the original is the implied rationale for the attempt at a faithful adaptation; Hodgson Burnett's work has not received the same kind of critical appreciation as those authors, and the fidelity of the film to its source can more plausibly be read as part of the rhetoric of timeless and authentic Englishness that these films tend to deploy. There are, however, some evident changes from the book to the film, changes which have the effect of heightening the representation of whiteness in the film, and diminishing or erasing the novel's critique of class inequalities and its implicit critique of imperialism.

Representations of whiteness

In his seminal text on whiteness Richard Dyer analyses how white women on film are frequently lit so that they appear to be 'bathed in and permeated by light' (Dyer 1997: 122). He also discusses the connections made in horror films between whiteness and death, and between white bodies and the undead (vampires and zombies). The connections between whiteness/light and virtue are long established in Western culture, as is the contrast between light and dark. My contention is that in *The Secret Garden*, in both the book and the film, whiteness is used as a signifier of health and power, and as a whiteness that illuminates; I also argue, however, that excessive whiteness is deployed as a signifier of death. The affordances of film for representing the scopic regime of race more effectively than written texts is particularly evident in these representations of whiteness as a power which is both illuminating and deadly.

In the film, in a scene that is reminiscent of many depictions of white women on film as the 'light of the world' (Dyer 1997: 122–42), the first time that Mary meets Colin she illuminates him from above: holding a lamp in her hand, she stands on a mezzanine balcony overlooking his bed. He is lying on the bed in a white nightgown, surrounded by white pillows. Beneath the light of the oil lamp he appears as an island of whiteness in the centre of a dark picture. Mary is also dressed in white, and the candle flame lights her white face. Evoking the connection between whiteness and death, they ask one another, 'Are you a ghost?' In making connections between whiteness, death and illumination, another connection is evoked: that of the spiritual world, of a connection between heavenly light and whiteness (Dyer 1997: 119–21).

There is another scene in the film which is striking for its use of whiteness. Here, Mary comes across a secret room in the house that has no parallel in the book. She is led to this room by a wood pigeon who hops before her up a short flight of stairs into a small room. The room is entirely white, bathed in light, and has trees growing inside it.

There, Mary finds a picture of her mother and her aunt (both wearing long white dresses), sitting on the swing that, she later discovers, is in the secret garden.

This secret room, bathed in a heavenly white light, is an innovation of the film. Here again whiteness is both desirable and deathly, but in contrast to the fearful deathliness of Colin discussed below, Mary's response to the discovery of the room is one of awe and respect. While Colin's response to light alludes to the undead whiteness of the vampire, the light in his mother's secret room evokes heavenly light. This contrast indicates the different significance of whiteness in relation to masculinity and femininity in which the (feminine) spirit of whiteness is evoked as 'the light of the world' and the (masculine) body of whiteness is located in the brute force of muscularity and the relentless and unstoppable horror of the undead (Dyer 1997: 146–83; 207–23).

Though these scenes depict whiteness as the (feminine) light of the world and as illumination and innocence, another scene, one of the most dramatic in the film, points to whiteness/light as a deadly power. In the book Colin is shocked out of his malaise by Mary's unsympathetic and angry response to being woken in the night by him screaming (1951: 150–56). Colin's tantrum has been provoked by an argument that he and Mary had earlier in the day about Mary's affection for Dickon (1951: 145). In the film Mary's unsympathetic response to Colin's tantrum is part of a long scene that begins with Colin being bathed in light. His windows have been barred shut to stop the air from coming into the room and contaminating his lungs. In this scene, Mary and Dickon have tied ropes to Dickon's white horse and to the shutters. Mary runs into Colin's room, where Colin is sitting in his wheelchair facing the windows. She stands next to him, and the next moment the shutters fall and the room is flooded with light. As Colin screams and covers his eyes with his arm, Mary calls to Dickon out of the window and then runs out of the room; Colin continues to scream and falls out of his chair. Mary runs out to Dickon and jumps up behind him on to his white horse. They ride for a few seconds and then Mary jumps off again and returns to Colin's room. On finding him lying on the floor she begins to shout at him.

This scene is dramatically very powerful; it is one of the most exciting scenes in a very slow-paced pictorial film, much of which is taken up with long shots of the English countryside. Colin's fear of light and air has been created for the film: how might it be interpreted as a representation of whiteness?

Colin is bathed by light. He has already expressed his fear of light and air, the fear that it will be the cause of his death. Like the scene which depicts shutters being pulled from the windows by Dickon riding his white horse, this phobia is an innovation in the film; it does not appear in the book, where Colin's only fear is that 'I shall have a hunch on my back and then I shall die' (1951: 152). The scene evokes both the power of whiteness/light, and the close association between death and whiteness that Dyer analyses in *White*. This tension between the desire for whiteness and its deathly effects is a tension that is also evident in the book. In the film, when describing Colin to Dickon, Mary says in a tone of faint disgust: 'He's not at all like you. His cheeks are whiter than ice or marble. Whiter than these little hairs' [pointing to the tiny roots at the base of a bulb]. 'Those are the roots,' Dickon tells her. Mary goes to place the bulb in the soil the wrong way up and Dickon corrects her. The metaphor in a film replete with visual metaphors seems clear enough: plant the roots of whiteness in English soil and it will flourish. For Colin, as for Mary, it is finding a place in the English garden that will empty his whiteness of its deadliness, leaving only light in its place. When Colin is brought into the garden for the first time by Mary and Dickon, we are told that 'Even his ivory whiteness seemed to change. The faint glow of colour which had shown on his face and neck and hands when he first got inside the garden really never quite died away. He looked as if he were made of flesh instead of ivory or wax' (1951: 186). In the film, Colin continues to wear white clothes in the garden with the effect that the whiteness of his skin is emphasized, but here because of his activity and the restoration of his health, it is white as the colour of innocence and light, not 'the marble pallor' of dead people which 'appals the gaze' (Dyer 1997: 212 citing Melville 1992: 208).

Class

Parsons (2002), discussing the book, claims that 'Class distinctions are undermined beginning with Mary's arrival at the manor and continuing in the garden' (2002: 259). This claim is based on Mary's recognition in the book that she cannot speak to the servants at the manor with the tyrannical tone that she used speaking to the servants in India. For Parsons this represents a 'breaking down of [class] barriers' (2002: 259). The textual evidence does not support the claim that class divisions are broken down, but rather it strongly and favourably contrasts rural working-class common sense and generosity with the despotism of the rural aristocracy. This should not be confused with a critique of class relations in themselves; Phillips, in an insightful discussion of class and empire in *The Secret Garden*, notes that there is a critique of despotism – but not of the right of the ruling class to rule. (Phillips 1993: 180).

In the book, the despotism of the English in India is established from the first page, where the narrator tells us that Mary

> never remembered seeing familiarly anything but the dark faces of her Ayah and the other native servants, and as they always obeyed her and gave her her own way in everything . . . by the time she was six years old she was as tyrannical and selfish a little pig as ever lived. (1951: 7)

On the next page, aged nine, she beats and kicks a servant (1951: 8). When she arrives in England she is puzzled by the behaviour of the servants. When she first meets the housemaid, Martha, the narrator observes:

> The native servants she had been used to in India were not the least like this. They were obsequious and servile and did not presume to talk to their masters as if they were equals. They made salaams and called them 'protector of the poor' and names of that sort. Indian servants were commanded to do things, not asked. It was not the custom to say 'Please' and 'Thank you', and Mary had always slapped her Ayah in the face when she was angry. She wondered a little what this girl would do if one slapped her in the face . . . Mary wonder[ed] if she might not even slap back – if the person who slapped her was only a little girl. (1951: 27)

Mary expects Martha to dress her, to which Martha responds:

> 'it's time tha' should learn [to dress yourself]. Tha' cannot begin younger. It'll do thee good to wait on thysen a bit. My mother always said she couldn't see why grand people's children didn't turn out fair fools – what with nurses an' being washed an' dressed an' took out to walk as if they was puppies!' (1951: 28)

After a further exchange in which Mary flies into a rage because Martha explains that she had thought that since Mary came from India she would be 'black', Mary breaks down sobbing, and Martha comforts her and then agrees to dress her (1951: 28–30).

How is the contrast between servants in India and servants in England, and the change of attitude required of Mary when she moves to England, represented in the film? In the opening scene Mary is standing in a room with two Indian women, one standing in the corner holding Mary's clothes, whilst the other dresses Mary. Throughout this scene Mary stands passively, and at the end the women holds Mary's arms at right angles to her body and turn her around to observe her. The tyrannical behaviour of Mary towards Indian servants is erased and, indeed, in this scene it is Mary who seems to be subjected to the control of the two women who dress her.

In England, when Mary is enraged by Martha's assumption that Mary would be 'a native' (as it is rendered in the film), far from wondering how Martha *might* respond if she slaps her, Mary starts beating Martha wildly. Similarly, Colin's despotic treatment of the servants is acted out in the film without negative commentary and is even responded to approvingly or, at the very least, as the order of things. In the book, Colin's lordliness is remarked on by the servants in either an irritated or bemused fashion; in the film the servants, under the tutelage of Mrs Medlock, are depicted as either frightened (although perhaps more of Mrs Medlock than of Colin) or content with their role, but never criti-cal. This can be illustrated by the contrast between a scene in the book, where Colin asks to speak with the head gardener because he wants to make sure that nobody is near the secret garden when the children go into it, and a scene in the film where Colin tells the entire body of servants that they are not to go into the garden whilst he is out. In the book, after giving his orders to the head gardener, Colin asks Mary:

> 'What is that thing you say in India when you have finished talking and want people to go?' 'You say, "You have my permission to go",' answered Mary. The rajah waved his hand. 'You have my permission to go, Roach,' he said. 'But remember, this is very important' . . . Outside in the corridor, being a rather good-natured man, he smiled until he almost laughed. 'My word!' he said, 'he's got a fine, lordly way with him, hasn't he? You'd think he was a whole Royal Family rolled into one – Prince Consort and all.' 'Eh!' protested Mrs Medlock, 'we've had to let him trample all over every one of us ever since he had feet, and he thinks that's what folks was born for.' (1951: 177)

In the film the collected servants, standing at the foot of the stairs in their black clothes covered with white aprons, and with white masks over their mouths for fear their breath might contaminate Colin, respond to Colin's imperious manner with a respectful demeanour, and without any suggestion that the assertion of class power by a young boy might be a legitimate subject for derision or sardonic remarks.

The class origins of Dickon's sensibility are a central aspect of his character in the book. Indeed the contrast between aristocratic tyranny and the common sense of the rural working class is one of the major themes of the book. In the book Yorkshire dialect is a signifier of a lack of artifice and a healthy attitude. In the film none of the characters speak in dialect and, most significantly, Dickon and Martha's mother, Mrs Sowerby, and the rest of their family are absent from the film. In the book it is through Mrs Sowerby's aphorisms that Dickon and Martha relay to Mary the values of the rural working class which provide the main critique of aristocratic despotism in the novel. No such critique is made in the film, which substitutes the book's disdain of class tyranny with a psychologizing about Mrs Medlock's influence over Colin. This refocusing on the psychology of the relationship between Colin and Mrs Medlock is made possible by the elevation of Mrs Medlock from a minor character in the book to a central character in the film.

Representations of empire

The film and the book were produced at very different moments in the history of 'race' and empire. In 1910 Frances Hodgson Burnett's romantic nationalism could also serve as a critique of empire. The book's narrator locates Mary's ill-health, emotionally and physically, in her separation from her homeland, to be sure, but the narrator also weaves into that nostalgia a critique of the despotic ways of the English in India. The thesis that Burnett was critiquing the British Empire cannot be taken too far, however; there is more than a suggestion in the book that Indian servants are attached to a tradition that reproduces their subservience and that, implicitly, makes imperial rule possible. Colin's aristocratic despotism is constantly semantically linked to 'Oriental despotism', through references to his being 'a young rajah'. Nonetheless it is difficult to read *The Secret Garden* and not find within it some discomfort with, or even contempt for, imperial rule.

The book opens with a description of Mary's upbringing in India. The main purpose of these opening pages is to establish that Mary is the unloved and unwanted child of colonial English parents, raised by Indian servants who, because she is an Anglo-Indian and notwithstanding her young age, have had to tolerate her rude and imperious manner. Within a few pages Mary's parents have died in a cholera outbreak, and the household servants have either fled or have themselves died of cholera. Mary is sent to England on a boat, accompanied by a colonial English woman who is taking her children to boarding school there.

The film also opens with Mary in India. Over the opening credits, Mary's life in India until her parents' death is shown as she narrates her story. Her narration begins as the dressing scene, described above, comes to a close. This sequence is worth attending to closely, because interesting comparisons can be made about the different ways that the book and the film represent the English in India. In particular, the film elides the fact of empire, and therefore omits the book's implicit critique of empire – a contradictory effect of the attachment of romantic nationalism to the idea of identity as rooted in blood and soil. In the following paragraphs I will describe the scenes and quote Mary's voiceover, before analysing the significance of the differences between the book and the film in their depiction of empire.

VOICEOVER: My name is Mary Lennox. I was born in India. It was hot and strange and lonely in India. I didn't like it.

ACTION: *Mary sitting on the sand trying to plant something in the soil. She loses her balance and falls.*

VOICEOVER: Nobody but my servant, my Ayah, looked after me.

ACTION: *Mary trying to reach her mother, who is getting ready for a party. Her Ayah is pulling her away. Mary is screaming.*

VOICEOVER: My parents didn't want me. My mother cared only to go to parties, and my father was busy with his military duties. I was never allowed to go to the parties.

ACTION: *An elephant with a carriage on its back comes into the room where the party is taking place.*

VOICEOVER: I wasn't allowed to. I watched them from my mother's bedroom window. I was angry but I never cried, I didn't know how to cry.
DIALOGUE: There goes the Maharajah! The Maharajah!
ACTION: *A young boy climbs down off of the elephant's back. Mary's mother and father approach the boy and bow to him with their hands held as if in prayer. A servant, a white man, stands behind them. All the other people in the room are Indian and attending on the young boy, 'the Maharajah'. Mary runs into her mother's bedroom, a sullen look on her face, and begins to throw things on to her mother's dressing table. She throws a small ivory elephant on to the floor, its trunk breaks off, and she picks it up and tries to repair it.*
The opening credits end.
Hearing sounds of laughter, she hides under the bed. Her mother and father come into the room. She watches from under the bed.
VOICEOVER: My parents always thought about themselves. They never thought about me. If only I could have known that in a few minutes I would lose them forever.
ACTION: *Her parents leave the room, and the room starts to shake. A lamp falls on to the floor and sets fire to the outside of the bed. The bed collapses. The cries of an elephant are heard.*

The sequence ends when the bed completely collapses, and Mary is left in the dark underneath the bed.

In the book Mary's father works for the English government. In the film he is an army officer, 'busy with his military duties'. In the book the servants are treated with utter contempt by Mary, and the very clear and strong implication is that this is how whites treat Indian servants, and that Indians are always in a servile relationship to whites. In the film there are only two scenes with servants, the opening dressing scene and the scene where her Ayah pulls Mary from her mother. In the first scene Mary does not speak at all and because she is being literally manipulated by the woman who dresses her it is the woman, rather than the child, who appears in control of the situation. In the second scene Mary is screaming at her mother, and again there is no depiction of the rudeness that Mary displays towards the servants in the book. Furthermore, the film shows Mary's parents at the periphery of a scene in which the young 'Maharajah' is at the centre and the other characters are attending to him, and not to the white people. The parents bow to him, suggesting that these white adults are in a subservient position to an Indian boy, whereas in the book it is Indian adults who are depicted in a subservient position to a European girl, Mary. In short, the film entirely elides the fact of British rule in India, obscuring the reason for her father's 'military duties' and implying that the family are in the service of an Indian Maharajah. One possible reading of the story as a critique of imperial rule is therefore lost. Instead, despotic rule, which is embodied in Colin's tyrannical behaviour towards English servants, is located in the context of Indian pre-colonial government.

Readings of *The Secret Garden* and its adaptations have largely focused on the representation of gender (Gunther 1994) to the almost complete exclusion of 'race' and class. All the characters in *The Secret Garden*, once Mary has left India, are white, and it is this, I would suggest, that accounts for the inattention to 'race' in readings of both film and book. Whilst film studies have recognized the importance of representations of black people on film in relation to the practices of racialization and racism, the same cannot be said of representations of whiteness. Studies of the representation of 'race' on film have been almost entirely studies of the representation of African Americans. This omission of the fact of whiteness as a racial category has the effect of naturalizing whiteness and white power (Frankenburg 1994).

In this chapter I have analysed the representations of whiteness in the book and in its film adaptation, and traced the connections between representations of whiteness and representations of class and empire. The film adaptation of the book was made nearly 40 years after the end of British rule in India, when Britain had become a multicultural society, and so might be expected to reassess its former colonial relations in a post-colonial context. My analysis suggests that the film does not take up this task, preferring to overlook the imperial context of the original story whilst maintaining an association between identity, blood and soil which collapses English national identity into whiteness. Whilst a critique of aristocratic tyranny that represents the rural working class as able to survive on the 'th'air of th' moor[s]' (Burnett, 1951: 31) is without doubt a critique that omits the immiseration of the rural working class in Edwardian England, the film abandons any critique of imperial or national despotism in favour of a psychologizing of Colin's relations with the bad mother, personified in Mrs Medlock, and the good mother figure in Mary and her dead aunt.

Bibliography

Dyer, R. (1997), *White*. London and New York: Routledge.
Frankenburg, R. (1994), *White Women, Race Matters: The Social Construction of Whiteness*. Minneapolis, MN: University of Minnesota Press.
Gunther, A. (1994), 'The Secret Garden revisited'. *Children's Literature in Education*, 25 (3), 159–68.
Hill, J. (1999), *British Cinema in the 1980s*. Oxford: Clarendon Press.
Hodgson Burnett, F. (1911/1951). *The Secret Garden*. London: Puffin Books.
A Little Princess (1995). USA, dir. Alfonso Cuarón.
Nayak, A. (1999), '"White English ethnicities": racism, anti-racism and student perspectives'. *Race, Ethnicity and Education* 2, 2, 177–202.
North, J. (1999), 'Conservative Austen, radical Austen: *Sense and Sensibility* from text to screen', in D. Cartmell and I. Whelehan (eds), *Adaptations: from Text to Screen, Screen to Text*. London and New York: Routledge, pp. 38–50.

Parsons, L. T. (2002), '"Otherways" into the garden: re-visioning the feminine in *The Secret Garden'. Children's Literature in Education*, 33, 4, 247–68.

Phillips, J. (1993), 'The Mem Sahib, the worthy, the Rajah and his minions: some reflections on the class politics of *The Secret Garden'. Lion and the Unicorn*, 17, 2, 168–94.

The Railway Children (2000). UK, dir. Catherine Morshead.

The Secret Garden (1993). UK, dir. Agnieskza Holland.

Webb, J. (2003), 'Walking into the sky: Englishness, heroism, and cultural identity: a nineteenth- and twentieth-century perspective', in R. McGillis (ed.), *Children's Literature and the Fin de Siècle*. Westport, CT/London: Praeger, pp. 51–5.

CHAPTER TWELVE

Taming the Velvet: Lesbian Identity in Cultural Adaptations of *Tipping the Velvet*

HEATHER EMMENS

'Lesbians hardly exist on the BBC,' a 2006 Stonewall report declared. Insofar as lesbian characters are represented, the report's authors found, they are overwhelmingly associated with negative stereotypes.[1] These conclusions highlight an important issue for queer identity politics: is negative stereotyping preferable to complete invisibility? And are these the only options for lesbian identities in mainstream media? I take up these questions in relation to *Tipping the Velvet*, a retro-Victorian novel published in 1998 by lesbian writer Sarah Waters. The BBC television serialization of the novel in 2002 marked a milestone for the mainstream portrayal of lesbian characters. The serial's widespread promotion, moreover, provoked significant and varied responses in the British media: discussions about *Tipping the Velvet* and, more broadly, sexuality, proliferated in tabloid and broadsheet newspapers, lesbian magazines, television talk shows, and straight and queer online sources. In this context I examine depictions of lesbian identities and lesbian sex in three of *Tipping the Velvet*'s cultural adaptations. I begin with the eponymous BBC serial, a page-to-screen adaptation which became the main intertext for two further versions of *Tipping the Velvet*: a semi-pornographic spread in *The Sun* newspaper, and a television parody by British comedy duo Dawn French and Jennifer Saunders.

Throughout this chapter I explore the ways in which dominant cultural forces seek to domesticate non-normative instances of gender and sexuality. Gender theorist Judith Butler differentiates between disruptive and domesticated cultural repetitions even in the case of parodic or ironic representations of gender (1990: 176–7). While *disruptive* repetitions constitute acts of identity that are 'truly troubling' to conventional gender norms, some parodic repetitions can become *domesticated* and 'recirculated as instruments of cultural hegemony' (177). Tamed, defused, they are emptied of subversive meaning. Although Waters deliberately depicts 'troubling' lesbian characters in her novel, the culture industry has no such investment in disrupting sexual stereotypes. I argue that the dominant response to *Tipping the Velvet* in British mainstream media was an impulse to deny lesbian subjectivity, and to repackage lesbian sexuality for a heterosexual male gaze. This domesticating impulse originated in the BBC serial but appeared most aggressively in *The Sun*'s 'tribute' to the serial. Perhaps more surprisingly, broadsheet reviews of the serial were similarly inclined; the only mainstream resistance to the domesticating impulse emerged in a parodic comedy by two heterosexual women.

Adapted by well-known screenwriter Andrew Davies, *Tipping the Velvet* aired on BBC Two between 9 and 23 October 2002. While the screenplay arguably domesticates Waters's lesbian characters in a number of ways, my focus here is the television serial's physical depiction of Nancy Astley. The most obvious – and problematic – change the serial makes to the novel is its visual feminization of Waters's protagonist. When Nancy first tries on a suit for the music-hall stage in the novel, she looks 'like a real boy' (1998: 118), so convincing in appearance and attitude that it worries her manager, Walter Bliss, who has her jacket altered to give her the illusion of hips and breasts. Looking like a 'real' boy is a disadvantage for Nancy because Victorian male impersonators are supposed to imitate masculinity rather than embody it.[2] By making Nancy a more 'feminine' male impersonator, Walter ensures that the gender performance retains a certain transparency. The modified costume in this way reassures the music-hall audience of Nancy's femaleness: her act becomes a domesticated repetition in Butler's sense, emptied of subversive meaning and 'recirculated as an instrument of cultural hegemony' (177). In a subsequent episode in the novel Nancy passes as a young man on the streets of London. Having cut its tucks to make it 'its old, masculine self again' (192), she wears the same jacket, its original fit emphasizing her own boyish angularities. Looking like a 'real' boy is no longer a liability but an advantage, and Nancy's attempt to pass is affirmed when she is solicited by a female prostitute who believes she is a young man (194).

Sally Head Productions, the production company for the BBC serial, cast Rachael Stirling in the lead role. Although she is tall and thin like Waters's Nancy, Stirling, I contend, lacks Nancy's 'real' boyishness. The oval-faced Stirling – who bears, as the press was fond of pointing out, a certain resemblance to her famous mother, Dame Diana Rigg – has what might be called 'delicate' features. These are emphasized in the serial by the production's make-up artists who darken her eyes and lips, highlight her cheekbones, and pluck her eyebrows into tapered arches. There is little change in her make-up when she apparently passes as a boy; in the words of one reviewer, Stirling is 'handicapped by . . . ever-present eyeliner and lipstick' (Lo 2004). Her appearance led Waters to comment, in a 2002 online interview, that Stirling '[is] great – but she never looks very boyish. She's too gorgeous, she's too girlish. She never looks like she could genuinely pass as a boy on the street' (*Moviepie*). Since television is primarily a visual medium, Nancy's appearance carries considerable meaning. While Stirling sounds like a boy – very convincingly, in fact, in one dimly-lit scene in which we can only hear her voice – she lacks visual masculine attributes. If the production company or the BBC had wanted to create a convincingly masculine 'look' for the scenes in which Nancy passes as a boy, they could have made her up differently, or even cast a different actress. The fact that they did neither suggests that a 'convincing' masculinity was not their objective; Stirling herself told *The Sun* that the only qualm Sally Head had with her appearance was that her forehead might be too big (Oglethorpe 2002).[3]

By casting Stirling the serial's production company provides the same reassurance for BBC viewers that Nancy's stage costume offers to Victorian music-hall spectators in the novel. Nancy's altered jacket disrupts any 'authenticity' in her masculine performance in the novel, just as Stirling's femininity undermines Nancy's identity in the serial. This discrepancy is particularly striking in scenes where Nancy passes as a boy. Here, Stirling's prettiness creates a disjunction between the other characters' acceptance of Nancy's masculinity and, as another reviewer put it, 'the inescapable fact that she is a girl' (Billen 2002). Thus Nancy's lesbian identity – emphatically described by Waters as 'butch' (Waters 2006) – is coded onscreen as feminine, and Stirling's 'girlish' appearance, like the tucks in the male impersonator's jacket, render the spectacle more transparent than transgressive.

The domestication of lesbian sexuality frequently takes the form of visual feminization. When they appear at all, popular or mainstream depictions of lesbian identities almost inevitably conform, like the numerous hyperfeminine characters of *The L Word* (2004–2009), to 'Hollywood' ideals of femininity. In contrast to these 'femme' stereotypes, 'butch' lesbians – who adopt a more 'masculine' image in terms of body, manner and dress – are virtually invisible on television. In Waters's novel Nancy combines aspects of femininity and masculinity in her identity, and can thus be read as disruptive – or 'gender troubling' – in Butler's sense. On television, however, Nancy resembled conventional visual conceptions of femininity. It is this specific representation of lesbian characters as feminine women that I call *femme-inization*. I contend that televisual femme-inization makes lesbian characters visually indistinguishable from the conventional heterosexual women on television who are coded as objects of heterosexual male desire. By femme-inizing its protagonist, the BBC serial brings Nancy's appearance into line with conventions of female desirability even as it forecloses on alternative (and thus 'undesirable') butch depictions of her character.

When viewers tuned in to the much-hyped first episode of *Tipping the Velvet*, they saw Stirling in sex scenes with Keeley Hawes (as Kitty Butler), an actress whose 'crisp beauty' and 'delicate sexiness' gave her, according to one television reviewer, 'the appeal of a younger Kristin Scott Thomas' (Anthony 2002). Waters's Kitty is hardly butch, but Hawes and Stirling in bed together evoke the pseudo-lesbian imagery of heterosexual pornography. Not surprisingly, Stonewall researchers Cowan and Valentine cite the characters in *Tipping the Velvet* as examples of 'very glamorous or very feminine' lesbian stereotypes which offer viewers a 'palatable form' of lesbianism (2006: 10). Rather than challenging femme stereotypes, then, the BBC *Tipping the Velvet* repackages lesbian sexuality for a heterosexual male gaze. In other words, as Andrew Davies told a press conference, 'men are going to love it' ('My TV Show is Absolute Filth' 2002).

Davies, the award-winning adaptor of BBC 'classic' adaptations such as *Pride and Prejudice* (1995) and *Bleak House* (2005), made this comment some three weeks before the first episode of *Tipping the Velvet* aired. It was reported in a *Sun* article which declared that Davies' 'new lesbian sex drama' would be, according to its dramatist, 'absolutely filthy' ('My TV Show is Absolute Filth' 2002). Beyond Davies' play for male viewers, the brief article is notable for the way in which it situates the adaptor as the author of *Tipping the Velvet*. Waters's name is not mentioned here; similarly, she is rarely acknowledged in other tabloid reporting on the serial. Writing of the 'classic serial' television adaptation, Paul Kerr contends that the position of the original author is 'an exceedingly ambivalent one: on the one hand she or he is foregrounded as guarantor of the cultural commodity on offer; but on the other, s/he often vanishes into the Classic Serial format' (1982: 13). In this case, Waters guarantees lesbianism but she does not guarantee prurient 'filth', so she is of little use to the tabloid writers. In *The Sun*, *The Daily Mirror* and other tabloids, then, straight male adaptor Davies supplanted lesbian novelist Waters as the creative power behind the production.

In the media conflagration that followed Davies' comments to the press, *The Sun* fanned the flames in various ways: one writer dubbed Davies a 'sex maniac' (Shelley 2002), others promoted the serial as outright pornography ('Keeley [Hawes] and Rachael [Stirling] are seen romping naked and using sex toys with – literally – gay abandon' [Iozzi 2002a]), but by far its most intriguing cultural contribution was *The Sun*'s own adaptation of the serial: between 12 and 18 October 2002, *The Sun* ran a five-part Page 3 series called 'Victorian Secrets'. Where each edition of *The Sun* features a young female model posing topless on Page 3, 'Victorian Secrets' adds corsets and frilly lingerie to the picture.

This was not the first time the British tabloids had appropriated lesbian sexuality for a heterosexual male audience. When the BBC serialized Jeanette Winterson's novel *Oranges Are Not the Only Fruit* in 1990, the tabloids, contends Hilary Hinds, 'made a concerted effort to construct a pornographic reading of the text' (1992: 166). Hinds analyses a review in *Today* newspaper which declared that '[i]n order to fully fulfil the "ultimate male fantasy"' the drama required 'a lot more tits' (166). The reviewer's 'male friend' opines that Samantha Fox and Maria Whitaker – two famous Page 3 models at the time – would more satisfyingly fill the lesbian roles, to which the reviewer quips that a more appropriate title might then be 'Melons Are Not The Only Fruit' (166). Hinds demonstrates that the acts of renaming the serial – from 'Oranges' to 'Melons' – and recasting it with Fox and Whitaker, force the 'ethos of "Page 3"' on the adaptation (166). In this way, she asserts, the *Today* writer 'reconstructs [the text] as a tabloid ideal . . . [to] emphasize more strongly its pornographic possibilities' (166–7). When *Tipping the Velvet* aired twelve years later, *The Sun* did not simply force the 'ethos of "Page 3"' on the serial; it completely reconstructed the text as a 'tabloid ideal'. In its renaming and framing of the serial, and by omitting all gender-troubling signifiers from the text, *The Sun* created its own soft-core pornographic adaptation.

The title 'Victorian Secrets' associates the BBC serial with the American lingerie store Victoria's Secret, a brand known for its print advertisements of scantily-clad female supermodels. *The Sun*'s title also cites the cultural connotations of the Victoria's Secret catalogue as an onanistic auxiliary for heterosexual pubescent boys.[4] Both the catalogue and Page 3 resemble what Jane Arthurs calls 'docuporn', her term for titillating late-night documentaries about the sex industry (2004: 46). Arthurs writes: 'Generic assumptions about what and who these programmes are *for* tie them into a long history of institutionalized reading practices for pornography in which sexualized images of women are coded for men's masturbatory pleasure' (98, emphasis in original). Page 3's invocation of Victoria's Secret might seem redundant since both texts are tied into similar pornographic reading practices, but the reference to the lingerie catalogue serves to shift *Tipping the Velvet* decisively into the realm of male masturbatory fantasy. 'Tipping the velvet' – a Victorian slang term for cunnilingus – is Waters's lesbian-coded title for a text which refuses to meet the expectations of Page 3's intended audience. *The Sun*'s alternative title, however, invokes the long history of sexualized images designed to appeal to its particular readership.

If the title hints at *The Sun*'s voyeuristic intentions, the captions accompanying the Page 3 images spell them out. These brief blurbs position readers as intruders gazing into the private spaces of the bedroom or the bathroom. The first 'Victorian Secret', of 12 October, explicitly establishes this dynamic with the phrase: 'Peep through the keyhole for a real frill [sic] . . .' Similarly, 18 October reveals 'what the butler phwoar [sic] . . .'[5] The pun on 'what the butler saw' invokes the classic voyeuristic scenario in which a butler observes upper-class female nudity by peeping through the bedroom keyhole. And what did the butler see? Page 3 typically features a single model of the day, but four of the five 'Victorian Secrets' depict two women posing together. The large-breasted, long-haired, lipsticked models in *The Sun* embody the *Today* reviewer's 'ultimate male fantasy' based on Samantha Fox and

Maria Whitaker; they are meant to be read as lesbians quite simply because there are two of them.

Film adaptation theorist Thomas Leitch describes how pornographic film adaptations 'empty their [source] stories of their original meaning in order to use them as a narrative framework for the sex scenes that are [pornographic films'] raison d'être' (110). In this case *The Sun* empties *Tipping the Velvet* of its original meaning in order to use the text's lesbian framework as the basis for its own pseudo-lesbian imagery. Once the BBC serial has been reconstructed as a 'tabloid ideal', however, it becomes potentially unrecognizable, so *The Sun* must name the original title in each image's caption. The models for 12 October, Anna and Sarina, are 'togged up like those girls in TV's *Tipping the Velvet*' in a 'tribute to BBC2's Victorian lesbian drama'; 16 October depicts a 'saucy scene inspired by BBC2's sizzling drama *Tipping the Velvet*'; and so on. Each image, we are told, has been 'inspired by' or 'pays tribute to' *Tipping the Velvet*. This repeated citation of the original title appropriates Waters's 'authentic' lesbian eroticism for the pseudo-lesbian scenarios offered up on Page 3, but the emphasis on 'BBC2's drama' invokes the version that 'men are going to love' and inscribes Davies as the text's author. These acts of renaming and framing package the lesbian eroticism of *Tipping the Velvet* as a commodity to be consumed by *Sun* readers.

Despite the claim that Anna and Sarina are 'togged up like those girls in TV's *Tipping the Velvet*', 'Victorian Secrets' bears little visual resemblance to the BBC serial. In both the novel and the screen version, Nancy's cross-dressing onstage as a male impersonator and offstage as a male prostitute drives the narrative. Male impersonation, however, clearly does not figure in the 'ultimate male fantasy', so it must be omitted from the tabloid ideal. This omission is evident in the 17 October 'Victorian Secret', which features Corina 'reflect[ing] on her saucy image [as she] adjusts her garter in a pose inspired by BBC2's drama *Tipping the Velvet*'. Corina's posing recalls an episode in Waters's novel and Davies' adaptation in which Nancy becomes the 'sex slave' (in tabloid parlance) of wealthy widow Diana Lethaby. Kept for nocturnal pleasures, Nancy spends the daylight hours artfully arranging herself while she waits for Diana to return. For her sojourn with the older woman, however, Nancy dresses in masculine attire; in both the novel and the television serial she passes as Diana's 'boy' when they go out in public (278). Her fine suits contrast sharply with the lacy white dressing gown in which Corina is draped. For Page 3, apparently, 'Secrets' signifies voyeurism while 'Victorian' signifies frilly knickers.

Male impersonation was not the only gender-troubling signifier omitted from 'Victorian Secrets.' *Tipping the Velvet* was notorious for the scene, translated to television, in which cross-dressed Nancy straps on a leather dildo to pleasure Diana. Described by a *Sun* television reviewer as a 'frightening-looking 10 in[ch] leather sex toy' (Iozzi 2002b),

Diana's favourite bedroom accessory would seem to be the stuff that tabloid fantasies are made of. Despite its titillating potential, however, the dildo, like Nancy's suits, is omitted from 'Victorian Secrets' because it disrupts the gendered coding of Page 3's images. Writing about pornography made by lesbians, Colleen Lamos states: 'the dildo flaunts its phallicism and in doing so throws into doubt received distinctions between male and female as well as between hetero- and homosexuality' (1994: 91). This troubling of gender and sexual binaries is at odds with what Hinds called the 'ethos of "Page 3."' Page 3 models smilingly pose as objects of heterosexual male fantasy, inviting male readers to penetrate them. If there are two models then both are equally available to the male gaze. The women in 'Victorian Secrets' are clearly not interested in each other's bodies or each other's pleasure; instead, they look out of the photograph, soliciting the reader's attention. A Page 3 'girl' wearing a dildo would evidently disrupt this equation: if she appropriates the phallic fantasy, her invitation becomes an offer to penetrate him. The dildo, then, potentially threatens male heterosexual phallicism and for this reason must be omitted from Page 3.

While the BBC serial femme-inizes its lesbian protagonist, *The Sun* constructs its own fantasy in 'Victorian Secrets'. In this way the newspaper can omit any elements that may disrupt or subvert its scopophilic economy. 'Victorian Secrets' recalls Butler's words on domesticated parody: through these images Waters's non-normative lesbian tropes become 'recirculated as instruments of cultural hegemony' (177). *The Sun* can therefore be seen to domesticate the lesbian text more thoroughly than the television adaptation; while the latter domesticates its lesbian characters visually, the former comprehensively assimilates the text's lesbian eroticism to its own heterosexual programme. In this way *The Sun* constructs a 'tabloid ideal' which replaces Waters's lesbian feminism with a heteronormative and anti-feminist agenda.

The British tabloids promoted *Tipping the Velvet* as a 'raunchy lesbo romp' ('The Scurra' 2002), *romp* being the tabloids' word of choice for lesbian (s)exploits. Following this 'hyperventilating advance publicity', as one reviewer put it (Joseph 2002), *The Sun* reported complaints that the BBC serial 'wasn't raunchy ENOUGH' ('Lesbian Show "Too Clean" Say Angry Viewers' 2002, emphasis in original). While some viewers predictably found the sex too explicit, others telephoned the BBC after the first episode to complain 'that [*Tipping the Velvet*] didn't live up to its billing as the "most explicit lesbian TV drama ever"'; a BBC spokesperson remarked that 'some viewers were "disappointed" at the lack of hot sex scenes' ('Lesbian Show' 2002). In a review for *The Times* Joe Joseph analyses this disappointment: '. . .by the time it came to actually watching the show our expectations were higher than Marge Simpson's beehive. Anything short of *What the Butler Saw* as filmed by Russ Meyer was at risk of seeming like rather an anticlimax' (Joseph 2002). What viewers got, according to Joseph, was '*Moulin Rouge* for beginners . . . spiked with a few cosy lesbian sex scenes that wouldn't have raised many eyebrows in a Fifties French art house movie' (Joseph 2002). Joseph's response is typical of broadsheet reviewers who adopted an intellectualized response to *Tipping the Velvet* in an effort to distance themselves from the tabloids' reputation for a vulgarity and carnality associated with the working class. While this is hardly more surprising than the tabloids' hyperventilation over the prospect of lesbian sex, there is a curious similarity among the broadsheet and tabloid responses: in attempting to distance themselves from the tabloids, certain broadsheet writers ended up aligning themselves with the latter.

This trend is exemplified by Roland White in *The Sunday Times*, who concludes, after describing the first episode:

> [D]espite its thin plot, *Tipping the Velvet* is as uplifting as a Victorian bustle. But shocking? No. I was only shocked at the way that middle age has wrapped me in its suffocating embrace. Two women squirming about in bed, panting and groaning, and it barely raised an eyebrow. (White 2002)

Instead he professes to have been 'much more interested' in a programme on London sewers. White employs a style of urbane wit marked by clever figurative language to distance himself rhetorically from the phew and cry of the tabloids. This distancing is mirrored by Andrew Anthony in The *Guardian*. Dismissing the lesbian sex for displaying the same 'standardized choreography' and 'carefully positioned bedsheets' as any other television sex scene, Anthony writes: 'The one novelty, and it was nothing to moan about, was that there were four breasts on show instead of the usual two' (Anthony 2002). Anthony's review is more thorough than White's: he is one of the few reviewers to discuss the novel in any detail, noting that Waters 'understood the erotic potential that lies between what is said and how it's said', a sexual tension that (he contends) the BBC serial lacks. Having made the comparison he gestures towards anti-fidelity criticism, admitting that it is 'an odious business comparing a screen adaptation with the original novel' (Anthony 2002). But for all his attempts to provide a balanced perspective, he, like White, remarks on the failure of the lesbian sex to titillate. Anthony concludes his review by declaring that 'next week's episode features a strap-on dildo', another 'novelty' which might succeed where the 'four breasts on show' failed.

The broadsheet stance is perhaps best illustrated by John Preston in *The Sunday Telegraph*. He writes:

> Like a lot of heterosexual men my attitude towards lesbianism goes roughly as follows: dead keen in theory; scared stiff of actual lesbians. *Tipping the Velvet* . . . was preceded by various windy pronouncements about how it revealed 'human nature in all its glory' and 'lifted the coat of Victorian sexuality.' Phooey! It's aimed squarely at robust male hypocrites such as myself; the sort of people who would come over very queasy at the thought of watching a porn film, but who are quite keen on those late-night Channel 5 movies

in which bored housewife, Nina, decides to improve her backhand by taking lessons from statuesque tennis coach, Helga. (Preston 2002)

Despite his expectations, however, Preston, too, is disappointed: 'The sex, when it eventually came, proved to be an extremely damp squib, carrying no erotic charge whatsoever . . . Better Nina and Helga any day' (Preston 2002).

These writers are eager to prove how *untitillating* they find the spectacle of Kitty and Nan 'squirming about in bed', as a way of affirming their own sophistication. It is in this very distancing, however, that they inadvertently align themselves with the tabloids. Anthony, Joseph, and particularly White and Preston, may find the women in *Tipping the Velvet* unsuccessful sex objects, but they still *expect* to be aroused by them. Lesbianism, they imply, should be inherently titillating for heterosexual men. In condemning *Tipping the Velvet* for its failure to raise more than eyebrows, these writers implicitly validate the lesbian objectification openly championed by the tabloids. While superficially the broadsheet reviews appear to have nothing in common with 'Victorian Secrets', they exhibit a similar impulse to domesticate the lesbian eroticism of *Tipping the Velvet*. The BBC itself, however, finally offered a version of the text which resisted this dominant impulse.

Two months after the serial aired on BBC Two, a third cultural adaptation of *Tipping the Velvet* appeared during *French and Saunders*'s 'Celebrity Christmas Puddings' special on BBC One.[6] The nine-and-a-half minute parodic sketch, called 'Tippin' o' the Velveteen', underlines the serial's cultural significance, for the comediennes are known for their elaborate parodies of television and film blockbusters such as *Harry Potter*.[7] That *French and Saunders* is itself a BBC production probably helped the comic duo recreate the look and sound of *Tipping the Velvet*; the *French and Saunders* theme tune, for example, is seamlessly incorporated into the *Tipping the Velvet* incidental music, while sets, costumes, hair and make-up appear almost identical to those in the serial. The bodies, however, are unmistakably those of Dawn French and Jennifer Saunders who play, respectively, 'Miss Nancyboy French' and 'Miss Titty Saunders' in a parody which ruthlessly mocks the BBC serial even as it subverts notions of male fantasy.

French and Saunders satirize the media's sensationalizing of the serial, beginning with the name 'Titty' which crudely foregrounds the expectations of nudity and lesbian sex that preceded *Tipping the Velvet*. The parody does indeed provide a lesbian sex scene replete with 'titties', but they happen to be enormous imitation breasts made of rubber. Feigning sexual excitement, Titty and Nancyboy rub their fake breasts together in a grotesque parody of sensuality; French tentatively pokes at one of Saunders's rubber nipples. The artefactual quality of the scene – the strap-on breasts and latex buttocks – codes the lesbian bodies themselves as fake, an artificiality paralleled by the actresses' deliberately unconvincing desire for each other. *French and Saunders*'s satirical critique of tabloid models of masculinity dates back to the 'Two Fat Men' sketches of their earliest days, in which the comediennes played unsavoury balding men in fat suits, driven by their unconsummated lust to hump inanimate objects. The Fat Men's frequent use of tabloid expressions such as 'phwoar!', 'I'd give her one!', and 'she's begging for it!' – whether discussing Page 3 girls or the Queen – explicitly ridicules tabloid modes of hypersexuality and the objectification of women. Read in this context, the Titty/Nancyboy sex scene not only parodies Davies' serial, but also deflates the sensationalist media treatment of lesbianism; it is a grotesque performance for a grotesque audience.[8]

Saunders further disrupts the sex scene by breaking character. Emerging from the blanket between French's legs, she asks: 'You're Diana Rigg's daughter, aren't you?' Temporarily abandoning her dubious Cockney accent, French replies in a posh voice: 'Yes, but I don't normally like to make a thing of it at work.' Saunders answers: 'She's a good friend of mine. Give her my love; tell her I'll call her. I've got my phone here somewhere, but I can't do it now, I'm busy.' Combined with the scene's inescapable grotesquerie, this alienation effect, which codes the scene as 'work' rather than carefree lesbian 'romping', undermines notions of lesbian sex as inherently titillating for heterosexual men. The parody is thus 'truly troubling', not to conventional gender norms as is Waters's protagonist, but to the domesticating impulse itself: 'Tippin' o' the Velveteen' interrogates those cultural mechanisms which seek to 'recirculate' non-normative instances of sexuality as 'instruments of cultural hegemony' (Butler 1990: 177). At the beginning of this chapter I asked whether negative stereotypes are preferable to complete queer invisibility. One might answer yes, provided it is French and Saunders who critique them.

Tipping the Velvet confirms that lesbians do indeed exist on the BBC. Davies' adaptation, however, reveals a clear if unconscious agenda to femme-inize the more disruptive aspects of lesbian identity in Waters's novel, while tabloid and broadsheet writers domesticate the serial by mediating its eroticism through their own fantasies. Moreover these writers, including Davies, foreclose on notions of female spectatorship by coding their audiences as heterosexual and male. French and Saunders, however, subvert the domesticating impulse on both counts: first, by satirizing this male appropriation of lesbian sexuality; and secondly, by embedding a female audience for their performance. This audience – one of several framing devices for the Christmas special – comprises two frumpy middle-aged women (also French and Saunders) with opera glasses sitting in an empty theatre. In the sketch's final scene the camera cuts to Nancyboy on stage singing Kitty's signature tune 'Oh Rosie' from the BBC serial. She throws a rose into the audience, which lands in Saunders's outstretched hand in the theatre. The Saunders spectator – who believes Nancyboy really is a boy – laughs: 'Thank you, young laddy! But if you think I'm taking my pants off, you've got another think coming.' French grabs the rose and exclaims: 'I will!' In this way the parody reinstates the female spectators erased by Davies' comment that 'men' would love the serial; in *The Sun*'s construction of the 'ultimate male fantasy'; and again in the broadsheet reviews written by men 'quite keen' on television lesbianism.

This brief interchange comes closest to establishing a non-stereotyped positive lesbian identity in the mainstream adaptations of *Tipping the Velvet*. French as middle-aged spectator responds to cross-dressed Nancyboy's performance in a queer way: brandishing the rose, she sticks out her tongue and wiggles it, imitating Nancy's explication of the act of 'tipping the velvet'. In her oversized glasses and shapeless clothes French defies femme-inized stereotypes, providing viewers with one alternative to invisibility and stereotyping in mainstream media. In its very brevity, however, this queer moment emphasizes the need for more positive representations of lesbian identities.

Notes

1. In 'Tuned Out: The BBC's portrayal of lesbian and gay people', a report published by queer British media watchdog Stonewall, Katherine Cowan and Gill Valentine found that during 168 hours of BBC One and Two television programming in 2005, lesbians were represented for a total of six minutes (2006: 6). Of those six minutes, they were represented positively for one minute and ten seconds (13).
2. See Ullman 2001: 197.
3. The novel's adaptor Andrew Davies was not responsible for casting, but had worked with Stirling, Keeley Hawes (Kitty Butler), and director Geoffrey Sax on his previous project, ITV's *Othello* (2001). He described them all favourably, and had no objections to the cast of *Tipping the Velvet* (Davies 2006).
4. For instance, the online *Urban Dictionary* – 'a slang dictionary with your definitions' – defines 'Victoria's Secret' variously as 'the best non-pornographic porn out there' and 'poor man's porn' (*Urban Dictionary*).
5. 'Phwoar': 'As an enthusiastic expression of desire, approval, or excitement, esp. in regard to sexual attractiveness: "cor!" "wow!"' (OED).
6. This special aired on 25 December 2002. Equal parts feminist and absurd, celebrated British comedy partners Dawn French and Jennifer Saunders have produced six series from 1987 to 2004, plus numerous seasonal specials.
7. 'Harry Potter and the secret chamberpot of Azerbaijan' (2003) featured Dawn French as Harry and Jennifer Saunders as Ron Weasley and J. K. Rowling. Other blockbusters parodied include, for example, *Lord of the Rings*, *Titanic*, *Braveheart*, and *Star Wars: The Phantom Menace*. Film auteurs get spoofed, as do horror films, film 'classics', television shows, and popular singers and bands.
8. I am indebted to Ellie Kennedy for bringing 'Two Fat Men' to my attention.

Bibliography

Anthony, Andrew (2002), 'Crushed velvet: while Andrew Davies' saga of lesbian love fell flat, *Faking It* scored again'. *Guardian*, 13 October.

Arthurs, Jane (2004), *Television and Sexuality: Regulation and the Politics of Taste*. Maidenhead, England: Open University Press.

Billen, Andrew (2002), 'Are lesbians really hilarious?' *New Statesman*, 14 October, 47.

Butler, Judith (1990), *Gender Trouble: Feminism and the Subversion of Identity* (second edn). New York: Routledge.

Cowan, Katherine and Gill Valentine (2006), 'Tuned out: the BBC's portrayal of lesbian and gay people'. London: Stonewall, 1–28. <http://www.stonewall.org.uk/media/tuned_out__gay_people_in_the_media/default.asp>. [Accessed 16 November 2006.]

Davies, Andrew (2006), Personal interview, 10 May.

Hinds, Hilary (1992), '*Oranges Are Not the Only Fruit*: Reaching audiences other lesbian texts cannot reach', in Sally Munt (ed.), *New Lesbian Criticism: Literary and Cultural Readings*. New York: Columbia University Press, pp. 153–72.

Iozzi, Giovanna (2002a), 'Keeley Hawes – the touch of velvet'. *The Sun*, 5 October, 12.

— (2002b), 'Tasteful? Corset is'. *The Sun*, 9 October, 26.

Joseph, Joe (2002), 'Andrew Davies' controversial adaptation of *Tipping the Velvet* ended up more like *The Good Old Days* as directed by Baz Luhrmann'. *The Times*, 10 October, 23.

Kerr, Paul (1982), 'Classic serials – to be continued'. *Screen*, 23 (1), 6–19.

Lamos, Colleen (1994), 'The postmodern lesbian position: *On Our Backs*', in Laura Doan (ed.), *The Lesbian Postmodern*. New York: Columbia University Press, pp. 85–103.

Leitch, Thomas (2007), *Film Adaptation and Its Discontents: From 'Gone with the Wind' to 'The Passion of the Christ'*. Baltimore, Maryland: Johns Hopkins University Press.

'Lesbian show "too clean" say angry viewers' (2002), The Sun, 10 October, 3.

Lo, Malinda (2004), 'Review of *Tipping the Velvet*', from 'After Ellen: news, reviews and commentary on lesbian and bisexual women in entertainment and the media'. <http://www.afterellen.com/Movies/92004/tippingthevelvet.html>. [Accessed 15 November 2006.]

Moviepie (2002), 'BBC2 dips into the sexy side of Victorian England: a chat with *Tipping the Velvet* author Sarah Waters'. <http://www.moviepie.com/filmfests/sarah_waters.html>. [Accessed 15 November 2006.]

'My TV show is absolute filth' (2002), *The Sun*, 20 September, 4.

Oglethorpe, Tim (2002), 'Corset is!' *The Sun*, 5 October, 21.

Preston, John (2002), 'Pedestrian Victorians'. *The Sunday Telegraph*, 13 October, 7.

'The Scurra' (2002), The *Daily Mirror*, 11 October.

Shelley, Jim (2002), 'Not such blue velvet after all'. *The Sun*, 10 October.

'Tippin' o' the Velveteen' (2002), in *French and Saunders: Celebrity Christmas Puddings*, BBC One.

'Tippin' o' the Velveteen' (2005), in *French and Saunders: On the Rocks*. DVD. BBC/ Warner.

Tipping the Velvet (2002), BBC Two.

Ullman, Sharon (2001), 'The "self-made man": male impersonation and the new woman', in María Carla Sánchez and Linda Schlossberg (eds), *Passing: Identity and Interpretation in Sexuality, Race and Religion*. New York: New York University Press, pp. 187–207.

UrbanDictionary<http://www.urbandictionary.com/define.php?term=Victoria%27s+secret>. [Accessed 4 November 2006.]

'Victorian Secrets' (2002), *The Sun*, 12 October, 3.

'—' (2002), *The Sun*, 15 October, 3.

'—' (2002), *The Sun*, 16 October, 3.

'—' (2002), *The Sun*, 17 October, 3.

'—' (2002), *The Sun*, 18 October, 3.

Waters, Sarah (2006), personal interview, 22 April.

— (1998), *Tipping the Velvet* (second edn). London: Virago.

White, Roland (2002), 'Girls just want to have fun'. *Sunday Times*, 13 October, 12.

CHAPTER THIRTEEN

'Who's the Daddy?': The Aesthetics and Politics of Representation in Alfonso Cuarón's Adaptation of P. D. James's *Children of Men*

TERRYL BACON AND GOVINDA DICKMAN

In 2006, Sony Pictures released Alfonso Cuarón's adaptation of P. D. James's 1992 novel, *Children of Men*, the apocalyptic story of human sterility leading to extinction. Reviews in the mainstream press, and online at sites like IMDb.com, describe a masterfully wrought Hollywood sci-fi blockbuster expressing worthy sentiments about race, postmodernity and globalization. Indeed, the film's well-meaning liberalism is attested to by a plethora of laudable neo-humanist signifiers. As the DVD bonus documentary, *The Possibility of Hope* (Sony Pictures 2006), explains, Cuarón aspires to elevate the diegesis of *Children of Men* above the simulacric space of desire conventional to Hollywood action movies. He re-presents, instead, the Present: this cinematic dystopia is no empty phantasmagoria, but rather a symbolic representation of failed late capitalism.

However, despite its ideological gravitas and the tightly packed symbolism of its mise-en-scène, the film is highly problematic in terms of the very historical and political themes it purports to explore. Under the guise of radical discourse, Cuarón reinforces flawed stereotypes of race, gender and class, and reiterates the historically constructed binarisms that maintain them.

Cuarón exploits cleverly the formal, cultural and ideological conventions of Hollywood action movies to create an aesthetic *ecstasis*, a transport into nightmarish exhilaration. His emotionally seductive film 'pulls the audience into' a megarealistic diegesis artfully recycled from atropic iconographic and symbolic references, popular culture and recent history which we term 'Here, Now'. He systematically subverts conventional media representations of contemporary Western society, transforming the neo-liberal 'global utopia', icon by icon, into a degenerate multicultural dystopia. Our worst reactionary tabloid nightmares are made manifest in dense, harrowingly recognizable references to corrupt or decaying fragments of the contemporary urban zeitgeist, beginning in a decrepit London-much-like-London: . . . a pavement covered with flowers, cards, teddy bears, reminiscent of public response to Diana's death, but in this case *ad perpetuam memoriam* a character whose death is a symbolic subplot, a recurring and evolving *leitmotif*, subliminally registered, background to the main action . . . on a train station platform, a cage of immigrants await deportation. From within, an old woman laments in an East European dialect, reminding us of the Holocaust . . . a field of burning cow carcasses, whose slaughter – divorced from the bleak pragmatism of the mad-cow disease to which this is a reference – makes no sense other than as nihilistic negation of the fecund . . . from a kneeling line of hooded and bound prisoners, armed soldiers single out and brutalize a cowering immigrant . . .

The crumpled habitus of the film's white male protagonist reflects the misery and futility of his habitat: Theo (Clive Owen) embodies the torpid disgust appropriate to the degenerate mise-en-scène and the historical crisis that it variously indicates or metaphorically signifies. The film begins with a news report on TV in the cafe where Theo buys his habitual fix of caffeine. The report highlights objections from the Muslim community to the continuing army occupation of mosques. We then learn of a Homeland Security Bill ensuring that an eight-year ban on immigration continues, illegal aliens are deported, and all UK borders remain closed.

The final news item is the only one without some clear resonance with contemporary British cultural and politics; while news stories about 'The Muslim Community' [sic] and 'The Immigration Situation' [sic] are both quite common in this country as we write, the sonorous announcement of the accidental death of the youngest person on the planet, eighteen-year-old Baby Diego, feels entirely new.

The newscast is closely followed by an apparently random bomb exploding in the street outside, ironically timed to illustrate and comment on the official version of events. Expressing the repressed passion that has been subtext to the horrifically bland news reports, it is yet another tabloid zeitgeist reference. Between what we have learned, what we know already, and the explosion, an entire history of social degeneracy is articulated, and a diegetic space coalesces, arising from the ringing in our ears.

This Gestaltist narrative strategy exploits the cultural background of the film's intended audience. It requires a spectator able to 'fill in the gaps', intuit the 'hidden pattern' that links this enigmatic news item to the others, and thus 'explain' the shift from contemporary liberalism to the harsh right-wing political milieu indicated by the newscaster's non-committal delivery of stories which convey racist attitudes, or tacitly accept violence toward Muslims and foreigners.

Cuarón's approach differs from the novel, which opens with a whimper rather than a bang, via the self-deprecating diary of the privileged relict of a decadent age: the literally and metaphorically impotent historian, Theodor Faron. As P. D. James herself observes, when History has come to an end, what could be more redundant? With wry reference to his own superfluity, Theodor writes to 'record the nothingness' (James, 1992: 1) and to fend off the torpor and apathy attending his condition:

> What possible interest can there be in the journal of Theodor Faron, Doctor of Philosophy, Fellow of Merton College in the University of Oxford, historian of the Victorian age, divorced, childless, solitary, whose only claim to notice is that he is cousin to Xan Lyppiat, the dictator and Warden of England. (James, 1992: 2)

This (grammatically impeccable) use of the third person in a first-person narrative form, the autobiography, demonstrates a sophisticated grasp of the genre, attesting to Theodore Faron's class and education.

Cuarón's re-characterization of Theo as an unassuming bureaucrat appears to 'democratize' the protagonist, making him less a figure of privilege, more an Everyman. Indeed, if one accepts this hypothesis, 'democratization' could be viewed as generally characteristic of the mutative logic informing the entire process of adaptation. The brutally ugly inner-cityscape, or the open-plan office where Cuarón's Theo works, with its anonymizing ranks of identical work-stations, are in stark contrast to the slowly decaying gentility of James's Oxford, whose dreaming spires are lexically and metaphorically indicative of an elite whose decay is anticipated, but distant.

Differences such as these might suggest that the film offers a more egalitarian perspective on social injustice, attested to by the overt thematization of terrorism and racism with which the film begins. However, while Cuarón's adaptation does present a more proletarian visual and cultural lexis in a more popular idiom (and medium!) than P. D. James's novel, it is by no means clear that the effect is to make the narrative more egalitarian.

Although their settings are geographically and formally distinct from each other, and they differ hugely in style, both novel and film are what Homi K. Bhabha might term *topologically* similar. Bhabha problematizes the notion of 'location' when he considers the role of narrative in the construction of a 'topology' of nation and national identity (Bhabha, 1994). In Bhabha's sense, both versions of the tale occur in very similar *topoi*: both Cuarón and P. D. James are speaking to the same anxieties, and *the location of those anxieties is in both cases identical.*

What are these anxieties, and to whom do they belong? Both book and film explicitly thematize 'foreignness', via a series of dichotomic relationships that structure, indeed propel, the narrative: Them and Us; Self and Other; Order and Chaos; Science and Belief; Law and Anarchy; Culture and Primitivism; Male and Female; Powerful and Abject; Fertile and Sterile, ad tragic infinitum. . .

In both the film and the novel, Theo is initially characterized through apathetic cynicism. Theodor's diary is an archly nihilistic reflection upon himself and recent history, a masochistic articulation of despair posing as an act of hope. The egotism of the diarist and the raison d'être of the historian are ironically subverted by self-loathing and the absence of any hope of posterity. In the film, Clive Owen's demeanour articulates the same message, enacted for an environment he clearly despises. His revulsion is performatively indexical of the privilege that Cuarón's strategy ostensibly rejects, because it can only arise from *despair* at the dissolution of a status quo wherein he was once happy. In this light, P. D. James's discourse on class is arguably more complex and explicit than Cuarón's, and the film's ostensibly egalitarian (multicultural, urban, spectacular) aesthetic actually masks a rather reactionary ideological topology, which both film and novel share.

And so we come to the only truly significant changes which Cuarón makes to the narrative. Firstly, in the book, humanity's decline is caused by the inexplicable drop in male sperm count; in Alfonso Cuarón's version, it is women who are mysteriously infertile. Secondly, in the book, the miracle child is born to a white middle-class woman called Julian, Theo's former student, and member of a not-quite-not-Christian resistance group called 'The Five Fishes'. In the film, the mother is a teenage African refugee called Kee (Clare-Hope Ashitey). Finally, Julian does appear in the film, as leader of a dissident group known as 'The Fishes'. She is Theo's ex-wife, who left him after the death by drowning of their infant son. In the novel, Theo is also divorced, but from a woman named Helena, who left him because she could not forgive him for accidentally killing Natalie, their infant daughter. The film's Kee is born out of a conflation of the characters of Julian and Helena in the novel.

Elspeth kydd, in a critique of the representation of multiculturalism in dystopic science fiction, observes:

> From the etymology of 'mulatto' in the word 'mule', hybridity and fertility have been intimately linked. The idea that an excess of hybridity leads to sterility is a legacy of the racist theories of the nineteenth century polygenesists. Even with the basis of scientific racism discredited, narratives of racial mixture often feature heightened anxieties around reproduction and a racialization of the processes of child bearing and rearing. (kydd, 2008)

Sterility and degeneracy are both explicitly and tacitly linked in every aspect of the film; the diegetic 'future' is 'now plus entropy', filmed in a pallet of dirty greys, smoggy browns, bruised blues and washed-out greens. Cities are concrete ruins filled with violence both sudden and perpetual; countryside, a decaying wasteland, devoid of all life (indeed, full of Death). According to kydd, this sterile world is:

> . . . a hybrid world, a place of multiculturalism imploded, representing a planet overly mixed and out of control. It is also a world where binarisms are re-established and the split between 'them' and 'us' re-inscribed. Here, in the urban decay, is a sterile, infertile humanity facing their pending end as a species. These elements of the dystopian fantasy are linked, as the world of hybridity and multiculturalism gone mad has led to the death of the future in the sterile world. (kydd 2008)

In the book, where even frozen sperm has become useless, the sterility threatening the end of humanity is attributed to men, yet we are only five minutes into the film when Theo's ageing hippy friend, Michael Caine, asks, 'The ultimate mystery: why are women infertile?' Later, a midwife recalls how eighteen years previously, all of her clients miscarried in the same week and she noticed that the appointment book was completely empty. Shortly afterwards, the world realized that women's inability to give birth had become a universal phenomenon. Human infertility is laid firmly at woman's door.

Woman, as Naomi Wolf (1991) has pointed out, has historically been made responsible for both beauty and emotion in the human race. Early in the film, a prominent headline on a public screen tells us: 'The World Has Collapsed – Only Britain Soldiers On'. And soldier on it does, in a militarized world where women, stripped of their procreative function, have little value. In this grim dystopian vision, women bear the blame for what is essentially the symbolic impotence of globalized capitalism: the abjection of the feminine is quietly implicit throughout society and its infrastructure.

In this context, perhaps the most eloquent of Cuarón's innovations is Kee, the African girl-woman whose fertile body offers messianic hope to the dying world. As kydd notes, 'The black-woman-earth-mother trope is the film's highly racialized comment on the nature of gender, race and difference and a stereotype that works in conjunction and in conflict with Theo as sterile white masculinity' (kydd 2008).

This is a morbid male fantasy, a wish-fulfilment drama in the tradition of the Arthurian legend. The death of the human race is in fact the projected fear-desire of the (white, male) subject. Fertility is embodied by Kee, object of desire and revulsion; impotence by Theo and Xan, his despotic alter ego.

Why Xan? Xan is the ubiquitously invisible antagonist of the film. As well as being the *sine qua non* of the action adventure genre, Bad Guys – as anyone who has considered Lacan's mirror will know – are the shadows of the Good Guys: narrative only occurs, *can only occur*, in the fermata caused by the schismatic dismemberment that separates Theo from his shadow, and in a sense creates them both. In the book, Xan is Theo's cousin, the dictatorial Warden of England. In the film, Theo's cousin is called Nigel (Danny Huston). Although clearly extremely powerful, he is not explicitly portrayed as the Warden and has almost no narrative function; Xan appears only as the background of the film, his paranoid will projected upon the landscape as the binarism 'them' and 'us'.

Cuarón understands that cinematic 'discourse' is *not* discursive. At the heart of cinema is *ecstasy*: a visceral, neurochemical discourse whose syntax is *pleasure*; a game where we pretend we do not believe what we are seeing so that we can believe it more perfectly. The film's intended audience *is* none other than the schizophrenic amalgam of Theo and Xan: the impotent neo-liberal who desires union with Kee, and the despot who fears and abhors her, who together face the causes and effects of their inability to (pro)create, or merge with (each) Other. In a sense, this differs from James's intended message and audience *not at all*, but the change in the source and idiom of the message very much changes its direction and its point.

'History,' writes Joshua Clover, 'is a nightmare from which movies cannot awaken' (Clover 2007: 6). To quote Frederick Jameson, 'History is not a text, not a narrative, master or otherwise, but . . . an absent cause' (Jameson quoted in de Lauretis 1987: 111), a cause which necessarily passes through its prior textualization, its narrativization in the political unconscious.

So we may ask what is missing from this narrative, what has been elided from the political unconscious? An interruption is required, some perspective upon the Gaze itself, or at least the phenomena of its perception; something that will allow the subject to question his own pleasures, and the objects of those pleasures.

In the book upon which the film is based, we are left in no doubt as to the relationship between pleasure and procreation. James writes:

> One might have imagined that with the fear of pregnancy permanently removed and the unerotic paraphernalia of pills, rubber and ovulation arithmetic no longer necessary, sex would be freed for new and imaginative delights. The opposite has happened. . . . Women complain increasingly of what they describe as painful orgasms; spasm achieved but not the pleasure. (James 1992: 168)

James seems to revive the link between female pleasure and procreation common to a pre-modern understanding of sexuality. Laqueur tells us that 'the view that women's orgasm was essential to generation was dominant throughout Europe until the late eighteenth century', and that 'the emergence of the Victorian era and its obsession with the passionless bourgeois wife and mother' (1987: 5) led to a repression of this view:

> Women, increasingly critical and intolerant of men throughout the 1980s and 1990s, have at last an overwhelming justification for the pent-up resentment of centuries. (Men) who can no longer give them a child cannot even give them pleasure. (James 1992: 168)

The allegorical resonance of this film is that of the sterility of modernity. But there is more, or less, going on. The miraculous pregnancy is revealed (of course) in a barn. The mother-to-be strips off to show our hero, a horrified Theo, her naked body. Repression, transgressed. *Repression* is what is missing from the political unconscious.

Theo moves from revulsion to something approaching awe as we grapple with the unacknowledged assumption of sexual difference. Her materiality reminds us of our own. His response reminds us of her abjection. The mother's body, even burgeoning with new life, is redolent of disintegration, decay and death: the defetishized body, reduced to the unspeakable Other.

Abjection, as theorized by Julia Kristeva, is associated with separation from the mother's body, the need to establish an autonomous, hygienic, 'proper' body, apart from bodily waste and inanimate bodily matter, the undifferentiated haptic chaos of infancy. The threat here is not just loss of separation, of subjectivity; it is ultimately a reminder of the mutability of the flesh: of death. In *Children of Men*, it is the threatened breakdown in meaning caused by the loss of the distinction between the white male subject and the objects of his desire/revulsion which is the centrifuge of all the pleasure the film has to offer, and which is also at the centre of the social breakdown it re-presents. As de Lauretis tells us:

> . . . there is indeed reason to question the theoretical paradigm of a subject-object dialectic, whether Hegelian or Lacanian, that subtends both the aesthetic and the scientific discourses of Western culture; for what that paradigm contains, what those discourses rest on, is the unacknowledged assumption of sexual difference: that the human subject, Man, is the male. (de Lauretis 2004: 192)

The primary mutative logic behind Cuarón's adaptation is *not* an egalitarian impulse to democratize P. D. James's themes and imagery, but rather the inevitable tendency toward *spectacularization*, which occurs as a result of its context within the Hollywood blockbuster tradition. The material and ideological exigencies of adaptation to the Hollywood screen (and the culture of its consumption) necessitates an aesthetic and ideological approach – a cinematics – appropriate to the expectations of a very specifically constructed audience. As an 'action adventure' movie, *Children of Men* conforms to the aesthetic and narrative conventions of *megarealism*, epitomized by Cuarón's deployment of the cinematic code, *ThereCam*.

In its current cultural context, ThereCam is part of an aesthetic and ideological framework that aims to construct in/for the appropriately conditioned Subject (the Spectator), the experience of a (sort of) roller coaster ride from HereNow-right-now into a megarealistic NowHere-nowhere-near-here. Megarealism aims to produce an *ecstasis* similar to that which all 'rides' exist to induce: the whole point is that the Subject of a megarealistic narrative fails to notice *anything* outside of the experience of immersion in the diegesis, because they are rendered physically and psychologically *ecstatic* by the cocktail of intense audio-visual stimulation, fantasy, their own neuropharmacopoeia (adrenalin, serotonin, dopamine), and of course the various stimulants traditional to the culture of consumption surrounding Hollywood action movies, including sugar, sex and status.

The implicit pact between Hollywood and the Spectator is that the ride will deliver them back to the HereNow 'once it's all over', a promise Hollywood cannot possibly break because, as everyone knows, roller coasters are a circular medium: they only go nowhere (NowHere). Crucially, the medium itself cannot break the pact: HereNow only exists as a dialectic construction of the NowHere that is its secret essence. The simulacric action of NowHeres is twofold: on the surface, they allow us to indulge the fantasy that they are not real, by being almost-but-not-quite-real instead; beneath the surface, they allow us to indulge the much more important fantasy that the world beyond the NowHere, the HereNow we walk into once we leave the cinema, is really real.

The truth is that NowHeres and HereNows are retroactive, mutually iterative. Žižek hints that the dialectics of fantasy, symbolism and reality are inextricable from the mutually constructive relationship of Self and Other, when he asks, '. . . is the Real not the traumatic kernel of the Same against whose threat we seek refuge in the multitude of virtual symbolic universes?' (Žižek, 2008).

As Bazin (1960) once noted, all photorealistic images, indeed all representations in any medium whatever, are at heart attempts to realize the unrealizable Other (Lacan's *Grand Autre*) by substantializing, and merging with, the fantasy other (*petit autre*).

ThereCam is a specific kind of immersive camerawork common to megarealistic film-making: a cinematographic code-set that fetishizes the phenomena indicative of *the continuity and presence of the camera in the diegesis*. It fuses the technological and the spectral gazes and tropes them as a pseudo-substantial 'thing' that can be physically affected by events occurring within the diegetic space, as when the camera shakes in 'realistic' simulated response to an explosion or when the scene is filmed through a blood-spattered lens. Despite its quasi-solidity, the gaze of ThereCam most often remains curiously immune to the situation, invisible, dedistanced, spectral. The NowHeres of ThereCam are, more often than not, explicitly phantasmagorical. In post-digital Hollywood, ThereCam is used to render the Spectator-Subject *ecstatic*, to transport them into the diegesis, and to dramatize its substance as well as its discourse for them. It is any approach to camerawork that attempts to substantialize and control Other by substantializing the spectator's presence within its space.

Nevertheless, the bloody lens has consequences: ThereCam casts the viewer as a silent witness to the NowHere, a spectral presence rather than a spectral absence, arguably culpable for his/her participation in the filmic fantasy. Is it possible to view *Children of Men* as an attempt to 'hijack the roller coaster' and take us instead on a nocturnal journey into the very HereNow that we go NowHere to escape? The first half of the film does indeed take place in a NowHere very like HereNow, but subjected to a systematic transformation: the future, it seems, is 'the view from the living room window', but older, and unloved; an England of tomorrow, as it is imagined by an imaginary Englander of today.

For example, note Cuarón's remediation of an object commonly found in English living rooms today: Large Demonstrations of Marching, Chanting, Angry Islamic Youths (henceforth LDMCAIYs), commonly featured in contemporary news reports. This stereotype is a leitmotif in Cuarón's mise-en-scène, whose entropic force remediatively dedistances it in a manner apparently intended to signify 'out of the TV screen and into reality'. However, due to the relentless simulacric action of a medium whose raison d'être is to mask reality (so that it can literalize fantasy), the strategy does nothing to reveal that LDMCAIYs are, in fact, stereotypes: Cuarón's remediation does not offer a new view of these demonstrations, just a terrifying close-up on the TV screen.

Where once Communist states were seen to be the opposite of liberal societies, neo-liberalism has substituted Islam (Treanor 2005). The film presents archetypes as atavistic in their simplicity as the tabloid iconography it so knowingly references. By not exposing LDMCAIYs as imaginary objects – myths that make sense only in the context of a living room On The Other Side Of The World from where LDMCAIYs occur – Cuarón simply makes them more frightening. Indeed, the film relies on the bogeyman quality of this stereotype, its dangerous Otherness, for the sense of apocalyptic threat (and concomitant thrill) it lends to the narrative space.

Far from subverting either the view or the gaze upon it, the likely effect is to invoke anxiety in those for whom the icons and objects of the deteriorated world have some value, whose living rooms are in question, inducing a reactionary response rather than inspiring a revolutionary one.

In the film, immigrants are derogatorily referred to as *fugees* – a contraction of the word *refugees*. Fugees are the Them whose relationship to the dialectally constructed Us is a version of the contemporary stereo-type of the 'economic migrant', a mythic character related to the equally mythic 'asylum seekers' who, according to the tabloid press, 'throng' or 'mass' or 'flow' towards Our Borders from the violent conditions of an undefined and ultimately unknowable Out There. Both myths implic-itly construct a set of discourses about Self, Other, and the Boundary that is meant to divide them. Discourses that invoke these stereotypes of Self and Other very often also directly reference our own repressed desire for the Other: our anxiety that 'We are in danger of being over-whelmed by Their desire or need' epitomizes both revulsion and desire.

In the book, immigrants to England are euphemistically called 'sojourners'; young foreigners lured to England under false pretexts to become the slave class whose exploitation allows English citizens their lives of luxury. Sojourners do everything considered beneath the dig-nity of proper citizens, and are consequently vital to society: without them, the infrastructure would rapidly degenerate into chaos. When their useful working life is over, they are forcibly expatriated or killed, hence 'sojourner': they are not here to stay.

The difference between a sojourner and a fugee is this: the simulacric action of the fugee is *not* only that the myth constructs a false distinction between Self and Other; rather, it is that it constructs a false Border, a non-existent Boundary between 'their' world and 'ours'. The inextrica-bility of the sojourner from the social order described in the book reveals that the Here/Us of capitalist culture is the centre of a mandala that exists only by dint of its (exploitative) relationship with its circumfer-ence: the rest of the world.

The most remarked-on scene in the film, the birthing scene, is prob-ably the shortest labour ever portrayed. It has been the subject of many tracts because of its clever use of CGI; it creates the illusion of a continu-ous real-time event captured in a single unbroken shot, but it is actually a composite of several shots and a CGI environment. The camera's dance reveals the birth in some detail, while completely obscuring female genitalia at all points; a rather coy mixture of prurience and voyeurism. This is almost a visual definition of the erotics of abjection, conforming entirely to the aesthetic and ideological tendency of post-modern (i.e. post-digital, post-domestic-video, post-cyborg) Hollywood cinema that we have been discussing. It attempts to substantialize fantasies and fantasy spaces by actualizing or substantializing sub-jectivity itself as various modes of 'presence' within those spaces: we feel we are 'there' with Kee and Theo. This 'feeling of presence' is the true simulacrum, rather than the spaces it reifies, although the faux-haptic phenomenological discourse of 'being in the space' does lend those spaces false externality and substantiality, masking both their fantastic nature and the directedness of the gaze upon them. However, the *true* simulacric action of megarealism is to trope the substantial as 'the real', absence as presence, voyeurism as immersion, being as existence.

The child is, of course, a girl. Born into abjection, legitimized by male presence, she will continue the cycle. In the final scene, mother and child at sea in a grey, undifferentiated mist, wait with a dying Theo for the promised rescue by the shadowy group, The Human Project. We will not explore the symbolism of the huge prow as it looms overhead.

Far from challenging the status of the female body as a signifier of a misogynist fantasy of femininity, this scene presents two polar feminine tropes that iterate conventional representations of femininity and race on nearly every level: Kee, near panic, enacts and embodies vulnerability and emotional reliance on the dying Theo, while the amorphous Other – the ubiquitous fog – threatens to consume them. This symbol is what Barbara Creed calls 'the monstrous feminine . . . the origin of all life threatening to reabsorb what it once birthed' (Creed 1990: 134). If we truly seek to challenge the status of any of the bodies that have been abjected by patriarchal hegemony, we must start by acknowledging difference not as threat, nor even as mystery, but as an inevitable compendium of our shared humanity (Mulvey, 1995).

Is there anything significantly new about Cuarón's version of the patriarchal allegory of male potency which fuels all Western cinema aimed at young white men, and is significantly (ubiquitously) absent even in films that are not?

Cuarón is counting on the fact that the audience who watch the film will consist predominantly of white male liberals who have come to the cinema to realize their secret fantasy of merging with the Other, wanting to become both the Oppressor and the Oppressed, to cease for a while being (Theo/Xan) and to become instead (Theo/Kee). Cuarón knows, he has to know, how racist and sexist the whole notion of Kee-the-fantasy-slave-girl-lost is, how perfectly she plays the role of abjected Child-Mother-of-the-future to Theo/Xan's Father, so that together we can pretend that Theo has not been Xan all along, and that escape is possible.

Perhaps Cuarón believes that he can free Kee's body from the web of fantasy that binds it, or induce the epiphany that she *is* a fantasy, from which might grow a sense of what that ramifies for everything else in the frame? This might, in turn, interrupt or dissolve the relentless simulacric action of a medium that substantializes fantasy in such a way that we do not notice that it *is* fantasy. Perhaps he is hoping that if someone can dissolve his megarealistic illusion and actually experience themselves experiencing Kee as a pseudo-reality, when in fact she is all fantasy, then maybe, just maybe, they will also grasp that not only Kee, but the entire World that Cuarón presents in *Children of Men*, *actually exists*. It has been made real, not by war and greed and lies and borders and History, as we might like to think, but by the violently performative and ineluctably *corporeal* Gaze of men like Theo, like Xan, like Cuarón.

Bibliography

Bazin, A. (1960), 'The ontology of the photographic image' (trans. Hugh Gray), *Film Quarterly*, 13, 4, 4–9.

Bhabha, H. K. (1990), *Nation and Narration*. London: Routledge.

— (1994), *The Location of Culture*. London: Routledge.

Bram, D. (1986), *Idols of Perversity: Fantasies of Feminine Evil in Fin-De-Siecle Culture*. Oxford: Oxford University Press.

Bynum, W. C. (1992), *Fragmentation and Redemption: Essays on Gender and the Human Body in Medieval Religion*. New York: Zone Books.

The Children of Men (2006). USA, dir. A. Cuarón.

Clover, J. (2007), 'All that is solid melts into war', *Film Quarterly*, 61, 1, 6–7.

Creed, B. (1990), 'Alien and the monstrous Feminine', in A. Kuhn (ed.), *Alien Zone*. London: Verso.

De Lauretis, T. (2004), 'Aesthetic and feminist theory: rethinking women's cinema', in P. Simpson, A. Utterson and K. J. Shepherdson (eds), *Film Theory: Critical Concepts in Media and Cultural Studies*. Oxford: Taylor & Francis, 193–212.

— (1987), *Language, Discourse, Society*. London: Macmillan Press.

Dovey, J. (2000), *Freakshow: First-Person Media and Factual Television*. London: Pluto Press.

Dutton, R. K. (1995), *The Perfectible Body: The Western Ideal of Physical Development*. London: Allen & Unwin.

Foucault M. (1976), *The History of Sexuality, Vol. 1*. London: Penguin Books.

— (1977), 'Nietzsche, genealogy, history', in Donald F. Bouchard (ed.), *Language, Counter-Memory, Practice: Selected Essays and Interviews by Michel Foucault*. New York: Cornell University Press, pp. 139–64.

Hunter, D. (1983), 'Hysteria, psychoanalysis, and feminism: the case of Anna O', *Feminist Studies*, 9, 3, 464–88.

Irigaray, L. (1985), *This Sex Which Is Not One*. New York: Cornell University Press.

James, P. D. (1992), *The Children of Men*. New York: Random House.

Kristeva, J. (1982), *Powers of Horror: An Essay on Abjection*. New York: Columbia University Press.

Kydd, E. (2008), *Children of Men: Infertile Multiculturalism, Degeneration and the Politics of Hybridity*. Publication pending.

Laqueur, T. (1987), *The Making of the Modern Body: Sexuality and Society in the Nineteenth Century*. Berkeley: University of California Press.

— (1990), *Making Sex: Body and Gender from the Greeks to Freud*. Cambridge, MA: Harvard University Press.

Marcuse, H. (1998), *Eros and Civilisation: A Philosophical Inquiry into Freud*. London: Routledge.

Mulvey, L. (1950), 'The Myth of Pandora', in L. Pietropaolo and A. Testaferri (eds), *Feminisms in the Cinema*. Bloomington, IN: Indiana University Press, pp. 3–19.

The Possibility of Hope (2006). USA, dir. A. Cuarón.

Schiebinger L. (1993), 'Theories of gender and race', in *Nature's Body: Sexual Politics and the Making of Modern Science*. London: Pandora, pp. 143–83.

Treanor, P. (2005), 'Neoliberalism: origins, theory, definition'. Accessed at www. inter.nl.net/users/Paul.Treanor/neoliberalism.html *on 3 January 2009*.

Wolf, N. (1990), *The Beauty Myth: How Images of Beauty Are Used Against Women*. London: Vintage.

Žižek, S. (2008), *The Cyberspace Real*. Accessed at *http://www.egs.edu/faculty/zizek/zizek-the-cyberspace-real.html* on 30 December 2008.

Part IV

Afterlives

Origin and Ownership: Stage, Film and Television Adaptations of Daphne du Maurier's *Rebecca*

REBECCA D'MONTÉ

Daphne du Maurier wrote *Rebecca* as a novel between 1937 and 1938, whilst living in Egypt with her husband, Major Frederick 'Boy' Browning, who was stationed there. It was her seventh book, her most popular bestseller, and it has been 'seen as the template for the modern gothic romance which flourished in the 1960s and 1970s' (Tuttle 1997: 196). It was itself inspired by Charlotte Bronte's *Jane Eyre* (1847), an important point, for here we can see the way in which one text generates another, without the need for complete fidelity. Indeed, the term 'adaptation' 'implies that there is more than one text and more than one author' (Whelehan 1999: 27). *Rebecca* has proved particularly malleable in this respect, having a long afterlife that stretches to the present day. It was first published in serial form in British and American newspapers, then as a book, before being turned into a radio play by Orson Welles's Mercury Theatre. Du Maurier herself adapted the novel for the stage in 1940, the same year that Alfred Hitchcock's celebrated film appeared. Thus, the stage and film versions were circulating at the same time in the public domain, with the novel still in the first flush of its success. There were two notable productions for television, one for the BBC in 1979 and another for ITV in 1997, and a stage adaptation by the Irish playwright, Frank McGuinness, in 2005. In the tradition of Jean Rhys' addition to Bronte's book, *Wide Sargasso Sea* (1966), female novelists have been fascinated with *Rebecca*, writing sequels (Susan Hill's *Mrs De Winter*, 1993; Sally Beauman's *Rebecca's Tale*, 2001), literary allusion (Maureen Freely's *The Other Rebecca*, 1996) and 'faction' (Justine Picardie's *Daphne*, 2008). By focusing here on the stage, film and television adaptations of *Rebecca* we can consider the ways in which notions of origin and authorial ownership can be problematized, as a means of exploring the effect of context and form upon subjectivity and meaning.

Staging Englishness during the Second World War

Daphne du Maurier was easily persuaded to adapt *Rebecca* for the stage by John Gielgud, who was originally to take the role of Maximillian de Winter. As her biographer tells us, she had no ideas for a new book, and needed distraction from the current political turmoil (Forster 1993). Immediately, she realized the difficulties of changing one form for another, especially as there was little scope on stage for the narrator's interior monologues or detailed descriptions of her surroundings. As it happened, the outbreak of the war allowed her, the director George Devine, and the set designer Roger Furse, to concentrate on another aspect of the novel, its encapsulation of Englishness. Just before the play opened in the West End, Norway and Denmark were invaded by Germany, and there were fears that this would have a detrimental effect on the theatre. Instead, what happened was that audiences were ripe for images of England's heritage, here represented by Manderley and the noble De Winter family. This meant that the play was an immediate and resounding success during much of the 1940s, with 380 performances in the West End of London, as well as touring productions around the country.

Significantly, Daphne du Maurier's stage adaptation can be seen as 'unfaithful' to her own novel. Whilst the original story was a way of representing difficult subjects such as fractured identity, dangerous sexuality, and the decline of the aristocratic house, the focus here is on its opposite: the importance of unity, stability and the defeat of threatening forces. The ambitious set design included a winding staircase at the side of the stage decorated with family portraits as reminders of the house's ancestral past (*The Bystander* 1940: 172–3). This imaginative construction of the aristocratic house, with its suggestions of tradition and history, followed on from contemporary propaganda in stressing the importance of English culture. Philip Page's review captured public opinion: 'to see on the stage in these days a stately home of England which is neither a war hospital nor a hive of evacuated children is something of a relief' (Page 1940: n.p.).

The script itself is efficient, but not startlingly original. It could be argued that this was because du Maurier's dramatic abilities were limited, even if they had been honed by the time of her next play, *The Years Between* (1945). Equally, though, this quality of theatrical conventionality can be seen as the play's strength. Several reviewers saw it as a melodrama, with exaggerated plotting and heightened emotions. This was a genre equally popular on stage and film during the Second World War, providing a release from everyday suspense and tension. Beyond this, the casting can be seen to place the melodrama within safe boundaries, helpful for a wartime audience. Owen Nares, a seasoned film and stage actor, and matinee idol of the 1920s, before Ivor Novello came on the scene, eventually played Max. He usually took roles that suggested a romantic solidity. Celia Johnson's ordinariness suited the role of the second Mrs De Winter, an attribute she exploited in future films like *In Which We Serve* (1942), *This Happy Breed* (1944), and *Brief Encounter* (1945). Actors known for their reliable competence also took lesser parts, and while Margaret Rutherford frightened audiences as Mrs Danvers, she was identified mainly with comic roles, and therefore her danger was destabilized.

Du Maurier's refashioning of her book can be seen most obviously in the eradication of the narrator, and consequent dispersal of that viewpoint amongst several characters. One paper saw the play as a 'psychological study of a nerve-wracked man' (*London News* 1940: n.p), and another described 'Miss Johnson's part [as] negative, the authoress having omitted to give the second Mrs de Winter any quality but that of being prettily terrified' (*Observer* 1940: n.p.). Her earlier role as companion to Mrs Van Hopper is excised, and the play starts from the perspective of Max's sister and brother-in-law as they wait for the arrival of the new bride. Any focus on the second wife that this would suggest is dissipated almost as soon as she appears, and the audience has its attention dispersed between the heroine 'very plainly dressed in grey' (du Maurier 1940: 14), Maxim and Frank Crawley, discussing the estate, and the stage business of Beatrice and Giles. The concentration on the external rather than the internal nature of the drama means that audience identification is not so readily available, and this is aided by the quick pace of the play. Whereas the novel unfolds slowly, with each mention of Rebecca divulged and dwelt upon, here the fateful costume ball is brought up in the first scene, and Jack Favell makes his appearance at the beginning of the next. The interiority of the young woman is replaced by dialogue between all the characters, and of necessity the play deals with the narrative, rather than the subtleties of underlying emotions. Whereas practically every chapter in the book ends on a new revelation, or the introspective comments of the narrator, who pulls the reader *into* her world of paranoia and delusion, the stage curtain pulls the audience *away* from their suspension of disbelief, and into an awareness of the theatrical world as a constructed one. Because the set is confined to the drawing room, in keeping with a number of other plays at the time, several crucial scenes are left out or altered, sometimes drastically: there is no confrontation between the heroine and Mrs Danvers in Rebecca's bedroom, the attempted suicide scene takes place at the top of the stairs, not at a window, and the inquest is reported, not created onstage. The ending itself is entirely different, so that a phone call is made to Rebecca's doctor to establish the motivation for her suspected suicide, rather than a last-minute dash up to London to receive the news about her cancer. Radically, there is also no dramatic fire, which destroys Manderley. Instead, Mrs Danvers attempts to threaten the de Winters, but her power has been dispelled, and as she is the one to be banished, husband and wife reunite in the family home where they will remain to weather the gossips, rather than going abroad. Here the evil is ousted from the stately home, which in this instance can stand in for Britain and its hoped-for victory over Germany. As the novel's framework of the exiled couple has been cut for dramatic simplicity, the bringing together of the couple at the finale follows through those conventions of romance that du Maurier was at pains to eschew in the novel. The critics of the time were certainly reassured by her new ending, which they felt was in tune with the turbulent times, so as husband and wife stand together in perfect accord, the aristocratic Manderley unravaged, the audience are faced with a potent symbol of Englishness at a time of renewed nationalistic pride.

Filming the feminine in the 1940s

Whilst the stage adaptation has been generally overlooked, Alfred Hitchcock's film has attracted a vast array of critical commentary. At the time it was lauded with praise, gaining 11 Academy Award nominations and winning two: one was for cinematography and the other was Hitchcock's only Oscar for best picture, but he lost out on an award for his direction to John Ford's *Grapes of Wrath*. Hitchcock's dismay over being given *Rebecca* as his first Hollywood film has been well documented. He thought it was nothing more than a melodramatic novelette, and did his best to add his own trademarks to it. That is, he wished to 're-author' it in his own fashion. Sometimes these efforts were stymied before they got off the drawing board. The producer, David O. Selznick, rejected Hitchcock's attempts to add humour to the story, and demonstrated a considerable understanding of du Maurier's intent, and of the relationship between female readers and the central narrator, even if this was reductive: '"little feminine things" like "nervousness," "self-consciousness," "gaucherie," and "embarrassment" that he believed made the novel's heroine so attractive to female readers' (Hollinger 1993: 18). Selznick's memo to Hitchcock tetchily states: '[Your changes in the script] have removed all the subtleties and substituted big broad strokes which in outline form betray just how ordinary the plot is and just how bad a picture it would make without the little feminine things which are so recognizable and which make every woman say, "I know just how she feels . . . I know just what she's going through"' (Modleski 1988: 43). Yet, if Hitchcock did try to distance himself from what he saw as the 'feminine' qualities of the book, it is therefore ironic that in filming *Rebecca* he was inspired 'to enrich' his later films 'with the psychological ingredients . . . initially discovered in the Daphne du Maurier novel' (Truffaut 1983: 129). This is done most succinctly in Hitchcock's film in the marrying of du Maurier's gothic elements (which in turn, of course, had been taken from Charlotte Bronte) with the 1940s woman's picture.

Here we can see the influence of the second 'author' of the film adaptation. Helen Hanson has described how Selznick 'can be seen as a key figure in initiating the transfer of the literary female gothic to the screen in the 1940s', influenced by a belief in the growth of female audiences (Hanson 2007: 44–5). This was a popular cinematic genre for just a decade or so, starting with *Rebecca* and continuing with films such as *Suspicion* (1941), *Jane Eyre*, and *Gaslight* (both 1944), three of which had Joan Fontaine as their unassuming heroine. Much has been made of the female gothic in cinema. Mary Ann Doane has referred to it as the paranoid women's film (Doane 1987), and Thomas Elsaesser describes it as the Freudian feminist melodrama (Elsaesser 1987). Misha Kavka suggests that this form brings together 'the tropes of the nineteenth-century haunted house story with the style and themes of the 1940s/50s *film noir*' (Kavka 2002: 219). The woman is uncertain whether her husband is a threat to her or not, as in films like *Rebecca*, *Suspicion*, *Dragonwyck* (1946), and *Secret Beyond the Door* (1948), and the romance plot turns into the nightmarish *Bluebeard*. The focus is on the way a woman is menaced in her own house. This is emphasized in *Rebecca* through the way in which Hitchcock dwelt on the brooding Manderley, rather than the surrounding Cornish landscape. This was partly because it was filmed in Hollywood, using miniatures of the house, but also because the lack of realism was used to heighten the setting's fairytale quality, often filmed shrouded in mist with a specific score to underpin the 'haunting impression' (Truffaut 1983: 131).

It is obvious that Selznick had an affinity with adaptations of popular classics for female audiences, as with *Anna Karenina* (1935) and *Gone With the Wind* (1939). In line with this, he allowed *Rebecca* to take its part in 'the gradual development of a "meta-text"', as Sarah Cardwell puts it, which 'recognizes that a later adaptation may draw upon any earlier adaptations, as well as upon the primary source text' (Cardwell 2002: 25). So, just prior to Joan Fontaine's role in *Rebecca*, her sister, Olivia de Havilland, had taken a similar role as the shy and long-suffering Melanie in Selznick's epic production of *Gone with the Wind*, a point that was made in several of the reviews. Indeed, the film was advertised as Selznick's *Rebecca* rather than du Maurier's, or even Hitchcock's, and specific reference was made to its place 'as a successor to *Gone with the Wind*' (Light 1996: 29). Four years after appearing as the second Mrs de Winter, Joan Fontaine also appeared in *Jane Eyre*, one of the influences on du Maurier's book, where her acting and appearance were deliberately exploited to emphasize similarities between the two literary heroines.

Yet though Selznick had a profound influence upon the making of *Rebecca*, history has rightly labelled it Hitchcock's film. He imbued it with his own directorial identity, thus bearing out his early declaration before the film went into production that it would 'reflect no personality other than his own' (Kapsis 1992: 24). The film included a number of

Hitchcock's key motifs, particularly anxiety about female sexuality, often expressed through the figure of the woman under threat. With this, we can identify a difference of subconscious intent between du Maurier and Hitchcock. The novel shows the heroine becoming obsessed with Rebecca, not just as a rival for the affections of her husband but also as someone who suggests a different, more transgressive, way of living. In part, this may have been to do with du Maurier's own same-sex desires, and her attraction to a number of strong and independent women (Forster 1993). The film gives a different view, best expressed in the erotically charged scene in Rebecca's bedroom. Here, as Alison Light has indicated, there is no encompassment of the female gothic's sub-liminal concern with female desire and empowerment. Rather, it 'shows Joan Fontaine's humiliation, disgust and nausea at being situated as voyeur. It conveys little of the voyeur's satisfaction' (Light 1996: 30).

In relation to this, we can observe how Hitchcock shifts the novel's viewpoint away from female subjectivity towards the male gaze. The film starts by imitating the narrator-guide; using Joan Fontaine's voice-over, the camera moves up the driveway as if we are seeing through her eyes. Other tracking shots continue this perspective, especially along the dark corridors of Manderley, emphasizing the role of woman as victim. This is also seen in the way that Fontaine's character 'is continu-ally dwarfed by the huge halls in which she wanders, and even the doorknobs are placed at shoulder-level so that the viewer receives a subliminal impression of her as a child peeking in on or intruding into an adult world that provokes both curiosity and dread' (Modleski 1988: 47). By the end of the film, though, the perspective of the narrator-guide is lost. The heroine is left behind at Manderley while it is up to the 'homosocial grouping' of five men – Maxim, Frank Crawley, Colonel Julyan, Jack Favell, and Dr Baker – to be privy to the final unravelling of the mystery (Wheatley 2002: 140). Maxim and Frank return to the burning house, whereupon the heroine is saved by her husband. By the last part of du Maurier's novel (which actually appears at the begin-ning in the 'framework' story of their life in exile), the heroine has grown in stature: she is the equal of her husband, even his saviour through the care with which she looks after him; this further references Bronte's heroine, where Jane leads the literally and figuratively blinded Rochester towards Christian redemption. In the film of *Rebecca*, how-ever, Fontaine's character is diminished through her assumption of a deeply traditional female role. There were a number of influences at work here. First, because it was released after war had already broken out, a depressing ending was not considered suitable. Again, the Hollywood Production Code meant Maxim could not murder his wife and get away with it, as he does in the book. Moreover, even whilst the gothic opens up issues of so-called 'perverse sexuality', censorship required the 'conventional reaffirmation of heterosexual marriage'

(Hollinger 1993: 19) at the end. Mary Ann Doane concludes that 'the ideological upheaval signalled by a redefinition of sexual roles and the reorganization of the family during the war years' (Doane 1987: 4) caused this peculiar situation, where films were made for a female audience, yet presented women as vulnerable or dangerous. So it is perhaps not surprising that Hitchcock opted to stress the gothic's paranoia about women, rather than female empowerment.

Sexuality, consumerism and heritage television

The television costume drama, including adaptations of 'classic' novels, has gone in and out of fashion over the last 40 years or so. Latterly there has been a seismic change in the way these novels have been approached, particularly in terms of the notion of 'fidelity' to the text. So the classic drama before the 1990s was more 'dialogue-based', whereas more recently it has become more 'televisual . . . and . . . less afraid to tamper with its source in order to create gripping television' (Giddings and Selby 2001: 82). This can be seen this with the two TV productions of *Rebecca*, in 1979 and 1997. The later version deliberately alludes to the earlier one through the casting of Joanna David's daughter, Emilia Fox, who takes the role of the second wife previously played by David nearly 20 years earlier. As with the *Rebecca* novels of Maureen Freely and Justine Picardie mentioned earlier, and Selznick's clever use of casting during the 1940s, the 'intertextual referentiality' of the classic drama exploits 'the viewers' capacity and willingness (their desire, even), to engage with the text as active readers' (Cardwell 2002: 93).

Fox's casting also shows a generational shift in the television audience. The earlier series draws on du Maurier's novel in concentrating on the gaucheness of the heroine, and on her role as class outsider, shown in her inability to act as hostess of the rather flatly replicated Manderley or as wife of the cold and forbidding Maxim. In the later version, however, with a society shaped by feminism and consumerism, and with changing notions of nationhood, the emphasis is on equality between the sexes, and on high production values which make much of cars, costumes and settings. The opening tracking shot is of the heroine, sketching a beautifully sunny coastline in Monte Carlo. The gentle music shows us that this will be a romantic drama. Indeed, the narrative focuses almost exclusively on the love between the central couple, with Maxim declaring his feelings early on, and the heroine reciprocating in kind. Several scenes show them in bed, making clear that theirs is a marriage based on mutual attraction. The heroine is much stronger than is usually depicted, meeting people's gaze with little evidence of shyness, appearing confused and upset by Maxim's outbursts, rather than fearful. Charles Dance works with his image of a sophisticated gentleman, as did Owen Nares, but imbues the role with more wit, becoming less mysterious and more available in the process.

Apart from the importance placed on the mutual love between the two main characters, and the confidence they gain from this, a major change is that for the first time Rebecca is literally shown. Rather than being represented fetishistically through a painting, her clothes, or her haunting presence at Manderley, she is seen in long shot, from the back, or in parts. Kim Wheatley notes that she is shown 'only in fragments – lips in one shot, eyes in another – as if to stress her power and attractiveness: she has to be fragmented in order to be held at bay' (Wheatley 2002: 135). It can be argued, though, that this literal embodiment saps her of potency; in du Maurier's novel and in Hitchcock's film, it is the heroine's imaginative construction of her that is more dangerous than her reality. So the director's introduction of an actress to play Rebecca runs counter to du Maurier's original intent: the more 'real' a person Rebecca becomes, the less firm her hold on the narrator.

Interestingly, the period has been moved back into the glamorous and decadent 1920s, an era redolent of F. Scott Fitzgerald's 'bright young things'. The reference point of war differs from that in the stage production, though. During the 1940s, the audience was able to make an explicit connection between the need to protect and preserve England's ancestral past and the war raging literally outside the London theatre; at one point, the production even had to be moved elsewhere after a bombing raid. In the 1990s television production, memories of the First World War and its aftermath seems to mirror contemporary interest with 'heritage' Britain, where the country has been 'packaged' for consumption by tourists: we see this in the selling abroad of British costume dramas like *Brideshead Revisited* or *Miss Marple*, or the way that the stately homes of England have been 'themed' in order that they may survive financially. Equally, though, in the 1990s production there is an opportunity to see Rebecca's sexual and social transgressions as less to do with her as an individual, and more to do with the general sense of a generation attempting to free themselves from the memory of the First World War: this rereading may also remind us of early feminist critiques of *Jane Eyre*, which posit the idea that the madwoman in the attic is a riposte to Victorian curtailment of female sexuality (Gilbert and Gubar 1979).

As with Hitchcock's film, the viewpoint is mainly that of the young woman, but once the location moves to Manderley there are several camera shots that are not from her perspective, particularly those that involve Mrs Danvers, played by Diana Rigg. Here Manderley looks like a National Trust property, not a foreboding, gloomy mansion which dwarfs the central character. The only part of the house that is not presented as light and comfortable is the west wing, where Rebecca's bedroom is situated. Jim O'Brien, the director, highlights this as a source of trouble, by copying Hitchcock's technique of looking down the dark corridors as if from the viewpoint of the second Mrs De Winter. In the open sexual climate of the 1990s, the lesbian relationship between Rebecca and Mrs Danvers can be made more explicit. Diana Rigg longingly holds the dead woman's clothes against her body, and after setting fire to the building, lies down on the bed next to Rebecca's spread-out nightdress. The ending provides yet another variation. Maxim enters the burning Manderley trying to save Mrs Danvers, in a literary and cinematic echo of Rochester trying to save Bertha Mason in *Jane Eyre*. The last scene is of Maxim with a walking stick somewhere abroad, being aided by his wife, the implication being that Maxim's 'resulting injuries accounted for the De Winters' childlessness' (Wheatley 2002: 141). Yet this ending is far more optimistic than any previous version, and it is significant that the couple's after-life abroad is dramatized at the end of the series rather than at the beginning. Emilia Fox's voiceover makes clear that the memory of Manderley will sweeten their time away, rather than poison it, with the suggestion that this is not a permanent exile in a foreign country, but rather a temporary period of rest. Interestingly, the scriptwriter Arthur Hopcraft seems to be following Daphne du Maurier's initial idea for an ending. Originally leaning heavily on Bronte's novel and conventions of Victorian fiction, du Maurier has her male character physically disabled in a car accident, and an epilogue reveals how his second wife looks after him (du Maurier 1981). The published account, of course, has far less focus on heroism and more on the stultifying existence that the two have to endure.

Critics have asserted that 'Historically, the novel succeeded the drama, but absorbed some of its qualities (character, dialogue) while adding possibilities of its own (interior monologue, point of view, reflection, comment, irony). Similarly, film initially followed the basic principles of narrative prose and copied stage drama' (Giddings, Selby, Wensley 1990: ix). What we can see with *Rebecca* is 'a continuity between source text and resulting text' (Cardwell 2002: 20), where alterations have been made due to the change of medium, but also adaptations to 'fit the cultural moment' (Brosh 2008: 4). So during the war years, the play focused on the notion of a controlled threat. Manderley embodied the play's meaning at a time when there was a concern with Englishness and when the country house represented, as Malcolm Kelsall says, 'a visible sign of "the ancient social order"' (Kelsall 1993: 303). Alison Light has also described this as a period expressing 'nostalgia for the waning of the British Empire and the decline of its aristocracy' (Light 1984: 7). The film, appearing at the same time as the stage version, and shortly after publication of the novel, shows a tension between Selznick's and Hitchcock's interest in the female: the former with what he saw as feminine traits, the latter with anxiety around the female figure, as filtered through the gothic genre. The 1990s television series is also influenced by society's more tolerant approach to sexuality, with Maxim and his wife able to forge a union based on equality and desire. There is also here what Robert Giddings and Keith Selby label the '*Pride and*

Prejudice effect', where the links between romance, consumerism and nation are tied into current socio-political concerns, and the British concern with repackaging their past is due to 'insecurity about the present [and] the undermining of national identity' (Gidding and Selby 2001: 124) in the 1990s. Daphne du Maurier's 'reauthorship' of *Jane Eyre*, then, foreshadows every other adaptation of *Rebecca*, where questions of fidelity, origin and authorial ownership are imaginatively interwoven in a way that sheds light on the original, as well as providing fruitful connections between written word and visual image, and between text and context.

Bibliography

Anna Karenina (1935). USA, dir. Clarence Brown.

Beauman, Sally (2001), *Rebecca's Tale*. London: Little, Brown.

Brief Encounter (1945). UK, dir. David Lean.

Bronte, Charlotte [Currer Bell] (1847), London: Smith, Elder.

Brosh, Liora (2008), *Screening Novel Women: From British Domestic Fiction to Film*. Basingstoke: Palgrave.

The Bystander (1940), 20 March. 171–3.

Cardwell, Sarah (2002), *Adaptation Revisited: Television and the Classic Novel*. Manchester: Manchester University Press.

Cartmell, Deborah and Imelda Whelehan (eds) (1999), *Adaptations: From Text to Screen, Screen to Text*. London: Routledge.

Doane, Mary Ann (1987), *The Desire to Desire: The Woman's Film of the 1940s*. Basingstoke: Macmillan.

Dragonwyck (1946). USA, dir. Joseph Mankiewicz.

Du Maurier, Daphne (1940), *Rebecca: A Play in 3 Acts*. London: Victor Gollancz.

— (1981), *The Rebecca Notebook and Other Memories*. London: Victor Gollancz.

— (1994/1945), *The Years Between*, in Fidelis Morgan (ed.), *The Years Between: Plays by Women on the London Stage 1900–1950*. London: Virago.

Elsaesser, Thomas (1987), 'Tales of sound and fury: observations on the family melodrama', in Christine Gledhill (ed.), *Home is Where the Heart Is: Studies in Melodrama and the Woman's Film*. London: BFI, pp. 43–69.

Forster, Margaret (1993), *Daphne du Maurier*. London: Chatto and Windus.

Freely, Maureen (1996), *The Other Rebecca*. London: Bloomsbury.

Gaslight (1944). USA, dir. George Cukor.

Giddings, Robert and Keith Selby (2001), *The Classic Serial on Television and Radio*. Basingstoke: Macmillan.

Giddings, Robert, Keith Selby and Chris Wensley (1990), *Screening the Novel: The Theory and Practice of Literary Dramatization*. Basingstoke: Macmillan.

Gilbert, Sandra and Susan Gubar (1979), *The Madwoman in the Attic: The Woman Writer and the Literary Imagination*. New Haven: Yale University Press.

Gledhill, Christine (ed.) (1987), *Home is Where the Heart Is: Studies in Melodrama and the Woman's Film*. London: BFI.

Gone With the Wind (1939). USA, dir. George Cukor, Sam Wood, Victor Fleming.

The Grapes of Wrath (1940). USA, dir. John Ford.

Hanson, Helen (2007), *Hollywood Heroines: Women in Film Noir and the Female Gothic Film*. London: I. B. Tauris.

Hill, Susan (1993), *Mrs De Winter*. London: Sinclair Stevenson.

Hogle, Jerrold E. (ed.) (2002), *Gothic Fiction*. Cambridge: Cambridge University Press.

Hollinger, Karen (1993), 'The female oedipal drama', *Quarterly Review of Film and Video*, 14.4, 17–30.

In Which We Serve (1942). UK, dir. David Lean.

Jane Eyre (1944). USA, dir. Robert Stevenson.

Kapsis, Robert E. (1992), *Hitchcock: The Making of a Reputation*. Chicago: University of Chicago Press.

Kavka, Misha (2002), 'The gothic on screen', in Jerrold E. Hogle (ed.), *Gothic Fiction*. Cambridge: Cambridge University Press, pp. 209–28.

Kelsall, Malcolm (1993), 'Manderley revisited: *Rebecca* and the English country house'. *Proceedings of the Bristol Academy* 82, 303–15.

Light, Alison (1984), '"Returning to Manderley" – romance fiction, female sexuality and class'. *Feminist Review* 16, 7–25.

— (1996), 'Gothic *Rebecca*'. *Sight and Sound* 6.5, 29–31.

London News (1940), 13 April, n.p.

Modleski, Tania (1988), *The Women Who Knew Too Much: Hitchcock and Feminist Theory*. London: Routledge.

Morgan, Fidelis (ed.) (1994), *The Years Between: Plays by Women on the London Stage 1900–1950*. London: Virago.

The Observer (1940), April, n.p.

Page, Philip (1940), The *Daily Mail*, April 10, n.p.

Picardie, Justine (2008), *Daphne*. London: Bloomsbury.

Pringle, David (ed.) (1998), *St James Guide to Horror, Ghost and Gothic Writers*. Detroit, MI: St James Press.

Rebecca (1940). USA, dir. Alfred Hitchcock.

Rebecca (1979). BBC Television.

Rebecca (1997). ITV Television.

Rhys, Jean (1966), *Wide Sargasso Sea*. London: Deutsch.

Secret Beyond the Door (1948). USA, dir. Fritz Lang.

Suspicion (1941). USA, dir. Alfred Hitchcock.

This Happy Breed (1944). UK, dir. David Lean.

Truffaut, Francois (1983), *Hitchcock*. New York: Simon and Schuster.

Tuttle, Lisa (1998), 'Daphne du Maurier', in David Pringle (ed.), *St James Guide to Horror, Ghost and Gothic Writers*. Detroit, MI: St James Press, pp. 196–98.

Wheatley, Kim (2002), 'Gender politics and the gothic in Alfred Hitchcock's *Rebecca*'. *Gothic Studies* 4.2, 133–44.

Whelehan, Imelda (1999), 'Adaptation: the contemporary dilemmas', in Deborah Cartmell and Imelda Whelehan, *Adaptations: From Text to Screen, Screen to Text*. London: Routledge, pp. 3–19.

CHAPTER FIFTEEN

The Post-feminist Biopic: Re-telling the Past in *Iris, The Hours* and *Sylvia*

JOSEPHINE DOLAN, SUZY GORDON AND ESTELLA TINCKNELL

The appearance of a number of British and American biopics released during the last decade suggests that the genre is enjoying something of a revival following the apparent decline after 1960 observed by George Custen (1992: 2).[1] Prominent in this resurgence have been three films about major women writers: *Iris* (UK/US, 2001, dir. Richard Eyre), *The Hours* (US, 2002, dir. Stephen Daldry) and *Sylvia* (UK, 2003, Christine Jeffs). Given that *The Barretts of Wimpole Street* (US, 1934 and 1957, Sidney Franklin)[2] is a rare precedent for such films, it might be assumed that a genre traditionally committed to the 'writing of public history' (Custen 1992) is now being re-imagined in relation to the interventions made by second-wave feminism around women's position within the literary canon. Stylistically, there is little to link these films: *Iris* offers middle-brow realism, *The Hours*, non-linear postmodernism, *Sylvia*, art-house aestheticism. All are, however, based to some degree on established sources, whether that is a memoir, a biography, or a literary novel about an author, and can therefore be read as 'adaptations' as well as offering a new take on the biopic. Yet worryingly, in a genre marked by its claims to 'truth-telling', the most powerful trope operating across all of these films is the articulation of a familiar and decidedly pre-feminist discourse: that of the profound connection between women's writing and mental and emotional instability. In short, creative passion is implicitly linked to female madness in ways that are familiar from the tradition of the literary biography. As Elaine Showalter argues, 'Biographies and letters of gifted women who suffered mental breakdowns have suggested that madness is the price women artists have had to pay for the exercise of their creativity' (1987: 4). In each of these films, the woman writer's success is systematically occluded by her mental collapse, while the price she pays for her creativity is presented as a high one. We therefore ask, why *this* version of women's creative production? Why now? And what is at stake in the complex relationship between feminist history, representational strategies, and the 'truth' status of the biopic?

Iris: heritage pictorialism retells 'the fifties'

Iris is based on two celebrated memoirs: *Iris: A Memoir* (1999) and *Elegy For Iris* (2000), by Iris Murdoch's husband, the literary critic John Bayley, written shortly after the novelist and philosopher's death as a consequence of Alzheimer's disease. These sources are a crucial factor in the film's production of meanings about Murdoch (Judi Dench), with Bayley (Jim Broadbent) occupying a central, controlling place in the story. Recounted through Bayley's perspective, the narrative overwhelmingly concentrates on Murdoch's intellectual and physical decline in the 1990s. Using flashback sequences, the film cuts between an ageing and increasingly unstable Murdoch and Bayley's memories of the younger 'Iris' (Kate Winslet). It is therefore structured around two key moments: the young Bayley's (Hugh Bonneville) first romantic encounter with her in 1950s Oxford; and the impact of Murdoch's illness on their relationship prior to her death in 1999. This emphasis on heterosexual coupledom positions Murdoch and Bayley as the Darby and Joan of intellectual companionship, while also obscuring Murdoch's individual significance. Furthermore, in switching between the 1950s and the 1990s the film moves seamlessly from 'pre-feminist' to 'post-feminist' moments without locating Murdoch within the enormous changes wrought by second-wave feminism on women's position in literary production. Instead, the humanistic emphasis on the couple and the intimate chimes with revisionist tendencies in contemporary accounts of gender relations, in which feminism is represented as both redundant and misguided because its demands were either initially unreasonable or were always already being addressed by benign patriarchy. However, this position cannot withstand the discursive tensions that can be traced through *Iris*.

For example, the younger 'Iris', first seen swimming naked in the Isis as the credits roll, is consistently represented as a mysterious and unknowable object of desire, a figure whose early philosophical attachment to existentialism is almost entirely conflated with control over her sexuality, as though women's actions, freedom and decision-making can only ever be about sex. This is important because of other ways in which *Iris* systematically reduces Murdoch to her body, even using dialogue to do this – 'Hang on and trust the body', she tells John. This corporeal emphasis problematizes Iris's status as a thinking, critical human subject, while simultaneously naturalizing male desire and the male gaze. The young Iris is primarily figured as a sexual free spirit – that is what attracts John – rather than a serious intellectual. And while this does establish her against the grain of stereotype (she is not a granite-faced, sexually repressed bluestocking), the film's ready deployment of sexualized tropes contradicts its apparent commitment to Murdoch's cerebral status. While *Iris* wants to show the interior depths of Murdoch's intellect, it fails to do this. The conventionally realist devices deployed to represent intellectual and emotional interiority – such as repeated shots of the domestic clutter and dirt unwittingly inhabited by Murdoch and Bayley – are absurdly inadequate. Unable (or unwilling) to use the tropes of surrealist or avant-garde cinema that might more effectively convey Murdoch's ideas, the film is left attempting to *tell* rather than show. Equally, because this is a biopic, there is a conventional trajectory towards narrative conclusion – an arc of achievement and ultimate death.

Iris's problematically overdetermined version of 1950s student bohemianism also stems from the tiresomely familiar tropes of Oxbridge intellectual, social and emotional rites of passage produced by countless British television and film dramatizations, exemplified by *The Glittering Prizes* (1976, BBC), *Brideshead Revisited* (1981, Granada and UK, 2008, dir. Julian Jarrold) and *Inspector Morse* (ITV, 1987–2000). Together with the tweed, trad and teashops that have become *de rigueur* for popular cinema's 'fifties' *mise-en-scène*, there are a couple of bicycling scenes in *Iris* that could, for example, be readily substituted for equivalents in *Sylvia*. Apart from the beautifully shot beach and river sequences which achieve a richer, more fully cinematic aesthetic, *Iris* is tightly focused on enclosed domestic interiors. In its 1950s scenes, 'period detail' and the special glow that apparently permeated that decade evoke the material world of gin and 'ciggies' rather than human interaction or moral dilemmas. Deploying the stagey pictorialism of 'heritage' cinema with its focus on *things* rather than events (clothes, furniture, props), *Iris* distracts from, rather than enhances, a complex sense of the past.[3] A British cinematic convention particularly linked with literary adaptations, such as *A Room with a View* (UK, 1986, dir. James Ivory) and *Howard's End* (UK, 1992, dir. James Ivory), the 'heritage' genre is associated with cinematic versions of upper-middle-class 'Englishness' (Monk 1995a, 1995b; Hill 1999). Here, these conventions efface any sense of place in 1950s Oxford, and its explicit hostility to women, thus disconnecting 'Iris's' dazzling brilliance from specific sets of gendered or class relations.

This 'Iris' thus seems a natural precursor to those contemporary young women who are now supposed to be the effortless winners in a post-feminist world, rather than a convincing figure from post-austerity Britain. Indeed, the 'Iris' of the 1950s is effectively figured as a romantic heroine (underlined by the casting of Winslet) caught in a love triangle between Bayley and his rival Maurice (Samuel West), someone whose playful wit simply underlines her desirability. Initially evoked in a flashback scene of an uncomfortable lunch between the three, this love triangle is ironically juxtaposed with a subsequent sequence when an exhausted Bayley, attempting to pacify the older, now ailing Murdoch by reading aloud to her, opens *Pride and Prejudice* at the point where Austen describes Darcy's growing sexual interest in Elizabeth Bennet. This sequence consolidates the presentation of 'Iris' primarily as a tragic romantic object, and slyly situates the Bayley-Murdoch relationship within the post-feminist preoccupation with Austen and with fantasies of chivalric protection (pace *Bridget Jones's Diary* and others), rather than within a chillier but more accurate set of gender relations linked to post-war liberalism and struggles over domestic responsibility. In this, as in its deployment of familiar 'heritage' conventions, *Iris* recognizably operates within the terms of middle-brow mainstream British cinema. Almost entirely character- and dialogue-driven, it is desperately respectful and respectable: anxious to establish Murdoch's fifties bohemianism with hints of a lesbian affair, while simultaneously reassuring its imagined audience of her later wifely heteronormativity. Its focus on material *objects* as signifiers of the past obscures the material *relations* of social hierarchies, sexual inequalities and class distinction, rendering them as picturesque and unchangeable as the dreaming spires themselves. In *Iris* continuity, not social and cultural transformation is emphasized.

Whose story is it, anyway?

Rather than exploring Murdoch's intellectual and creative flowering in the manner of conventional biopics, *Iris* centralizes Murdoch's intellectual *decline*, whilst the cultural significance of her novels is reduced to mere gesture. There is little to suggest how her books were received, why they are regarded as significant, or what their relationship has been to a wider literary culture. Instead, the film's emphasis on the domestic relationship between Bayley and Murdoch returns the female writer to the private sphere and to a humanistic conception of authorship in which gender specificity is denied. This might suggest an ideal of companionate marriage, in which gender difference is important only insofar as it mediates desire. But the film also implies that it was Bayley's *special* tolerance of his wife's compulsion to write and live 'inside her head' that was the defining characteristic of Murdoch's successful career. Without him, it appears, she could not have achieved what she did. Bayley is represented as contentedly playing second fiddle: a position signified through flashback in the film's main visual *leitmotif* – the adventurous youthful Iris bicycling downhill, cautiously followed by the plodding young John. Yet while Bayley is cast as a proto-new man, emotionally and intellectually nurturing Murdoch, the film's resolution presents a curious and troubling form of ideological closure. While the conventional biopic naturalizes and rewards female support for the heroic creativity of masculinity, and reminds the viewer of that genius in its closing moments, *Iris* stages *John's* increasingly heroic role in supporting a wife whose creative importance already seems obscure.[4]

'Iris's' growing confusion is dramatically enacted in scenes that contrast television interview appearances made by the young and the ageing Iris. In the first, 'original footage' shows a young, confident Iris (in the form of Winslet) being prepared for inclusion in an arts programme, while in the other, the older Murdoch is presented as muddled and uncertain. Later scenes show her confusion terrifyingly intensified as she can no longer remember who friends are, or as she weeps and screams uncontrollably. This is framed in terms of tragedy, potentially of Shakespearian magnitude: it is 'Iris's' love of words, her pleasure in the linguistic construction of meaning, which is her mark as a writer – and is therefore the first casualty in her downfall. As the film proceeds, the poignancy of the contrast between the 'two Irises' – the physically decrepit older woman and her desirable but troublesome younger version – is developed and intensified. 'Iris' increasingly *becomes* her body as the Alzheimer's takes hold, no longer cerebral but physical. Murdoch's status as a highly intellectual writer is eroded by the image of her as an abject female body – and by the pathologization of that body as a site of mental and moral decline. The figure of the active, independent and fiercely intellectual younger woman is systematically replaced by that of the passive and dependent older one. The narrative is riven by powerful textual and discursive contradictions as a struggle to represent Murdoch the writer as someone with physical and social agency is recuperated by an opposing desire to fix 'Iris' the woman as an object of love, and then of abjection.

Notwithstanding its apparent status as the biopic of a woman who writes/wrote, *Iris* is actually a film about a woman who *cannot* write. Discomfort with Murdoch as a writer and intellectual, and efforts to recuperate her for normative femininity are as evident in the publicity and marketing strategies as in the film itself. For example, the front cover of the DVD casing for *Iris* features two close-up images of the 'young' and 'old' writer in the conventional pose of challenging femininity – looking directly at camera . But this is countered by the maudlin strap-line, 'her greatest talent was for life', a statement that relocates Murdoch's creativity into the acceptably feminine condition of *being* rather than doing. Due to its underlying and unacknowledged gender politics, the film struggles to reconcile the idea of artistic genius with conventions of appropriate femininity. *Iris* thus fails to establish Murdoch as an agent in her own story, and substitutes Bayley as the *real* protagonist, the real hero – the person who survives the chaos. Consequently, the film's erasure of second-wave feminism takes on a darker meaning. Not only does heritage pictorialism obscure very real obstacles to women's writing in its depiction of the 1950s, but the representation of Bayley as somehow 'always already' a nurturing, supportive partner also erases the real strength of patriarchal power – even as it reasserts it.

The Hours: heritage pictorialism meets (post)modernism

Where *Iris* is highly conformist in its deployment of biopic conventions, *The Hours* (US/UK, 2002, dir. Stephen Daldry) can be more closely aligned with postmodernist narrative techniques, not least in its complex inter-leaving of biographical and fictional characters. The film weaves together three storylines which are variously set in the London suburb of Richmond-on-Thames during the 1920s, 1950s suburban Los Angeles, and the cosmopolitan urbanity of 2001 New York. The 1920s storyline depicts Virginia Woolf (Nicole Kidman, sporting that highly publicized prosthetic nose) as she writes *Mrs Dalloway*, succumbs to depression and eventually commits suicide. Threading through this account are stories of two fictional readers of *Mrs Dalloway*. The first, Laura Brown (Julianne Moore), is a depressed pregnant housewife, the mother of a young son, planning her husband's birthday party in 1951 Los Angeles. The second is Clarissa Vaughan, affectionately known as 'Mrs Dalloway' (Meryl Streep). Based in contemporary New York, Vaughan is a lesbian publisher planning a birthday party for her depressed friend, an award-winning writer who is dying of AIDS.

Shifts in time and place between writer and readers are registered through cinematic conventions associated with three readily recognizable film genres – 'heritage' film, Sirkian melodrama and urban noir, each of which are highly determined in their articulation of place. As with *Iris*, *The Hours* employs 'heritage' costume drama in its formulation of a suburban literary milieu. In the hands of Stephen Daldry, the over-determined Englishness of the genre's mise-en-scène is filtered through the muted pastels of faded photographs or English landscape paintings. In striking contrast, the 1950s plot references the Technicolor excesses of Sirkian melodrama (e.g. *All That Heaven Allows*, US, 1955, dir. Douglas Sirk), representing post-war America through suburban architecture and spaces, fetishized cars and restrictive, domestic femininity, whilst twenty-first-century New York is figured by dystopian city locales filtered through the grainy colour palettes of contemporary noir (e.g. *Taxi Driver*, US, 1976, dir. Martin Scorsese; *Fatal Attraction*, US, 1987, dir. Adrian Lyne). These generic conventions fix time and place, even as the fragmented narrative shifts between storylines.

An adaptation of Michael Cunningham's novel, *The Hours* (2000), inventively reworks Woolf's *Mrs Dalloway* – referentially appropriating her working title. As this suggests, the film mobilizes a complex literary intertextual web that includes Cunningham's novel, Virginia Woolf herself, her diaries and letters, her biographies and biographers, *Mrs Dalloway* and its characters, and all the critical legacies that adhere to the reputations of Woolf and Cunningham. The narrative complexity of *The Hours* is not simply the product of its rich literary seam: its use of genre to stage time and location is also implicated. Equally, a non-linear time-frame integrates biography and fiction, past and present, effectively blurring the boundaries between experience, memory and fantasy. This temporal and spatial blurring is also facilitated by the iconographic codes of 1950s melodrama: images of women framed by doors, close-ups of eyes in strategically lit faces, the swell of evocative music to signal contained high emotion and moments of deep introspection

(Gledhill 1987: passim). When these features combine with the film's sparse dialogue and its insistent musical score, the boundaries between exterior identity and interior subjectivity are effectively dissolved.

Feminist links

In the blurring of boundaries between Woolf and her two 'readers' (Clarissa and Laura), recurring motifs also forge links to broader social patterns and experiences that suggest the film's post-feminist positioning. Although not overtly introduced, Woolf's reputation as a feminist intellectual shapes the film's intertextual mesh, whilst the narrative establishes Woolf's resentment that *her* writing, rather than her husband Leonard's (Stephen Dillane) publishing, is interrupted by the demands of domesticity. However, the ways in which this feminism might be understood are highly problematical. Woolf is represented as a woman unable, rather than unwilling, to manage either domestic arrangements or servants, thus obliterating any feminist resistance to 1920s normative middle-class femininity. At best, Woolf's failure at household management is registered as the price of female genius, the consequence of a creative imagination that inhabits its own fictional worlds with greater ease than everyday, domestic realities. This genius is pathologized as the *cause* of her fragile mental health, with the restoration of her well-being dependent on rationing her opportunities to write. Throughout, Leonard, rather than Virginia, is the established object of sympathy. In the film's opening sequence Virginia carefully writes whilst a voice-over articulates her inner anguish, then, walking through a dew-damp garden, she calmly places stones in her pockets before wading into a fast-flowing stream. This sequence is intercut with shots of an anguished Leonard discovering the letter, and his desperate race to prevent the suicide. With Leonard's grief prefigured, sympathy is consistently secured for this husband of a nervy and difficult woman. As with Bayley in *Iris*, Leonard's tenderness, patience and concern for his wife's physical and mental well-being combine to demonstrate a palpable love, whilst conveniently glossing over the horrors of the 1920s 'rest cure', thus rendering Virginia's repeated desire to escape Richmond House as the petulant whim of an over-indulged wife.

This equation between the feminist Woolf and the pampered wife becomes crucial during the unfolding stories of her two 'readers', a liberal feminist narrative of women's progress from post-suffrage idealism, through the myth of enforced post-war domesticity and on to feminism's ultimate triumph following second-wave activism. For instance, a patterning of same-sex kisses initiated by each female character forges an alignment between lesbian desire and the film's implied feminist triumphalism. Undoubtedly, the kiss that Woolf presses on to Vanessa Bell (Miranda Richardson) could be passed off as sisterly affection. However, the violence of the gesture suggests that more is at stake. Crucially though, the uncertain status of this kiss evokes what Adrienne Rich (1980) calls the lesbian continuum: a second-wave concept that includes the entire range of woman-identified experience. Later in the film, Laura Brown offers a comforting embrace to her neighbour Kitty (Toni Collette), as the latter reveals her impending surgery for cancer. What starts as a neighbourly hug transforms into a lingering kiss. Yet within minutes the kiss is denied, excised from the repertoire of memory, its threat to normative heterosexuality rendered an inexpressible desire. But no ambiguity, no inexpressible longing, adheres to a kiss exchanged between Clarissa and her live-in lover, Sally Lester (Alison Janney). Clarissa and Sally are out and proud, ostensibly the benefactors of decades of feminist activism. Without doubt Clarissa, a mother, a successful publisher, and an economically independent woman at ease with her non-heterosexual orientation, can be read as the successful embodiment of second-wave feminism – and therefore of its redundancy. Clarissa stands for the post-feminist moment.

Trauma and post-feminism

Feminism's triumph is also registered in gendered role reversals that differentiate the three temporalities. Where the 1920s and 1950s stories have economically successful men concerned for the well-being of much-loved, 'nervy', dependent women, the 2001 storyline has an economically successful woman concerned for the well-being of a much-loved, 'nervy', dependent man – who, like Woolf, is a writer. In a highly problematical reworking of gay stereotypes, Richard Brown (Ed Harris) has AIDS, is hopelessly depressed, self-loathing, inhabiting a dystopian environment that magnifies and compounds his total collapse. His suicide seems an inevitable end, whilst its enactment suggests he is more the victim of feminist achievements than the HIV virus. Reversing the gender dynamics of Woolf's suicide sequence, a distressed Clarissa fails to prevent Richard's despairing slide from a high apartment window to a violent death on the street below. The contrast between the aesthetic register of Woolf's suicide – a romantic reference to Millais' painting, *The Death of Ophelia* – and the sickening brutality of Richard's death leaves little doubt that masculinity pays a high price for the gendered reversals of feminist achievement.

   Ultimately, Richard's suicide links to the 1950s storyline where Laura leaves her son Ritchie with a babysitter and goes to a hotel with a bottle of pills. She reads *Mrs Dalloway*, the scene cuts to Woolf planning that novel and deciding not to kill a female character, then a cut back to Laura registers an emotional sea-change visually realized through a fantastical sequence of breaking waters: the reference to Woolf's watery suicide being as self-evident as is the recognition of rebirth. Later, driving home after collecting Ritchie, she lovingly calls him 'my guy'. This touching scene abruptly cuts to a black-and-white photograph of Laura on her wedding day. Left of screen, in close-up, a hand fingers blue pills. The camera pulls back, revealing the hand to be Richard's – the adult Ritchie is Laura's son. The juxtaposition of Richard, Laura's image and the medication forces a connection between her survival and Richard's condition. There follows a series of rapid cuts between close-ups of the agonized Ritchie screaming for his mother and the adult Richard with tears streaming down his cheeks as he gazes at Laura's image. Throughout, a crescendo of music adds emotional intensity as the flow of tears dissolves child and adult into a single, traumatized identity. The terms of the trauma are not revealed here, but there is little doubt of Laura's culpability.

The dénouement comes after Richard's suicide. Clarissa is in her apartment clearing debris from a party that never happened. The door-bell rings; on opening the door Clarissa comes face to face with an ageing Laura. At this stage, nothing is known of her life following the dramatic 'rebirth', but dialogue rapidly establishes that she abandoned family life as a means of psychic survival. This revelation draws together the traumatic photograph scene, the wreckage that was Richard's life, and his violent suicide, thus rendering Laura's refusal of 1950s domestic femininity (a refusal that prefigures second-wave feminism) as the underlying trauma. Once Laura is configured in terms of feminist resistance, her face-to-face encounter with Clarissa becomes a meeting between feminism and its post-feminist conclusion. By extension, the multiple traumas of Richard's life and death are attributed to those feminist successes that link Woolf and her readers, and women's refusal to be confined within heteronormative regulations. *The Hours* therefore constitutes an insidious attack on feminist politics in its reproduction of those post-feminist discourses that, via Clarissa, declare the triumph of feminism and its attendant redundancy; and, through Richard, in its equation of feminism with the violent traumas of masculinity.

Knowing *Sylvia*[5]

Like *Iris* and *The Hours*, *Sylvia* has a relationship to a literary source, albeit a less direct one. The publication of his last collection of poetry, *Birthday Letters*, in 1998 was supposed to have 'successfully rehabilitated worldwide' the 'unfairly maligned Ted Hughes' (Moses 2003). This rehabilitation depended upon the collection's status as a delayed confessional. Because Hughes had refused for more than 30 years to speak about his relationship with Sylvia Plath or about her suicide, his turn to an autobiographical mode at the end of his life seemed to recast his silence as an act of dignity (no longer of guilt or obstinacy) and his confession as a mark of courage. The autobiographical turn in Hughes's poetry thus brings a powerful legitimacy to his voice, as well as to his version of 'Plath'. As with *Iris*, *Sylvia* is told and controlled through the male viewpoint. But here, the capacity to refuse the category of the personal and instead to offer disclosure *at will* is staged as the privilege of the male writer. In contrast to this version of male privilege, the closing moments of *Sylvia* lay bare the extraordinary vulnerability of the woman writer when her writing is read as self-exposure.

With the conventions of a 1950s domestic mise-en-scène in place, Ted Hughes (Daniel Craig) stands alone in the empty flat in which his estranged wife, Sylvia Plath (Gwyneth Paltrow), has recently committed suicide. He leafs through the manuscript she has left on her desk, and a close-up reveals his mournful touch. At first he brushes his fingertips against the paper as though it is flesh, then moves to press his palm with gentle force into the stack. In the next shot the camera pans down as Hughes bends to kiss Sylvia's still, white forehead. Pulling away, he leaves his hand to rest there, her dead face alone in centre frame. The final cut completes the movement, revealing Hughes's hand as it draws away from the manuscript. This sequence vividly establishes the connection between the woman's writing and her body, the editing literally transforming her words into her (dead) flesh. This visual articulation of Hughes's loving touch indicates how risky the idea that the woman writes her 'self' may prove to be. Crucially, the woman's death, her self-destruction, brings into focus the man's emotional complexity and profundity. In this incarnation of the Plath narrative, Hughes is also cast as a 'new man', utterly at the mercy of the woman he loves, a victim of her tortured and destructive genius.

This film can be situated – like *Iris* and *The Hours* – within a range of cultural discourses which serve to legitimize male power by offering up the 'feminized' man as an explicit – and appropriate – response to feminism's critique of patriarchal power. The ways in which *Sylvia* inflects the new man have clear implications for the representation of the woman writer, too. The film regenerates the figure of Hughes and rehabilitates masculinity, while simultaneously falling back on powerful conventions in which women's writing is cast inexorably as autobiographical, conventions which portray women's psychological instability both as symptom of their creativity and as individual pathology. Engaging the tropes of romance and melodrama, the film casts Hughes as the tragic hero, his sexual and emotional magnetism conjured by the depths of his capacity for love. These same generic modes re-invoke the spectre of the female writer as madwoman. But it is the form of the biopic, its relationship to 'history', and its presentation of the biographical subject as 'knowable', that underpin the ideological power of this narrative. From the outset, *Sylvia* presents Plath as utterly knowable. She is framed within a very conventional cinematic iconography of women's madness. She wrings her hands, her mouth quivers, she stares vacantly into space; her drab and faded clothes immerse her in an oppressively grey mise-en-scène. The opening shot announces the film's perspective on the way she can be known. Plath's apparently dead body lies in the foreground, her face, eyes closed, in close-up. In voiceover she breathes lines from 'Lady Lazarus': 'Dying / is an art, like everything else. / I do it exceptionally well. / I do it so it feels like hell.'(1965: 17). There is no gap between this woman and her writing, between language and subjectivity. This is a woman utterly known through the destructive creativity that materializes in her body. The film is insistent that Plath's creativity is read as psychological instability – only at the very end, when she is at her most disturbed, is she shown able to write.

It is specifically in the context of its realist re-telling of the 1950s that *Sylvia* effaces the significance of feminism. By inserting a contemporary masculinity – the 'new man' – into this recent past, the film suggests that men have always been loving and supportive, always on women's side. Equally problematically, the film reiterates the familiar tropes that there is no distinction to be made between a woman and her writing, between her body and the body of her work, and between madness and female creativity. As with *Iris* and *The Hours*, female authorship is employed to screen out the feminist sensibility that adheres to the lives of iconic women writers, whilst they themselves are displaced from their own stories by a controlling masculine perspective.

In the biopics discussed here a recuperative move is taking place. The pre-feminist discourse of female creativity as a form of self-destructive madness is stitched into an equally powerful representation of self-effacing masculine support for women that only post-feminism has now made visible. In all three films the mise-en-scène of recent history becomes a distracting spectacle that substitutes period artefacts for women's struggles to achieve literary recognition, male control of the literary canon for male support of the lives of women writers, and self-destruction for the tensions which women writers face in reconciling public reputation with domestic responsibility. In articulating the redundancy of feminism through women's success and the destructive consequences of that success, these biopics' rewriting of the public history of authorship therefore also offers a profoundly troubling re-telling of feminism's project.

Notes

1. See, for example, *The Aviator* (US, 2004, Martin Scorsese), *Beyond the Sea* (US, 2004, Kevin Spacey), *Ray* (US, 2004, Taylor Hackford), *Capote* (US, 2005, Bennett Miller).
2. Bizarrely, Sidney Franklin directed both the 1934 and the 1957 versions of this film.
3. If you find yourself thinking 'mmm, nice curtains', chances are you're watching a heritage film.

4. See, for example, *Walk the Line* (US, 2005, James Mangold), the biopic of Johnny Cash (Joaquin Phoenix) in which the figure of June Carter (Reese Witherspoon) is represented as unremittingly supportive, while Cash himself is cast as a tortured but redeemed figure of universal significance. Similarly, in *The Glenn Miller Story* (US, 1954, Anthony Mann), Miller's wife (June Allyson) is comforted and rewarded for her fidelity by the promise that his music will never die, as she hears it playing over the radio in the final scene.
5. Of necessity, unpublished papers presented by Suzy Gordon in conference-panel collaborations with Josephine Dolan and Estella Tincknell are paraphrased here. Health problems have prevented Gordon from developing her ideas, although she is fully credited as a co-author of this chapter.

Bibliography

Custen, George (1992), *Bio/Pics: How Hollywood Constructed Public History*. New Brunswick, NJ: Rutgers University Press.

Gledhill, Christine (1987), 'The melodramatic field: an investigation', in C. Gledhill (ed.), *Home Is Where the Heart Is: Essays on Melodrama and the Woman's Film*. London: BFI, pp. 5–39.

Hill, John (1999), *British Cinema in the 1980s*. Oxford: OUP.

Monk, Claire (1995a), 'The British "heritage film" and its critics', *Critical Survey* 7, 2, 16–24.

— (1995b), 'Sexuality and the heritage', *Sight and Sound* 5, 10, 32–4.

Moses, Kate (2003), *Wintering: a Novel of Sylvia Plath*, London: St Martin's Press.

Plath, Sylvia (1965), *Ariel*. London: Faber and Faber.

Rich, Adrienne (1986), 'Compulsory heterosexuality and lesbian existence', in *Blood, Bread and Poetry: Selected Prose 1979 –1985*. New York: Norton.

Showalter, Elaine (1987), *The Female Malady: Women, Madness and English Culture*. London: Virago.

CHAPTER SIXTEEN

For the Love of Jane: Austen, Adaptation and Celebrity

BRENDA R. WEBER

A collection that uses the word 'infidelities' in its subtitle, as this one does, at some level tacitly suggests that there might be a faithful form of adaptation, a relationship between original and ancillary texts that does not depart from or multiply potential modes of representation and analysis. It is a similar connection to that established between the terms 'fiction' and 'non-fiction', or between memory and history, as if the first is entirely created and the second only and always about facts, which are perceived to be in some way inviolable and outside of time. Although we know that things are always more complicated than such linear relationships presume, there endures a sense that a documentary or biography about the life of a famous person might be more authoritatively 'accurate' than a fictional account. If the famous person under consideration is none other than the literary great Jane Austen, the notion of original and adapted text becomes all the more vexing, since relatively little is authoritatively known about Austen's 'real' life.[1] Her consequent construction as a figure of fame, as with all celebrity profiles, both relies on and distorts links to an actual everyday life. Yet if, as Pablo Picasso once famously quipped, 'art is the lie that tells the truth', then great storytelling always stands with only one foot in any one of these categories of 'fact' and 'fiction'.

In the myth that is Jane Austen, much has been made of the fact that she wrote about romantic love and yet can be credited with no specific historically verifiable amorous relationship. How is it, many have wondered, that an author could so powerfully evoke the exigencies and desires of romantic love when she herself led a sheltered and short life, unmarried and dead at a relatively young age? How, in turn, can the celebrant of Austen's fictions revel without guilt in the romantic plots and outcomes each book provides, all the while knowing that the creator of such storybook concoctions never experienced the love-into-marriage of which she writes? As the host of PBS's *Masterpiece*, Gillian Anderson, remarks in the introduction to the 2008 biopic *Miss Austen Regrets*, answers to these questions might have been lodged in Austen's journals and letters. But since these papers were burned (by her sister Cassandra) after Austen's death, we are left with no alternative but fiction: 'We can only imagine.'

And imagine we have – our collected cultural speculations, both historical and contemporary, have been desperate to provide Austen with a satisfyingly consummated love connection. The driving force behind these adaptive representations of the author's life and loves seems to be this: if we are to believe that love is 'real' and thus trust the romantic unions Austen builds, if we are to surrender to her rendering of that most effable of feelings, then there must be narrative assurance, if not historical evidence, that Jane herself both loved and was loved. Otherwise, a fondly held truism that affective epistemology stems from ontology – that you will know love when you feel it – is placed perilously at risk.

Although Austen wrote about many other topics – among them political economy, the rights of women, and class prejudices – by and large, when Austen is referenced as wise in the ways of human nature it is as the keeper of love's secrets. Such a regard for Austen has often translated into the idea that anyone (and usually this person is a woman) wanting to know how to find a spouse need only consult Austen to meet with success. Dierdre Lynch speculates that this focus on Austen as the mistress of all things love-related stems from a hopeful reasoning, whereby readers become assured that after reading Austen they will have gleaned the tools necessary to demystify the ways of the heart. Reading Austen will therefore 'guide them toward love' (Lynch 2007). In imagining Austen as a mentor and escort and thus creating a celebrity profile of her whereby she is both loving and beloved, readers invest in the idea that she too enacted and experienced the emotions of which she is a putative expert.

In the context of adaptation, the curious case of Jane Austen asks that we further consider what happens when we think about adapting a life, since a life-text arguably has some stronger tether binding it to authenticity. Rather than using this chapter to chart the many film adaptations of Austen's work, then, I want to analyse the cultural figure represented by and made intelligible through the image of the celebrated Jane Austen herself, particularly in our own post-millennial iterations about, and investments in, the nature of experience and love. In particular, I will argue that the enigma of Jane Austen's heterosexual romantic history opens a hermeneutic space that might be filled by an equally powerful affective bond, the sorophilia she experienced with her sister, Cassandra.

'Few so gifted were so truly unpretending'

Even including such famous transatlantic literary celebrities as Charlotte Bronte, Lord Byron, Harriet Beecher Stowe, Mark Twain and Charles Dickens, no writer of the nineteenth century has been more immortalized, personalized and adapted than Jane Austen. Claudia Johnson credits the rise in 'Janeitism', or the 'self-consciously idolatrous enthusiasm' for all things Jane, to the last two decades of the nineteenth century with the 1870 publication by Jane Austen's nephew, James Austen-Leigh, of the *Memoir of Jane Austen*, and Bentley's deluxe *Steventon Edition of Jane Austen's Work*, published in 1882, which put 'Austen's famous little "world" into a tidy bundle' (Johnson 1997: 211). Much to the chagrin of authors such as Joseph Conrad or Charlotte Bronte, who famously critiqued Austen's works as passionless, Austen's novels have been ardently embraced, studied and adapted for nearly 200 years.[2]

The concern over the state of Jane's romantic life has raged as long as her celebrity, scholarship and curiosity, co-mingling to create a passion for Jane. To offer an early-twentieth-century example, Rudyard Kipling centred his 1924 poem *Jane's Marriage* on a central driving question: 'Who loved Jane?' Kipling's poem imagines 'England's Jane' entering the gates of heaven, where she is met by such literary luminaries as William Shakespeare and Sir Walter Scott. When asked by one of the holy attendants what she yet desires, the spectral Jane declares that her most ardent wish is for love. The angels immediately canvass heaven and realize that a 'Hampshire gentleman' sitting off in the corner reading Austen's *Persuasion* is the man for her. Who loves Jane? 'I did – and do!' the man exclaims, thus bringing Jane connubial bliss, if not on earth, then in heaven (no matter that he is Captain Wentworth, the hero of *Persuasion* meant for Anne Elliot, making his suitability as a love interest to the book's author a bit of narrative fancy worthy of postmodern narratology). Kipling's poem offers the certainty that what Jane Austen missed in life, she may yet experience in death.

This fascination with Jane is particularly acute in our present moment. Indeed, as a way of describing both the contemporary reader's pleasure in reading Austen and our larger culture's voracious desire to learn more about her, metaphors of obsession and addiction are often invoked, eclipsing their paler cousins, admiration or affection. Laurie Viera Rigler's 2008 novel *Confessions of a Jane Austen Addict* emphasizes that readers of Austen are never tepid, through continual statements about a fan's 'ungovernable addiction to Jane Austen novels' (Rigler 2008: 64) that can be used, like a pharmacological antidepressant akin to Xanax or Prozac, for 'beating the blues' (Rigler 2008: 204). The supplementary material included on the DVD for the feature film *Pride and Prejudice* extends such addiction to identification, suggesting that each of the film's actresses responded instantly to Austen out of a feeling of recognition and personal ownership – the ideas which she renders are so close to each of us who read her, the mini-documentary attests, that we can make no separation between her thoughts and our own (2005).

Although Austen's own literary output – six books published in a seven-year period from 1811 to 1818 – is slight compared to her more prolific peers, Austen has been claimed in the contemporary public imagination, according to *Becoming Jane*, a big-budget Hollywood film that attempts to fill in the romantic gaps in Austen's life, as 'one of the greatest writers in the Western world' (2007). Surely, not only the ubiquity of her presence in the literary canon but the sheer amount of cultural fascination attached to her life and her novels further attest to her significance. With *Pride and Prejudice* and *Emma* leading the way, Austen's novels have inspired a veritable second canon of Jane-inspired materials that include novels, plays, feature films, radio dramas, television mini-series and made-for-TV movies, making of her both a producer of commodities and a commodity for consumption.[3] In preparing to write this chapter, I threw myself with abandon into a stockpile of Jane-aphilia. Reading all six of her novels was only a small start, for I also travelled through a good many film and television adaptations of her books and her life, from Hollywood to the BBC and the RSC to Bollywood, and back again. I read books 'inspired' by Jane Austen, including *Austenland*, *The Jane Austen Book Club*, *Lost in Austen*, *Confessions of a Jane Austen Addict*, and *Emma in Love*. I watched documentaries and fictional interpretations of Austen's life such as *Miss Austen Regrets*, *Becoming Jane*, and *The Life of Jane Austen*. I also travelled in real time and space to find Jane. In England I visited Bath, the site of so many steamy and steam-room encounters in the novels, as well as Chawton House in Hertfordshire, where she lived with her sister and mother and wrote or edited her later novels.

In each encounter, I experienced a different person in Jane Austen. In her own works, she was the witty and wise implied-author, leading me through her heroines' maturation, as each developed an improved capacity to read personalities that resulted in a happy love-match. In literary works inspired by Austen, she was often a God-like figure: the luminous, almost spiritual entity that had brought all her characters together and conspired to create (and bless) endless imaginary variations based on the relationships she draws in her novels. In films about her life she emerges as a beautiful, if often flirtatious and irreverent, young or middle-aged woman, who experienced many of the romantic tensions described in the novels, without their resolution in love and marriage.

Certain elements of an Austen-inspired story are intrinsic, and perhaps obvious: there must be heterosexual romantic tension, confusion and misunderstanding, and eventual accord and love. There must be a vast stock of colourful surrounding characters. There will be letters (or texts and e-mails) written and exchanged, essentially communication – and often foreplay – through the written word. There will be dancing and big houses, punctuated by minute gestures of finger against finger or meaningful gazes. But also, there will be many walks across pastures and moors (or dense urban spaces), often in the rain. There will frequently be incompetent and missing fathers, loving sisters, some sort of domestic tragedy, and a mandate for familial solidarities. Fidelity to Jane, then, can often mean creating narratives, no matter how far removed from her actual subject matter, where the text offers finely observed interactions among people within a simultaneously expanding and shrinking domestic world – what Austen herself described as 'the little bit [two Inches wide] of Ivory on which I work with so fine a Brush' (*Jane Austen's Letters*, L 146 Jane Austen to James Edward Austen, 16 December 1816: 323).

Along with the insistence and seeming ubiquity of fascination for all things Jane across film, literature, and various Jane-inspired gift shops across the globe, there is a concomitant and equally ubiquitous version of Austen as shy and retiring, unused to and unwelcoming of fame's attention or celebrity's glaring spotlight. Some of this understanding of Austen's retiring ways was undoubtedly established by her brother, Henry Austen, whose foreword to the posthumously published *Northanger Abbey* and *Persuasion* emphasized the terms of sentimental nostalgia by reminding the reader that the 'the hand which guided the pen' was now 'mouldering in the grave' (Henry Austen 1817: 3). Henry Austen's reminiscences of his sister are noteworthy for many reasons, the least of which are his thinly veiled attempts to properly gender Jane by emphasizing her 'true elegance', graceful 'carriage and deportment' and refined talents for music and dancing (Henry Austen 1817: 4–5). Austen also carefully assures the reader that his sister 'became an authoress entirely from taste and inclination' (Henry Austen 1817: 5). It was 'neither hope of fame nor profit mixed with her early motives' that compelled her to write, he emphasizes, thus deftly suggesting that fame and fortune might be acceptable if passively achieved, but that a stigma accrues to she who too actively seeks such rewards (Henry Austen 1817: 5–6).[4]

Twenty-first-century filmic imaginations of her life in *Becoming Jane* and *Miss Austen Regrets* heighten this notion of Austen's uneasy relationship with renown by including scenes where she is depicted as uncomfortable with acclaim, even if, as in *Miss Austen Regrets*, they afford her opportunities for mild flirtation. Remarkably, in our present age – so seemingly comfortable with celebrity – such depictions reinforce a notion that cultural greats are unmoved by the lures that fame offers. Indeed, this regard for fame heightens the notion that an author practises her craft for the love of art alone, and that readers, in turn, should admire greatness when it is not knowingly predicated on popular affection and applause.

Hopelessly devoted to Jane

Laurie Viera Rigler begins *Confessions of a Jane Austen Addict* with a dedication to fellow 'Austen addicts past, present, and future', and to the creator/pusher/source of their addiction, 'Jane Austen, whose bit of

ivory is an endless source of wisdom and joy for this humble admirer'
(Rigler 2008). Rigler continues the dedication, shifting to second-person
direct address: 'If there is any justice in the world, Miss Austen, then
there is a parallel reality in which that lovely young man from the seaside didn't die young, you lived to write at least six more novels, and
the two of you grew happily old together, preferably without children'
(Rigler 2008). In these statements filled with equal parts approbation
and veneration, Rigler aptly prepares the ground over which much of
Jane-aphilia is trod and on which the myth of Jane is largely predicated.
Austen is thought to be the shy and retiring denizen of the domestic
sphere, who wrote secretly on a small round table (even requiring a
squeaking door that would alert her to visitors), and who wrote of
romance but herself never married. She died at the age of 41 of a mysterious ailment (see Upfal 2005), at that time the famous, though still
anonymous, author of four novels, with two more to be published after
her death.

Rigler's dedication references a man met at the seaside, a person with
whom Jane experienced a form of romantic attachment. Austen-Leigh
reports that Jane's sister, Cassandra, dropped her 'habitual reticence'
many years after Jane's death and indicated, even if vaguely, that:

> [W]hile staying at some seaside place, they became acquainted with a gentle-
> man whose charms of person, mind, and manners was such that Cassandra
> thought him worthy to possess and likely to win her sister's love. When they
> parted, he expressed his intention of soon seeing them again; and Cassandra
> felt no doubt as to his motives. But they never again met. Within a short time
> they heard of his sudden death. (Austen-Leigh 1870: 29)[5]

Austen-Leigh opines 'if Jane ever loved, it was this unnamed gentleman', dismissing other accounts of romantic connection to Thomas
Lefroy (depicted as the love of Jane's life in the film *Becoming Jane*
and the book on which it was based, Jon Spence's *Becoming Jane Austen*),
or to the Reverend Brook Bridges (represented as the long-enduring,
though married, devotee of Jane in *Miss Austen Regrets*), or to Harris
Biggs-Wither (with whom Jane had an overnight engagement in
1802, apparently calling it off, as might one of her heroines, for lack
of affection).

These filmic and textual speculations on Jane Austen's love life each
endeavour to answer that most pressing of questions – in the words
of *Masterpiece*: 'What about the lively, attractive, flirtatious Jane? Was
there no one charming enough, handsome enough, or rich enough for
the clever Miss Austen?' (*Miss Austen Regrets*, 2008). Such issues of
Jane Austen and love become more pressing if framed in the thematics
of adaptation that serves as the cornerstone to this book. If the 'real'
experience of love is the original, and our artistic representations of it
somehow the adaptation, can it be possible for an author to concoct this
most desired of emotional states if she herself has not experienced it?

Although cultural studies scholarship would suggest that any given historical moment offers critical instruction in these matters – so that Jane Austen would have been just as likely to know the ways of love from reading Shakespeare or Richardson, or through the ambient discourse to which she was exposed, as she would from forging her own bond of love – the question of her relative romantic experience refuses to die. Indeed, in its endurance as a matter of speculative fascination about Jane Austen, there is evidence of a greater cultural fixation on these tenuous matters of originals and adaptations.

Such an issue increases in urgency if we consider a core popular, if not always scholarly, belief about Austen, reiterated so often that it has become sacrosanct: Austen's artistry was one of faithful observation, rather than of tempestuous imagination. As *Jane Austen's Life*, an extensive if often tedious three-part documentary, attests, everything and everybody in Jane's Georgian world existed 'just as she described them' in her novels (1997). Further, the documentary declares, the affective realities experienced by Jane's female (though apparently not her male) characters, such things as Elizabeth Bennet's sardonic satire or Fanny Price's shyness, were described 'only as someone who has experienced these feelings can do' (1997). The supplementary material to the 2005 film *Pride and Prejudice* makes a similar claim, when both the director and cast members declare that Jane Austen created scenes predicated only on what she had herself seen. According to these accounts, we can thus be assured that Jane was a faithful scribe to life rather than an artistic interloper who wrote from imagination. Unlike the Bronte sisters or even Austen's contemporary Ann Radcliffe, Austen's work is renowned for its deft realism, social commentary, and subtle characterization. Jane's genius, we are made to understand, dwelt in her powers of observation rather than imagination.[6]

Ironically, the very publication that cemented Austen's star-text in the public imagination, Austen-Leigh's *Memoir*, strikes against this very claim that Jane had to know of what she wrote. Austen-Leigh refers to an 1821 *Quarterly Review* column written by Richard Whatley 'concerning the attachment of Fanny Price to Edmund Bertram' in *Mansfield Park*, quoting from the review:

> The silence in which this passion is cherished, the slender hopes and enjoyments by which it is fed, the restlessness and jealousy with which it fills a mind naturally active, contented, and unsuspicious, the manner in which it tinges every event, and every reflection, are painted with a vividness and a detail of which we can scarcely conceive any one but a female, and we could almost add, a female writing from recollection, capable. (Austen-Leigh 1870: 28)

Austen-Leigh responds to this passage by arguing that the reviewer's 'conjecture' is 'wide of the mark', insisting that Jane drew her portrait from 'intuitive perceptions of genius not from personal experience. In no circumstance of her life was there any similarity between herself and her heroine in *Mansfield Park*' (Austen-Leigh 1870: 28). That his aunt Jane did not experience the exact relationship of which she writes, Austen-Leigh hastens to add, does not mean she was bereft of 'being the object of warm affection' (Austen-Leigh 1870: 28). Indeed, before the paragraph has run its course he reassures his readers of Jane's romantic legitimacy through the anecdote of the mysterious seaside gentleman referred to above. So even in this context, where Austen-Leigh argues for the imagination of genius over the mimesis of personal experience, he buttresses Austen's credibility by alluding to biographical accounts.

'Her peculiar attachment to her sister'

Perhaps one reason why Jane Austen's love life has been considered an enigma that must be filled through her characters, or through passing flirtations along England's southern coast, is that we have looked too intently for an exact approximation of the kinds of love she depicts in her novels. In this final section, then, I want to explore the possibility, poignantly if tentatively rendered in *Miss Austen Regrets*, that Jane Austen may have experienced a complete and totalizing love of a most profound and epic nature with her sister Cassandra. To call theirs a woman-woman love is not to suggest that these sisters shared a sexual life together, though often during the eighteenth and nineteenth centuries the domestic bonds of friend-to-friend or sister-to-sister offered the only achievable means of living in a passionate same-sex union (see Smith-Rosenberg 1995). Indeed, the actual state of Jane and Cassandra's sexual lives, whether separately or together, is completely immaterial to my argument here that the contemporary filmic representation of Jane's life in *Miss Austen Regrets* introduces the possibility that Jane could well have been informed in the ways of love through the intense sorophilia she experienced with her sister – or, as Austen-Leigh described it, their 'peculiar attachment' (Austen-Leigh 1870: 28).

The 2008 made-for-TV *Miss Austen Regrets* (a co-production between the BBC in London and WGBH in Boston) offered viewers a version of their heroine, Jane Austen (Olivia Williams), previously never seen and seldom imagined. This Jane is irascible, flirtatious, and often bitter; she can be rude, indifferent, and even cruel, but she is always very witty and funny. *Miss Austen Regrets* establishes the author Jane as more of a theorist about love than its practitioner, as the Austen character herself opines at various times throughout the film: 'Good Lord, what do I know about any of it? I'm simply the mistress of theory.' She is 'like someone who can't cook writing a recipe book'. This biographical rendering of Jane Austen's life, so very concerned with the state of her heart, meanders its way through various conjectures about the author's attachments to men, offering along the way several palliatives that might account for her single status at the end of her life. Marriage and children would have been a distraction from writing, it argues, or would have brought an unwelcome cessation to the enjoyments of courting: 'I never found one [man] worth giving up flirting for,' remarks the Austen character. The film is so broadly understood as a reckoning about the author's romantic life that in recommending it to readers, *The Daily Express* described *Miss Austen Regrets* as a 'poignant look' at the men who 'got away' (*Television Express* 2008).

Throughout the film, the character of Cassandra (Greta Scacchi) is played with consistent, if unremarkable, resolve. She is the quiet contrast to Jane's zest, the sober long-suffering soul to the author's tipsy glee. But as the film and Jane's life simultaneously move to their end, *Miss Austen Regrets* offers the viewer an intense scene, lasting only a matter of minutes. In this tableau, set up as a private moment between the sisters that their niece Fanny – and through her the at-home viewer – observes without the sisters' awareness, a sick and dying Jane shares the screen with a concerned and sympathetic Cassandra. Jane is mostly undressed, her body weak, and Cassandra offers both support and closeness, their hands clasped tightly, their eyes conveying their deep reverie. For those attentive to filmic conventions, this extended series of moments depicting the physical proximity between the sisters is captured in a tight two-shot close-up, a camera angle largely reserved for evoking the intimacy of lovers.[7] The character of Jane tells her sister in whispers: 'Everything I am, and everything I have achieved, I owe to you. To the life we have made here, to the love that we have together. This life I have, it's what I needed. It's what God intended for me. I'm so much happier than I thought I'd be. So much happier than I deserve to be.' The character Cassandra, borrowing language from a letter that the actual Cassandra wrote to her niece Fanny, speaks about her love for the lost Jane: 'She was the sun of my life. The gild of every pleasure. The soother of every sorrow. I have not a soul to conceal from her. And it's as if I lost a part of myself.'[8] If this is not a depiction of consummating love, I am at a loss to know what else might suffice. In the realm of love, this film suggests, Jane Austen harboured no regrets. In sum, *Jane Austen Regrets* offers contemporary Austen addicts/viewers/readers a version of this author's life that through its representation of sorophilia might well contain the spirit of Austen's idea that there are as many kinds of love as there are moments in time.

But sorophilia itself does not encompass the extent to which a profound and meaningful love fits into the world of Jane Austen. The love between these sisters is not limited to their own passionate twosome, for the love of Jane is open to a broader sisterhood created by the enduring and ongoing ardour that her male and female lovers – in the form of fans, academics, film producers, television producers, biographers, and writers of fiction – express through their adaptations of her work. This collective ardent homage is what fully extends the affective registers of Austen's fiction – and may account for a character in Rigler's novel, who invokes the bonds of marriage to describe her relationship to Jane: 'Men might come and go, but Jane Austen was always there. In sickness and in health, for richer, for poorer, till death do us part' (Rigler 2008: 33). For really, it may well be because we believe Austen shows an uncanny understanding of the human heart, and that her own heart seems to so profoundly need what fans/readers/scholars/lovers/addicts have to offer, that we create in union, and across the particularities of time and place, the beloved object of which love and legends are made.

Notes

1. *Remembering Jane Austen*, a four-part radio play, declares: 'We know more about Shakespeare in some way than we know about the only English writer with the indisputable right to stand beside him in the history of literature' (2008).
2. For an excellent and comprehensive study of the workings of fan-culture, see Dierdre Lynch (ed.), *Janeites: Austen's Disciples and Devotees*. Or simply consult Amazon.com, where one can purchase upwards of 30 variations on Austen novels.
3. Such commodification is rendered literally in the opening scenes of *Jane Austen in Manhattan*, when a previously unknown Austen play is auctioned for what the film considers to be an exorbitant sum: $55,000.
4. Jan Fergus persuasively argues that this image of Jane Austen as retiring, uninterested in notoriety or professionalism, and in all ways unaware of her public persona or her literary celebrity, was one studiously cultivated by Henry Austen, rather than by Austen herself (Fergus 1997).
5. For a novelized account of Jane's attachment to the mysterious man at the seaside, see Constance Pilgrim's *Dear Jane*.
6. This distinction is critical because it keys into larger debates, which expanded during the Victorian period, about women's capacities to imagine, and thus depict, experiences such as debauchery, adultery or incest.
7. Indeed, one blogger certainly understood the filmic conventions when she wrote: 'Very uncomfortable with the last scene where Fanny spies on the sisters, the insinuation of lesbism/incest [sic] between the sisters . . . is this why Cassandra burned some but not all Jane's letters?' (Barbara, 4 February 2008). *http://www.pbs.org/nights/blog/2008/01/ the_complete_jane_austen_miss.html*. [Accessed 28 August 2008]
8. Days after Jane's death, Cassandra wrote to her niece Fanny: 'I have lost a treasure, such a Sister, such a friend as never can have been surpassed, –She was the sun of my life, the gilder of every pleasure, the soother of every sorrow, I had not a thought concealed from her, & it is as if I had lost a part of myself" (*Jane Austen's Letters*, CEA/x From Cassandra Austen to Fanny Knight, 20 July 1817: 343).

Bibliography

Austen, Henry (1817), 'Biographical Notice'. Foreword to Jane Austen's *Persuasion*. New York and Oxford: Oxford University Press, 2004.

Austen-Leigh, James (1870), *Memoir of Jane Austen*. London: R. Bentley.

Becoming Jane (2007). UK, dir. Julian Jarrold.

Fergus, Jan (1997), 'The professional woman writer', in Edward Copeland and Juliet McMaster (eds), *The Cambridge Companion to Jane Austen*. Cambridge: Cambridge University Press, pp. 12–31.

Fowler, Karen Joy (2004), *The Jane Austen Book Club*. New York: Penguin.

Hale, Shannon (2007), *Austenland*. New York: Macmillan.

The Jane Austen Book Club (2007). USA, dir. Robin Swicord.

Jane Austen in Manhattan (1980). USA, dir. James Ivory.

Jane Austen's Life (1997). USA, dir. Liam Dale.

Johnson, Claudia L. (1997), 'Austen cults and cultures', in Edward Copeland and Juliet McMaster (eds), *The Cambridge Companion to Jane Austen*. Cambridge: Cambridge University Press, pp. 211–26.

Le Faye, Dierdre (ed.) (1995), *Jane Austen's Letters*. Oxford and New York: Oxford University Press.

Lynch, Dierdre (2007), 'See Jane elope: why are we so obsessed with Jane Austen's love life?' *Slate*, 3 August. *http://www.slate.com/id/2171615*. [Accessed 26 August 2008]

— (ed.) (2000), *Janeites: Austen's Disciplines and Devotees*. Princeton: Princeton University Press.

Miss Austen Regrets (2008). UK, BBC.

Pilgrim, Constance (1989), *Dear Jane*. New York: Hyperion Books.

Remembering Jane Austen (2008). UK, BBC Radio.

Rigler, Laurier Viera (2008), *Confessions of a Jane Austen Addict*. London and New York: Penguin.

Smith-Rosenberg, Carroll (1995), *Disorderly Conduct: Visions of Gender in Victorian America*. New York: Alfred A. Knopf.

Spence, Jon (2003), *Becoming Jane Austen*. London and New York: Hambledon Continuum.

Television Express (2008), 'Miss Austen regrets', April 27. *http://www.express.co.uk/posts/view/42627/Miss-Austen-Regrets*. [Accessed 9 April 2008]

Upfal, Annette (2005), 'Jane Austen's lifelong health problems and final illness: new evidence points to fatal Hodgkin's disease and excludes the widely accepted Addison's'. *Journal of Medical Ethics; Medical Humanities* 31, 3–11.

Webster, Emma Campbell (2007), *Lost in Austen: Create Your Own Jane Austen Adventure*. New York: Riverhead Books.

Whately, James (1821), 'Modern novels', *Quarterly Review* 24 (48, January), 352–76.

CHAPTER SEVENTEEN

Glamorama, Cinematic Narrative and Contemporary Fiction

RUTH HELYER

In a collection about adaptation in contemporary culture it is apt to consider a book which dares to suggest that celluloid is more life-like than novels, indeed more life-like than life. The action of Bret Easton Ellis' cinematic novel *Glamorama* (1999)[1] plays out in the facile world of beauty and fame, using the appearance-focused characters to display the slippery connections between what is seen, what has been experienced already, and what might be perceived to have actually happened or be happening now. Robert Stam's description of filmic adaptation also equally sums up Ellis' narrative, as an 'ongoing whirl of intertextual reference and transformation, of texts generating other texts in an endless process of recycling, transformation, and transmutation, with no clear point of origin' (Stam 2000: 66). It is impossible to differentiate between original and adapted; there is no original, only layers of copying, repeating, amending, breaking up, altering, putting back together. Adaptations are 'modelled' on existing versions, so Ellis' idea of populating his book with 'models' seems an apposite way to ask questions about originality and intertextuality.

The narrative's play between levels of actuality makes very apparent the difficulties for any claims to originality and, subsequently, fidelity. What and who can claim to be adapted (and from where) is far from straightforward, as it is suggested that everyone and everything are modified from multiple sources, and constantly adapting further to survive; improvements and enhancements are open to question and opinion, and reliability and faithfulness somehow irrelevant. As all texts are incomplete, fragmentary and rewritten within the reader's interpretation and experience, the best an adaptation can hope to do is to refract these experiences and beliefs through the mirror it holds up, with any so-called original only ever loosely cited, due to its own inherent incompleteness. The adapter can, after all, only guess at what has been left out.

On the surface *Glamorama* is a comedy, a spoof deriding the vacuity of the celebrity social scene, where your status depends upon 'A smart suit . . . being buff. A cool haircut. Worrying about whether people think you're famous enough or cool enough or in good enough shape' (Ellis 1999: 410). The mockery is aimed at those who fear not being beautiful enough; however, running alongside this pathetic anxiety is the very real panic that contemporary society is hurtling towards a violent and bloody disorder, ending in torture and death perpetrated by terrorists. The narrative's major premise is that models and terrorists can easily be the same group of people. David Punter refers to this as 'a constant sliding between two worlds, between a sense of the real and a sense of the filmic; of being an actor in another script, of the *virtual*' (Punter 2001: 68, emphasis in original). This slippage and avoidance of categorization is present in Ellis' earlier novels, but, Punter maintains, reaches a 'remarkable pitch' (Punter 2001: 68) in *Glamorama*. The exaggerated staging of this narrative results in the reader scrutinizing the relationship between textual and visual representations, and as a consequence the narrative illustrates the impact which cinematic culture has on both human experiences of reality and the construction of fictions about these realities. Linda Seger comments on the commonly held belief that films are more commercial than literature, often exaggerating this commerciality by, 'adding a car chase and a sex scene' (Seger 1992: 4); *Glamorama* has both in abundance and, as a cinematic narrative about celebrities, has the capacity to attract a large audience. Throughout *Glamorama*, characters are identified by their physical similarity to famous models and actors – 'you look just like Uma Thurman, baby' (Ellis 1999: 8) – and, furthermore, are tailed by competing camera crews, eager to capture their 'performances':

> A film crew I haven't seen before enters the room. A large Panavision camera is wheeled in, lights are positioned. The first AD tells me where to lie on the bed while Jamie confers with the director and script supervisor. (Ellis 1999: 308)

There is no differentiation between existing celebrities and ordinary people who look like celebrities. The entire cast are equally authentic (or inauthentic) and they are all shown as both adapted and adapting, on a continuum of imitation. The only characters who are not compared to celebrities are recurring and future characters from Ellis' other fiction. These characters frequently disagree about when they last saw each other, indeed whether they actually *know* each other, and if so from where. These confusions could be attributed to their cross-novel connections; they have met in different places and timescales as parts of various different plots. Sometimes what happened before matters and has a relevance in this new scenario, but often it does not. Several of Ellis' characters, for example Victor Ward, Patrick Bateman and Jayne Dennis, have evolved from their fictional status to come to life as adaptations on the internet, with fan sites and profiles on networking webspaces such as MySpace. Within *Glamorama* the misfit happens when characters' readings of situations differ, for example one of Victor's ex-girlfriends feels aggrieved that he is ignoring her, but the incident to which she is referring actually took place in a novel other than *Glamorama*, accentuating how priorities and memories vary greatly from person to person due to conflicting interpretations and influences.

The frequent mis-recognition of characters, and the ease with which different personas are adopted throughout the narrative, is ironically juxtaposed against the adulation of the rich, famous and good-looking, both fictional and real. Victor Ward/Johnson, the beautiful central protagonist, first seen in *The Rules of Attraction* (1987), with his 'high cheekbones, ivory skin, jet-black hair, semi-Asian eyes, a perfect nose, huge lips, defined jawline' (Ellis 1999: 16), is frequently spotted at events he did not attend: even those closest to him wrongly identify him. He denies these sightings, but cannot resist asking 'Did I look good?' (Ellis 1999: 80), eager for confirmation that his appearance is acceptable even as he is, to quote Imelda Whelehan, 'burdened by the weight of interpretations' (Whelehan 1999: 7).

Cases of mistaken identity proliferate throughout the text; characters discuss themselves in the third person, appear where they claim not to have been, and return, re-packaged in differing formats. As Palakon, the mysterious diplomat, suggests, 'There are different truths . . . we adapt' (Ellis 1999: 406). Meticulous mediated construction has created subjects honed to such an intense state of 'perfection' that they have become deeply iconic. Even the person believed to be the 'original' cannot sustain the required level of finery required for this impossibly lofty position. Famous individuals are constantly told that they look 'like' themselves, though never enough to actually be themselves: in a contemporary culture predicated on adapting, nobody can fulfil that revered role. Supermodel Chloe is resigned to hearing, 'You look *just like* Chloe Byrnes' (Ellis 1999: 37, emphasis added). In much the same way that her fans emulate her appearance, so must she work hard on her image if she wants to sustain (and retain) it. Her mute acceptance of such comments illustrates her realization that it is impossible to live up to her own image. She and Victor should make the perfect celebrity couple, capable of matching each others' allure, and indeed their personal interactions appear occasionally to be spontaneously genuine, only to be undermined by a director, part of the continuous filming, asking them to repeat their actions: 'I start relaxing but . . . a camera starts panning around us and we're asked to "do that" once more. Someone yells "Action". Someone yells "Cut". I stop crying and we do it again' (Ellis 1999: 409).

Glamorama is peopled with models who flaunt their ability to adapt chameleon-like to multiple outfits and scenarios, already adapted from what is currently deemed attractive. This propensity to adapt and evolve is what determines whether or not they survive. The title 'model' has implications beyond a fashion mannequin who displays clothes to prospective buyers: a model can also be someone to imitate or to follow. 'To model' can be to mould to a particular design or type; also to plan, adapt or create a different version. Victor eventually notices: 'I think they double people . . . I don't know how, but I think they have . . . doubles. That's not Sam Ho . . . that's someone else . . . they have doubles' (Ellis 1999: 373). When Sam Ho is tortured to death Victor tries to reassure himself that the object of Bobby Hughes's (the world's most successful male supermodel) electrical torture is a dummy, imagining 'the camera aimed solely at the mannequin' (Ellis 1999: 283), until he sees the body leap, contort and haemorrhage.

Alison Poole has migrated into the narrative from *American Psycho* (1991), a rare survivor of one of Patrick Bateman's attacks and originally a Jay McInerney character from *Story of My Life* (1989). Patrick himself also appears (Ellis 1999: 38) as the differing narratives comment on each other and interweave. When, in *Glamorama*, Mica the DJ is found dead in Hell's Kitchen, beaten with a hammer and eviscerated (Ellis 1999: 149), there are distinct echoes of Patrick's (*American Psycho*) methods of murder and mutilation, and uncomfortable re-memories of his apartment in Hell's Kitchen, kept specifically for disposing of bodies. Texts are not merely quoted, they are incorporated, the incongruous result of this being that the action is both more and less real. Patrick's (*American Psycho*) obsession with graphic visual images, and aptitude for using his vast resources to facilitate evil, would make him an eager backer for films, like those being made in *Glamorama*, where people physically have sex, and actually die. In the film of *American Psycho* (2000, dir. Harron) Patrick is played by Christian Bale, an actor frequently cited by Victor as resembling the man who is tailing him throughout *Glamorama* (Ellis 1999: 322). *Glamorama* was published before the film version of *American Psycho* was cast. Bale the actor has now transformed again from psychotic Bateman to a dark and disturbed Batman, simply by losing one letter.[2] Victor relies on this celebrity-similarity for clarity, asking his Bale lookalike stalker whether they are in the same movie (Ellis 1999: 279). The complex layers of intertextual relationship and identity remind the reader of the created, fictional nature of the adaptive culture they are both analysing and occupying.

The permanent presence of camera operators, film editors and make-up technicians throughout the novel reiterates that contemporary adaptation culture, with its visual fixations, requires constant 'acting'. As in Dziga Vertov's *Man With a Movie Camera* (1929) there are multiple film crews and it is never clear who is filming whom. When Jamie, one of Victor's girlfriends, says her nail polish is for 'the movie', Victor asks which movie and she replies 'both' (Ellis 1999: 243). The borderline between versions becomes increasingly hard to define until the act of filming takes on the role of validation, causing Victor to ask 'is this for real? . . . I mean, is this like a movie? . . . Is this being filmed?' (Ellis 1999: 373). There are echoes of *Man Bites Dog* (1992), in which a film crew tailing a serial killer become embroiled in his gore-soaked world, where murder and rape are acceptable parts of life, further reflected in Ellis' *American Psycho*, where the murderer is witty and entertaining. This level of detail and intimacy (Ellis treats sex scenes and murder scenes with the same level of nauseatingly detailed voyeurism, allowing his cinematic imagination free rein) leads to the formation of extremely ambiguous relationships, both with other characters within the narrative, and with the audience themselves.

Adaptations are copies of copies: multi-faceted creations consisting of everything their interested parties (author, characters, readers/viewers, screenwriters, costume designers, make-up technicians, and so on) have invested in them, and this includes influences they are unaware of. One of the major preoccupations of the characters of *Glamorama* is sex.[3] This seems fitting in a narrative examining contemporary adaptations culture, as sex is a copy of a copy ad infinitum – perhaps the archetypal simulacrum, capable of sustaining (déjà vu-like) endless memories, and layers of adaptation which have no actual event to refer back to. As Jacques Lacan has suggested, sexual desires are never fulfilled because the ideal sexual scenario is always already a tissue of fantasies, in much the same way that readers will never be fulfilled by subsequent adaptations of a familiar narrative. Humans endlessly strive to re-enact something that never existed in the first place. This is why Lacan feels that so much significance is attached to the surrounding scene and setting of sexual activity (Lacan 1977).[4] There is reliance on scripted material from the multifarious, hybrid pieces already in existence, as William Simon suggests: 'a complex text, the script of the erotic . . . the costuming and posturing of desire often, but not always, in the culturally available idioms of the sexual' (Simon 1996:29).

Such 'posturing' proliferates throughout *Glamorama*, where the models/actors follow various scripts. Victor describes clothes and objects in such obsessive detail that their necessity for his 'posturing' is in no doubt: 'white jeans, leather belts, leather bomber jacket, black cowboy boots, a couple of black wool crepe suits, a dozen white shirts, a black turtleneck, crumpled silk pajamas' (Ellis 1999: 143). His closet is replenished unwitnessed, for forthcoming scenes; the level of detail makes him easy to imitate. The intense value placed upon appearance by Victor and his contemporaries leaves them vulnerable to being misled and confused. When Victor has sex on board the ocean liner, it seems obvious that it is not with Marina (Ellis 1999: 220). However, Victor has been coached to see what he wants to see. Desire is 'Costumed and occasioned', dressed up 'in the style of', to the extent that the biological sex of the other person no longer matters (Simon 1996: 137). This reliance on adapted identities ensures that part of arousal is always false. Paradoxically, the falsified and restricting mapping of sexual activity makes what passes for reality feel 'real'; so what is acted out and adapted facilitates actuality: in this example, the created face of sex leads to the physicality of orgasms and discharges, the tangible factors.

In *Glamorama* sex works in this formulaic way. Fantasies involve certain favoured scenarios which include the mannerisms and speech patterns of lovers, 'replaying imaginary conversations with her while on the StairMaster, rehearsing the words I'd use during sex' (Ellis 1999: 211–12); the action centres on sensation and pre-agreed ideas of perfection, and cuts from one sustainable interlude to the next. Freud described this phenomenon as 'the conceptual scaffolding we have set up to help us in dealing with the psychical manifestations of sexual life' (1905; 1991: 138). In other words we 'play the game' and restrict our adaptations within safe, predetermined parameters designed to detract from the potential poverty of our actuality. In *Glamorama* Victor demonstrates the way that the messy 'joining' sections, those pieces which might challenge or overthrow the fantasy, are not focused upon but instead skipped over. Sex can be seen as the activity linking humans most firmly with the acting required by contemporary adaptation culture; sex is marketed as emotionally engaging and real, yet actually contains vast quantities of that which has been acted out on an imaginary level, at some previous time, as with the process of adaptation – it is always made from fragments of other things and is trying, impossibly, to live up to what has already played out in multiple imaginations.

Adapting to what society expects means that during sex the participants re-invent themselves for that particular partner, and through the expectations and view of that partner assist in their *own* creation by using the correct responses. As Victor demonstrates:

> At first I'm able to look as if I'm concentrating intensely on what she's saying and in fact some of it is registering, but really I've heard it all before; then, while talking, she moves closer and there's a quickening and I'm relieved. Silently focusing in on her, I realize that I've been activated. I stare into her face for over an hour, asking the appropriate questions, guiding her to certain areas, mimic responses that I'm supposed to have, offer sympathetic nods when they're required, sometimes there's a sadness in my eyes that's half real and half-not. (Ellis 1999: 209)

Chapter 28 in its entirety is dedicated to a sexual marathon between Victor, Bobby and Jamie. The action is multi-genre combining sex manual, soft-pornography and formulaic romance and, like random shots from a movie, dispenses with beginnings, ends, and consequences. In this scene explicit sexual activity between two men and one woman is presented to the reader in a way reminiscent of a screen adaptation of a narrative previously only read; graphic, vivid details replace what a human mind might only imagine as a brief snapshot. The detailed description is fragmented, highlighted by the frequent use of ellipsis between sections, and constant new paragraphs. This method of representation reiterates the impossibility of keeping a fantasy running continuously, and chronologically. Cinematic devices abound – such as zooming in on the action, cutting from one character to another, and providing masses of visual detail, to the point of creating feelings of claustrophobia rather than lucid pictures. The sex act is usually imagined in non-chronological fragments, with detailed focusing on the segments particularly enjoyed, or coped with, like sections of a roll of film, framed shots from a movie, to be edited, cut and pasted, re-ordered. As David Jays suggests, 'we need to edit experience in order to find meaning' (Jays 2007: 2). As 'self' is shaped and adapted in the shadow of the awareness of what others desire, 'self' becomes a continuous production.

Fantasy is supposed to present what somebody would like to be doing, some idealized version, rather than tediously and mundanely re-running the mechanics of what *actually* happens in 'real' life. Supposedly fulfilling, sex also has a huge capacity to frustrate. Victor recalls that in his early relationship with Jamie, 'I'd try and fuck her into some kind of consciousness, desperate to make her come' (Ellis 1999: 182). This desperation leads to created stories, played out in minds, and to the need for manipulation. There is an inherent impossibility in ever adequately representing 'fantasy', in much the same way that Colin MacCabe discusses the problems of adequately representing what is purportedly 'real', concluding that 'no discourse can ever be equal to the multifarious nature of the real'(MacCabe 1993: 53). He claims that the 'notion' of the real is what is settled for instead, and this is what must be settled for in the terrain of living up to others' fantasies, because what is desired, and seen as real, is illusory: 'Reality *is* an illusion' (Ellis 1999: 9, emphasis in original).

Victor's clone-like girlfriends emphasize this: they are all beautiful, tall, thin, with short blonde hair, large breasts (usually implants), bright blue eyes and endless interchangeability. Victor cannot remember them all, or which order they came in (Ellis 1999: 249). Chloe, his current girlfriend as the narrative begins, spends hours performing such mind-numbing feats as practising how to wink (Ellis 1999: 40–41), exemplifying Mike Gane's assertion that 'The distinction between the real and its representation (is being) effaced'(Gane 1991: 101–2). Her death is gruesome, insides flooding out of her in a tide of blood, bodily tissue and chemicals, in a 'massive haemorrhaging due to the ingestion of fatal quantities of Mifepristone' (Ellis 1999: 456). She is tended not by an ambulance, whose paramedics may have tried to help her from the inside, but by a film crew, only interested in capturing the surface (Ellis 1999: 429). Her graphic physical loss of depth symbolically represents the manner in which she has been reduced to a brittle shell by her facile life, profoundly reproducible. Similarly, when Jamie is dying Victor describes her as 'just a shell, and something huge and shapeless is flying over us in the darkness, hanging above the courtyard, and a voice says,

You all are' (Ellis 1999: 425). This emptiness is underlined by the ease with which all characters are doubled. Victor's much-repeated catch phrase, *'We'll slide down the surface of things. . .'*, reiterates this lack of form and substance (Ellis 1999: 145, emphasis in original).

The prioritization of surface recalls Jean Baudrillard's suggestion that there is nothing else (1983); whatever may appear to be under this surface is only placed there by that particular interpreter/adaptor. When Victor is trapped on an ocean liner he complains that the surface appearance of his surroundings are dull, grey and bland – again giving priority to surface stimulation: 'Surrounded by so much boring space, five days is a long time to stay unimpressed' (Ellis 1999: 189). Towards the narrative's end, he rebukes Damien – 'You're just looking at the surface of things' – to which Damien retorts: 'There's something else?' (Ellis 1999: 453). When one of the film crews require Victor to fight to the death with Bobby, the scripted nature of the action and presence of the cameras associate the action with surface falseness; however, the blood and pain are in keeping with ancient gladiatorial pursuits. The director's words of comfort to Victor articulate the scripted nature of the situation: '"Don't worry, nothing's broken" . . . "You're just badly bruised"' (Ellis 1999: 436). Victor has already 'wonder[ed] if the third slap was in the script' (Ellis 1999: 170), drawing attention to the ill-defined nature of the divisions between differing scripts and versions. Although the action is filmed – the 'Steadicam operator is unable to keep up' (Ellis 1999: 170) – the blood and pain are real. Victor's narration of the fight places him in the position of a spectator, watching and describing, able to include aspects he would not be aware of whilst being punched. This distance gives the action a surreal, glassy feel. Even Victor can look at 'Victor'. The present is endlessly scripted and re-scripted, argued – even fought – over. There is no indication of which might be the most real script or the most authentic film crew – even those tools of reproduction are blatantly, and repeatedly, reproduced.

Victor's appropriation of the narrative's soundtrack exemplifies this. Victor continuously quotes lyrics closely relevant to his life, creating an incestuous, circular environment where it becomes impossible to ascertain who is adapting who. The lyrics are rarely referenced, but situations compromise themselves to accommodate them and the action evolves to the atmosphere of the track playing. As Victor sums it up, the music gives 'the footage an "emotional resonance", that I guess we are incapable of capturing ourselves' (Ellis 1999: 193). Victor's huge repertoire of lyrics echo his willingness to assume a pre-given identity, experience his life via media simulation and reproduction, and act out the emotions and ideas of others. As Neil Bartlett suggests: 'Most people are other people. Their thoughts are someone else's opinions, their lives are mimicry, their passions a quotation' (Bartlett 1988: 190). Victor's appetite for the words of others is reflected in contemporary culture's fascination with re-issuing, re-mixing and re-recording records, and in the use of sampling, a technique which produces songs containing portions of the lyrics and/or music of other songs. Such recycling of influences, appropriation of sentences and sections of tunes, both mirrors and encourages Victor's penchant for taking song words, out of context, and re-making them into a part of his present. He uses the words of others to finish his sentences, and to sign cards and gift-tags. This creates an eerie sense of déjà vu and ambiguity; the reader knows what the lyrics remind them of, without knowing what they mean to Victor. This play of meaning, created by multiple implications and similar sounds, ensures that communication can never be straightforward; definition, interpretation and understanding overlap. Victor's habit of adapting song-words ensures that he in turn is easily quotable, and therefore his double, Victor Mark II, is instantly plausible – sending flowers to Chloe with a message which quotes two songs, both adapting and outdoing in a brief plagiarized sentence: 'Ain't no woman like the one I've got . . . baby I'm a want you, baby I'm a need you' (Ellis 1999: 66).

The ghostly images and frequent occurrences of déjà vu scattered throughout *Glamorama*, where characters metamorphose between narratives and levels of reality, as a consequence blurring and obscuring which side of the camera they inhabit, were preceded by the gothic nature of *American Psycho* (1991), and live on to be substantiated by the contemporary ghost story *Lunar Park* (2005). In *Lunar Park* the author himself is finally haunted not just by his fictional past characters, but also by his past personal selves. This transmission between levels of what can be experienced and articulated allows Ellis' intertextual style to travel full circle, as he reveals himself to be an author adapted by his own texts: his youth, his success, his wealth, his family circumstances – all run intermingled throughout whatever he creates. His past characters reappear and mutate, he appears personally (as do some of his life events and his acquaintances), he refers to other narratives and uses filmic traits to capture the action, his work is adapted into films and inspires other films and narratives who may or may not cite this inspiration. His favoured themes jostle for centre stage: identity, vanity, wealth, surface, decadence, surveillance, social control and breakdown. As Cecile Guilbert suggests, 'although his vision has grown more acute over the years, Ellis has always written the same book . . . His heroes are always young, beautiful, rich, narcissistic and ignorant' (Guilbert 2000: 3). This suggests self-adaptation and reiterates the idea that the boundaries between authorship, ownership and identity are permeable and evolving, and therefore changing. Ironically, whilst Ellis is happy to 'adapt' celebrity identities (including his own), he wishes to protect his own work from similar borrowings, illustrated by his attempts to sue Ben Stiller, the director, co-writer and star of *Zoolander* (2001), for copyright infringement. Ellis suggested that the film's plot ideas, which focus on fashion models, celebrity culture and terrorism, had been lifted from *Glamorama*; the case was settled out of court. Both narratives have undoubted similarities, and both are incestuously self-referential. To claim that Stiller is 'copying' seems to be somewhat missing the point of contemporary adaptations culture, which admits, indeed embraces, its mongrel derivation.

Notes

1. Cartmell and Whelehan discuss the phenomenon of the cinematic novel, 'a book which is, arguably, more cinematic than its filmic adaptation, and more comfortable with its status as fantastic narrative' (Cartmell and Whelehan 2005: 48, re: *Harry Potter and the Philosopher's Stone*).
2. Christian Bale now stars as Batman in the Batman series of movies, 2005 and 2008.
3. Simone Murray, in her essay 'Materializing adaptation theory: the adaptation industry', points out the 'sexually loaded vocabulary [used to critique adaptations], with its accusations of "unfaithfulness", "betrayal", "straying", "debasement", and the like' (Murray 2008: 5).
4. Lacanian theory states that desire can never be obtained, due to the impossibility of ever knowing what is 'true' desire amongst the endless layers of social conditioning which humans are exposed to, and therefore the background or setting of fantasies becomes the main focus.

Bibliography

American Psycho (2000). USA, dir. Mary Harron.

Aragay, Mireia (2005), *Books in Motion: Adaptation, Intertextuality, Authorship*. Amsterdam, New York: Rodopi.

Bartlett, Neil (1988), *Who Was That Man?* London: Serpent's Tail.

Batman Begins (2005). USA, dir. Christopher Nolan.

Baudrillard, Jean (1983), *Simulations* (trans. P. Foss and P. Patton). New York: Semiotext(e).

Cartmell, Deborah and Imelda Whelehan (2005), 'Harry Potter and the fidelity debate', in Mireia Aragay (ed.), *Books in Motion: Adaptation, Intertextuality, Authorship*. Amsterdam, New York: Rodopi, pp. 37–49.

Beckett, Andy (1999), 'Leader of the Bret pack' – January 9, books.guardian. co.uk.

The Dark Knight (2008). USA, dir. Christopher Nolan.

Easton Ellis, Bret (1987), *The Rules of Attraction*. New York: Vintage Books.

— (1991), *American Psycho*. New York: Vintage Books.

— (1999), *Glamorama*. London: Picador.

Freud, Sigmund (1905, 1991), *Three Essays on the Theory of Sexuality*. London: Penguin.

Gane, Mike (1991), *Baudrillard's Bestiary: Baudrillard and Culture*. London and New York: Routledge.

Guilbert, Cecile (2000), 'The blindness of the spectacle', *Art Press* 258, 58–60. Je vnweb.hwwilsonweb.com.

Jays, David (2007), 'First love, last rites', *Sight & Sound* 17 (10), 34–5.

Lacan, Jacques (1977), *The Four Fundamental Concepts of Psychoanalysis*. London: Hogarth.

Leitch, Thomas (2007), *Film Adaptation and its Discontents*. Maryland: Johns Hopkins University Press.

Man Bites Dog (1992). Belgium, dir. Rene Belvaux.

Man With a Movie Camera (1929). USSR, dir. Dziga Vertov.

MacCabe, Colin (1993), 'Realism and the cinema: notes on some Brechtian theses', in Anthony Easthope (ed.), *Contemporary Film Theory*. London: Longman.

McInerney, Jay (1989), *Story of My Life*. New York: Vintage.

Murray, Simone (2008), 'Materializing adaptation theory: the adaptation industry', *Literature Film Quarterly*, 36 (1) 4–20.

Naremore, James (ed.) (2000), *Film Adaptation*. London: Athlone.

Petersen, Per Serritslev (2005), '9/11 and the "problem of imagination": *Fight Club* and *Glamorama* as terrorist pretexts', *Orbis Litterarum* 60, 133–144.

Punter, David (2001), 'E-textuality authenticity after the postmodern', *Critical Quarterly* 43 (2), 68–91.

Seger, Linda (1992), *The Art of Adaptation: Turning Fact and Fiction into Film*. New York: Henry Holt and Company, LLC.

Simon, William (1996), *Postmodern Sexualities*. London and New York: Routledge.

Stam, Robert (2000), 'Beyond fidelity: the dialogics of adaptation', in James Naremore (ed.), *Film Adaptation*. London: Athlone, pp. 54–76.

Welsh, James W. and Peter Lev (eds) (2007), *The Literature/Film Reader: Issues of Adaptation*. Maryland: Scarecrow Press.

Whelehan, Imelda (1999), 'Adaptations: the contemporary dilemmas', in Deborah Cartmell and Imelda Whelehan (eds), *Adaptations: from Text to Screen, Screen to Text*. London and New York: Routledge, pp. 3–19.

Zoolander (2001). USA, dir. Ben Stiller.

Index